INTRODUCTION TO DATA PROCESSING

Second Edition

MARTIN L. HARRIS, Ph.D.
California State Department of Education

in consultation with
NANCY B. STERN, Ph.D.
Hofstra University

JOHN WILEY & SONS
New York • Chichester • Brisbane • Toronto • Singapore

Editorial Supervisor: Martha Jewett
Manager: Ken Burke
Editor: Judith Fillmore
Artist: Carl Brown
Composition and Make-up: Wendy Welsh

Library of Congress Cataloging in Publication Data

Harris, Martin L
    Introduction to data processing.

    (Wiley self-teaching guides)
    Bibliography: p. ix
    1. Electronic data processing—Programmed
instruction. 2. Electronic digital computers—
Programmed instruction. I. Stern, Nancy B.
II. Title
QA76.H293 1979   001.6'4'077   78-21161
ISBN 0-471-04657-4

Printed in the United states of America

79 80 10 9 8

For: Ann, Mary Louise, and Megan Lee

Acknowledgments

The following organizations have kindly supplied photographs and permission to reproduce illustrations.

Control Data Corporation
Figures 3-7, 3-9, 3-10, 3-11, 3-14, 3-15, 3-30

Data 100 Corporation
Figure 4-11

Eastman Kodak Company
Figure 3-22

International Business Machines Corporation
Figures 2-6, 2-10, 2-11; 3-1, 3-4, 3-8, 3-16, 3-18, 3-20, 3-21, 3-23, 3-24, 3-28; 4-4, 4-8; 5-5, 5-10, 5-11; 7-1; 11-1; A-1, A-2, A-8, A-9, A-13, A-14

Lockheed Electronics Company, Inc.
Figure 3-27

NCR Corporation
Figures 4-9, 4-10

Radio Shack, Inc.
Figure 3-26

Sperry Univac
Figures 3-13, 3-29; 9-2

Tektronix, Inc.
Figure 4-6

Teletype Corporation
Figures 4-2, 4-5

Texas Instruments, Inc.
Figure 4-7

John Wiley & Sons, Inc.
Figures 5-13, 5-14, A-7, A-15, A-16 from Arnold, Robert R., Harold G. Hill, and Alymer V. Nichols, Modern Data Processing. Figure 10-2 from Stern, Nancy B., and Robert A. Stern, COBOL Programming.

Preface to Second Edition

Data processing with computers is here to stay. From birth to death information about each individual is gathered, stored, and used in many ways—for good or ill. Many of the things we take for granted—charge cards, college registration, automatic telephones, airline reservations—would be quite different, if not impossible, without electronic data processing.

The purpose of this book, then, is to give you some basic understanding of what data processing is, how it is organized, what types of equipment are used, and how a data-processing system is designed. Since the first edition was written, there have been major advances in the field of data processing. This edition incorporates many of these advances, such as telecommunications, microcomputers, integrated circuits, and intelligent terminals, as well as more discussion of the uses of computer systems.

Chapter 1 describes the basic cycle, or series of steps through which data passes, and the basic principles of data processing are discussed in Chapter 2.

The types of equipment used in computer systems and their relationships to each other are discussed in Chapter 3. An all-new Chapter 4 covers the increasingly important topic of telecommunications. The representation and storage of data in computer systems is covered in Chapter 5.

Chapters 6, 7, and 8 describe the major steps in preparing a computer program—the series of steps that tell a computer exactly what it is to do with any data it is given. Chapter 6 is a general overview of the process, and Chapter 7 gives practice at drawing flowcharts to specify how certain data-processing tasks are to be performed. In Chapter 8 you will see how instructions are written for a computer using one particular language, BASIC.

In Chapter 9 we look at ways in which computer systems can be made more efficient through the use of software and operating systems. Chapter 10 describes how a complete data-processing system is designed.

Chapter 11, also completely new, is designed to get you thinking about the impact of the computer on our daily lives. It is not written in the self-instruction format as is the rest of the book, but is a discussion of some of the important issues raised by new applications of computer technology.

Appendix I describes the use of punched-card equipment which, although generally obsolete, can still be found in many organizations as a supplement to electronic computers. Appendix II is a chart showing characteristics of selected computer systems.

My thanks are due to Judy V. Wilson, publisher of the Self-Teaching Guides, for her continued patience with missed deadlines. Nancy B. Stern again provided invaluable help with suggestions for revisions and on technical matters. Any errors of fact are solely my responsibility. Finally, thanks to my wife and daughters for enduring those "lost" weekends while this revision was under way.

Davis, California   Martin L. Harris
December, 1978

How to Use This Book

The material in this book is presented so that you will be actively applying what you learn as you go along. Each chapter is divided into numbered sections called <u>frames</u>; each frame presents a discussion of some new information. You will be asked to apply your understanding in some way—by choosing or filling in the best answer to a question, calculating a result, drawing a chart, or writing a program. You may write the answer in the book or on a separate piece of paper. The correct answer is given below the dashed line. If your answer is different from the one given, review the previous few frames to see why. When you're sure you understand the material, go on to the next frame.

Each chapter includes an introduction describing what you can expect to learn and a Self-Test that will help you evaluate your progress. (If the material described in the introduction looks familiar, you may want to try the Self-Test first. If you do well, you might skip that chapter or skim it lightly.) A Final Test appearing at the end of the book can be used as a final evaluation. Answers to both the chapter Self-Tests and this Final Test are provided.

Chapter 11, "The Impact of Computers," is not written in self-instructional format. This chapter is designed to raise issues for thought and discussion rather than to impart new technical material. For this reason, it is also the only chapter without a Self-Test.

A Cross-Reference Chart correlates chapters in this book with some popular course texts; this will be useful if you wish to learn more about a particular area or if you are reading this guide along with a textbook.

Cross-Reference Chart to Some Popular Data-Processing Texts

REFERENCES

Awad, Elias M., Business Data Processing, 4th ed. (Englewood Cliffs, N.J.: Prentice-Hall, 1975).

Couger, J. Daniel, and Fred R. Mcfadden, A First Course in Data Processing, (New York: Wiley, 1977).

Dock, V. Thomas, and Edward Essick, Principles of Data Processing, 3rd ed. (Chicago: Science Research, 1974).

Feingold, Carl, Introduction to Data Processing, 2nd ed. (Dubuque, Ia.: Brown, 1975).

Fouri, William M., Introduction to the Computer: Tool of Business, 2nd ed. (Englewood Cliffs, N.J.: Prentice-Hall, 1977).

Stern, Robert A., and Nancy B. Stern, Principles of Data Processing, 2nd ed. (New York: Wiley, 1979).

Chapter in This Book	Awad	Couger & McFadden	Dock & Essick	Feingold	Fouri	Stern & Stern
Introduction	1, 2	1	1	1	1	1
1. The Data-Processing Cycle	3, 14	10	4	1	3	1
2. Data-Processing Principles	8	10	4	3	3	2
3. An Overview of Computer Systems	5, 9-13	2, 5-7	6-10 Mod A*	5, 6, 18	4, 5	5, 6
4. Tele-communications	13	8	16	16	5, 13	8
5. Data Representation and Storage	6, 7	4	7	7	6	4
6. Development of Computer Programs	14-16	12	12 Mod C	9, 10	7	7
7. Flowcharting	15	11	Mod B	–	8	8
8. Writing a Computer Program in BASIC	19	13	Appen**	17	10	12, 13
9. Software	16	9	13, 15	18	7	3, 7, 12
10. Systems Analysis	14, 21, 22	16, 18	3	8	11	15
11. The Impact of Computers	–	1	Mod D	1, 2, 16	1	17
Appendix I	8	–	4, 5	3, 4	2	1

*Mod means Module
**Appen means Appendix

Contents

INTRODUCTION
What Is Data Processing?

A piece of <u>data</u> is simply a fact about something. Among the pieces of data that describe me are: 5 ft. 9 in. tall, brown eyes, married, has a daughter called Mary and a daughter called Megan. Notice that not all this data is numeric (composed of numbers). Data does not have to be numerical, although much of the data we process is.

Individual pieces of data are rarely useful on their own. We usually have to perform some kind of <u>data processing</u> in order to answer a specific question or arrive at some meaningful decision on a course of action. For example, suppose someone asks: "How much will 14 widgits cost if you airmail them to me?" To find the answer, we would have to multiply the cost of a single widgit by 14, find the cost of airmailing them, and then add the two amounts together. Deciding whom to invite to a party also involves data processing. We have to run through a list of possible names and for each one use some pieces of data such as age, sex, habits, interests, and so on, to select the people we want to invite. We may not write anything down. And much of the processing may be so fast that we are unaware of it. Nevertheless, we are using data to reach a decision. Here's another example. If you go into a restaurant with a limited amount of cash (and no credit card), you would have to process some data before you order. You would add together the prices of what you would like to order and compare the total with the amount of cash you have. Again, you probably don't have to write anything down, but you are processing data nevertheless. As you can see, data processing does not have to involve calculating machines, computers, or wizard mathematicians.

But it can. For example, to decide how long to burn a moon lander's rocket motor in order to put it in the same orbit as the command ship also involves data processing. The data used include such things as the weight of each vehicle, their distance apart, speeds, orbits, and so on. This example of data processing involves wizard mathematicians and, because of the short time in which the calculations must be made, large and very fast computers.

In each of the examples given so far, data was processed to reach some kind of decision—what answer to give, whom to invite, what to order, how long to burn the rocket motor. Data processing involves manipulating data into an arrangement that is more meaningful for decision making. In the restaurant, you probably could find more than one combination of dishes that you could afford. In this case, data processing reduces the total amount of data (different foods and their prices) to a few combinations from which to choose. In the case of the rocket burn or the price of the widgits, data processing produces only one piece of data as an answer.

Data processing falls into two broad types—business and scientific. The difference between these types is not so much in the way processing is done but in the relationship between the amount of data to be processed and the number of calculations to be performed on the data. In the example of the moon lander, only a few pieces of data are used, but many thousands of calculations are performed on them to produce the answer. Relatively few pieces of data and a large number of calculations are typical of scientific data processing. In business data processing, however, we usually have large amounts of data but perform relatively few different calculations. To calculate the payroll for 2,500 employees for example, the same few calculations have to be performed 2,500 times. Relatively few calculations and a large amount of data are typical of business data processing.

Although the basic processes are much the same in business and scientific data processing, in this book we will generally use examples from business since they are easier to understand.

All the data processing that is done today could be done by human beings with paper and pencil, although not very quickly nor very accurately. However, our world has become so complex, and decisions have to be made so often and so quickly, we cannot afford to spend time processing data by hand (even if we had enough trained people). So, automated data-processing systems have been developed, which use hand-operated calculating machines (requiring much human time to operate), electronic accounting machines, and computers (requiring very little human time to operate).

The development of computers not only has allowed us to do many things faster and more efficiently than before, it also has allowed us to do many things that were previously impossible. We could not have put a man on the moon without the aid of computers—not because we didn't know how, but because the complex mathematics involved would have taken years to do by hand. Many things that we take for granted today, such as automatic telephone dialing and the convenience of credit cards, would be impossible without the aid of computer systems.

In addition to performing calculations very rapidly, computer systems can store and retrieve vast quantities of data. Thus, computer systems are essential to the operation of large, modern business organizations, since management decisions need to be based on as much up-to-data and accurate information as can be gathered. The storage capacity of computers also makes them increasingly useful in education. It becomes possible to store, cross-reference, and retrieve information about books, articles, and papers on a scale that would be impossible by hand. It is also possible to computerize instruction in schools and colleges, making it possible for a student to work through only material that is related to his or her particular interest.

Of course, this vast storage capacity can also be put to bad uses. There is a growing concern over the vast amounts of data on individuals which have been gathered and stored by federal, state, and local governments, as well as by credit bureaus. Although most of this data was gathered with good intentions—to ensure accurate and timely social-security payments or to protect society against criminals—there is always the chance that the data can be used as tools of repression by unscrupulous individuals or agencies.

This leads us to the human element in computer systems and automated data processing. No data processing can take place unless an individual, or a group of individuals, wants it done and designs a way to do it. By themselves computer systems are incapable of doing anything. A human mind must determine in advance everything that computers do. Even the mistakes that are blamed on the computer are usually the result of a human error in the designing of the system or in the handling of data before it is put into the computer. So the use of computers for good or ill depends on the people who control them, not the systems themselves.

Whether we like it or not, computerized systems of all kinds will play a larger part in our lives as time goes on. The purpose of this book is to give you a basic idea of the way these systems work. The more people who understand the way computers work, the more likely it is that computers will be a great benefit to society.

CHAPTER ONE
The Data-Processing Cycle

However large or small a company may be, or whatever method it uses to process data, it follows the same general steps. This series of steps is called the data-processing cycle, a systematic method of handling data and producing desired information. In this chapter we will look at this cycle and some of its functions. Detailed discussion of the steps will be given in later chapters.

After completing this chapter you will be able to:

- list the main steps in the data-processing cycle;
- describe what happens at each step of the cycle; and
- give descriptions of documents and procedures, identify the steps to which they belong.

1. Figure 1-1 shows the basic data-processing cycle.

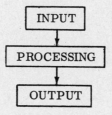

Figure 1-1. The Basic Data-Processing Cycle

The first step, input, refers to the gathering together of all the data required in a form convenient for processing. For example, in order to calculate how much to pay a student for yard work at my house, I must have two pieces of data—the number of hours worked and the hourly pay rate. These two pieces of data will be the _____ for my data-processing cycle.

- - - - - - - - - - - - - - - - - -

input

2. Once the input has been gathered, it has to be <u>processed</u> to produce the desired output. In the preceding example, what must I do with the input data to determine how much to pay for the yard work?

_____

- - - - - - - - - - - - - - - - - -

multiply hours worked by hourly pay rate

3. Processing is the step at which all necessary calculations are performed on the input data in order to produce the desired output. The multiplication of hours worked by hourly pay gives the number of dollars to be paid—the desired information, or <u>output</u>. If the student worked for 5 hours at an hourly

rate of $2.00, how much would I have to pay? _____

- - - - - - - - - - - - - - - - - -

$10.00

4. Of course, this is a very simple example of the data-processing cycle at work. Here's a slightly more difficult one. At the end of another day of yard work, the student says to me, "I worked from 9 until 5 and took an hour out for lunch. You said you would pay $2.50 an hour today because it has been heavy work. Oh yes, I owe you $3.00 from last week." My job is to calculate how much to give the student this week. The data given to me will serve as

the _____ to the data-processing cycle.

- - - - - - - - - - - - - - - - - -

input

5. The next step in the cycle is the _____ step.

- - - - - - - - - - - - - - - - - -

processing

6. This time the processing of the data is a little more complex. It goes something like this:

_____

9 until 5 is 8 hours
Hours worked = 8 - 1 (for lunch) = 7
Money earned = 7 × $2.50 = $17.50
Give to student $17.50 - $3.00 (owed) = $14.50

There are four separate calculations, each with a separate result. Which result will I choose as output from my data-processing cycle?

_____

- - - - - - - - - - - - - - - - - -

$14.50, the amount to pay

7. Match the following

_____ (1) input

_____ (2) processing

_____ (3) output

(a) the desired information
(b) gathering the required data
(c) performing calculations on the data

- - - - - - - - - - - - - - - - - -

(1) b; (2) c; (3) a

8. This very simple three-step data-processing cycle describes how to solve very complex problems as well as very simple ones. We could take 50 pieces of data as input, perform 1,000 calculations with them at the processing stage, and produce 16 different pieces of output.

However, it is convenient to add two more steps to the data-processing cycle shown in Figure 1-1. This expanded cycle is shown in Figure 1-2.

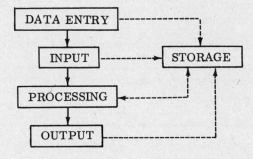

Figure 1-2. An Expanded Data-Processing Cycle

The first step in the expanded cycle is <u>data entry</u>, which refers to the "birth" of a piece of data and how it is recorded. For example, when a customer buys an ice-cream cone, a piece of data is generated. This is recorded on a roll of paper in the cash register.

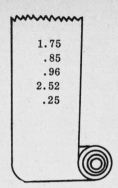

This roll of paper is called the source document for that piece of data. It is the document to which we would refer at a later time to find out how much the ice-cream cone cost. Of course, it is also the source document for many other transactions.

A restaurant check, which is normally handwritten, is also a source document, usually for only one transaction.

JAX'S		
1	fries	.15
1	CB	.95
1	cola	.20
		1.30
	TAX	.07
	TOTAL	1.37

The data on it tells the customer how much is owed and tells management what the customer ordered and what it cost.

Thus, a source document is anything that contains data needed for a processing cycle. The nature of the document (large, small, handwritten, printed) is unimportant. If the document contains data needed for some data-processing cycle, then it is a source document.

Try to match the following:

_____ (1) data

_____ (2) source document

(a) time card
(b) number of miles traveled
(c) invoice
(d) cost of goods sold

- - - - - - - - - - - - - - - - - - -

(1) b, d; (2) a, c

9.   Which of these statements is correct?

_____   (a) A source document contains only one piece of data.

_____   (b) Data that is to be processed is found on a source document.

_____   (c) both

_____   (d) neither

- - - - - - - - - - - - - - - - - - - .

b

10. Once data has been entered on a source document, it has to be introduced into the processing cycle. As you recall from the basic cycle, this is

done at the _____ step.

- - - - - - - - - - - - - - - - - - -

input

11. At the input step data must be <u>recorded</u> in a form suitable for the processing system being used. If a manual system is being used, data from the
source documents is entered by hand into ledgers or journals before it is
processed. Electronic data-processing systems can accept data to be processed in many forms—punched card, punched tape, magnetic tape, and the
like. Some source documents can be used directly as input into electronic
systems. For example, data may be entered through the keyboard of a terminal directly into a computer that is hundreds of miles away. (How this is
done will be discussed in Chapter 4.)
    After the data is recorded, it must be <u>verified</u>. To verify data is to check
its accuracy in recorded form. Thus, handwritten entries in a journal are
verified by checking each entry against the source document. Input recorded
in other ways may also be verified, as you will see in a later chapter.
    Data is:

_____   (a) verified before being punched into cards.

_____   (b) recorded from source documents for introduction to the system.

_____   (c) recorded after being verified for input to the system.

- - - - - - - - - - - - - - - - - - -

b

12. Which of these statements is true?

_____   (a) Data is verified after it is recorded.

_____   (b) Data must be punched into cards before it can be verified.

_____ (c) Data is recorded only after it has been verified.

- - - - - - - - - - - - - - - - - -

a

13. At the input step one other operation may be performed on the data from the source document. It may be <u>coded</u>. Coding is convenient for two reasons. First, it allows a piece of data to be reduced in size. For example, sales receipts might have the name of a department printed on them—hardware, millinery, appliances, and so forth. Rather than record the whole name, a number would be assigned to each department: Hardware—01; Millinery—02; and so on. Second, sorting numerical data (numbers) is much quicker than sorting alphabetic data (letters). The person recording the data applies the appropriate code where necessary.

What three operations may be performed at the input stage of the data-

processing cycle? _____

- - - - - - - - - - - - - - - - - -

recording, verifying, coding

14. At the processing step, data:

_____ (a) is verified.

_____ (b) has calculations performed on it.

_____ (c) both

_____ (d) neither

- - - - - - - - - - - - - - - - - -

b

15. As you can see from Figure 1-2, the next step in the expanded processing

cycle is the _____ step.

- - - - - - - - - - - - - - - - - -

output

16. Output is the information that is required of the data, prepared in the most useful format. The monthly sales figures of each department of a large store could be produced in several forms. A printed summary may be given to the store manager. The same information might also be punched into cards or put on magnetic tape for delivery to the head office of the store chain. This would then become the source document for another processing cycle that

prepares department totals for the whole chain of stores. Output is the goal
of all data processing—the communication of useful information derived from
data sources.

Output from a data-processing cycle:

_____ (a) may be produced in different forms.

_____ (b) communicates desired information.

_____ (c) both

_____ (d) neither

- - - - - - - - - - - - - - - - - -

c

17. You will see from Figure 1-2 that each step in the data-processing cycle
is connected to another step by a dotted line. This step is called

_____.

- - - - - - - - - - - - - - - - - -

storage

18. Data may be stored in many different ways. It may be written or typed
on a piece of paper, punched into cards, or written onto magnetic tape or a
magnetic disk. Just how it is stored depends on which method of data processing is used and how long the data is to be kept.

Refer to Figure 1-2 again and list the steps at which data might be stored

in the data-processing cycle. _____

_____

- - - - - - - - - - - - - - - - - -

data entry, input, processing, output

19. The lines are dotted because storing data at each step is not essential to
the data-processing cycle itself (except in one instance) but is very important
in running an efficient business. The length of time data will stay in storage
varies according to the type of data, how the business is organized, and other
factors.

The original data, in the form of source documents, is usually stored in
case a question should arise about the final output. For example, a monthly
bill may include an item which the customer claims not to have bought. It
could be that someone else bought the item and the customer was billed by
mistake. Or perhaps the customer forgot about buying the item and lost the
receipt. The source document will normally serve as a proof of purchase
when such discrepancies occur.

After the data has been recorded, it is usually stored in the same form in which it was recorded. For example, if data is recorded on a magnetic disk, it will be stored on a magnetic disk. If data is recorded on punched cards, it is stored on punched cards. This allows the data to be used in more than one data-processing cycle without returning to the data-entry step.

Results of calculations at the processing step may also be stored. In a billing job, if a customer bought more than one of a certain item, the cost of these items must be calculated (unit cost × number purchased). This result is stored as a subtotal until the final total for the customer is calculated by adding all the subtotals.

Finally, output is stored until required. The weekly summary of sales by departments may be stored on magnetic tape for use in preparing a monthly summary. It is far quicker to make a tape with the weekly summary data and use it as input for the monthly report than it is to go back to all the original source documents.

Data is stored:

_____ (a) to save having to print a report.

_____ (b) because it is useful in checking apparent errors in output.

_____ (c) only following the output step of the data-processing cycle.

- - - - - - - - - - - - - - - - - - -

b

20. To review the data-processing cycle, consider how it might be applied to the customer-billing operation in a small store that uses a manual method. When a customer charges something, the signed receipt becomes the

_____ for the data-processing cycle.

- - - - - - - - - - - - - - - - - -

source document

21. The clerk will _____ these source documents until ready to begin the next step of the cycle, the _____ step.

- - - - - - - - - - - - - - - - - -

store, input

22. Assume the clerk performs an input operation at the end of each week. What does the clerk do?

_____ (a) Calculate the total spent by each customer during the week.

_____ (b) Record the data in a more convenient form for processing.

_____ (c) both

_____ (d) neither

- - - - - - - - - - - - - - - - - - - -

b

23. In the manual system, the clerk would record each transaction in some kind of ledger arranged by customer name. When the data is recorded, what would the clerk do? _____

- - - - - - - - - - - - - - - - - -

verify the recorded data

24. Each entry is checked against the source document to ensure its accuracy. When the verification is complete, what will the clerk do with the source documents? _____

- - - - - - - - - - - - - - - - - -

store them

25. The next step in the data-processing cycle is the _____ step.

- - - - - - - - - - - - - - - - - -

processing

26. Although the data is recorded each week, the clerk probably performs the processing step only at the end of each month to prepare a bill for each customer. The total bill for each customer will be calculated by adding up the individual charges. An amount representing a returned item or the payment of last month's bill may be subtracted, or the interest on the unpaid balance from last month may have to be calculated.

At what step in the process would the bill for a customer be written?

_____

- - - - - - - - - - - - - - - - - -

output

27. At least two copies of the bill for each customer would be made, one to be sent to the customer and the other to be _____ for future

reference.

- - - - - - - - - - - - - - - - - -

stored

It should be noted that the data-processing cycle described in this chapter is very broad and general. The various operations performed at each step may overlap in some systems and not occur in others. For example, if the clerk had a large number of receipts to record, the receipts might be sorted into alphabetic order before the input step is begun. However, if a computer system was being used, the data might be recorded on cards in the order that the source documents were created and then sorted into alphabetic order on the computer. But whatever data is to be processed, and whatever method is used, all these main steps—data entry, input, processing, output—are required to go from raw data to some meaningful output.

This is the end of Chapter 1. You should now work the Self-Test that follows.

SELF-TEST

Answer all the questions and then check against the answers that follow.

1. List the three basic steps of the data-processing cycle.

_____

2. After which of these steps in the data-processing cycle may data be stored?

_____ (a) data entry

_____ (b) input

_____ (c) processing

_____ (d) output

_____ (e) · all of the above

3. What is the purpose of verifying recorded data? _____

_____

4. Sometimes numbers, letters, or letter-number combinations are substituted for data on the source document. What is this operation called and at what step of the data-processing cycle does it take place?

_____

5. Data is stored:

_____ (a) only for the purposes of producing output.

_____ (b) in order that apparent errors in output may be checked.

_____ (c) both

_____ (d) neither

6.   Match the following.

_____ (1) data entry

_____ (2) processing

_____ (3) output

(a) a monthly statement
(b) signing a sales receipt
(c) calculating payment due
(d) filing copies of statements

Answers to Self-Test

The numbers in parentheses after each answer refer to the frames in which the appropriate answers can be found. If you have a wrong answer or are not sure why your answer is correct, read that section again before going on to the next chapter.

1.   input, processing, output   (frame 1)

2.   e   (frame 19)

3.   To ensure its accuracy before proceeding to other steps of the cycle. (frame 11)

4.   coding, input   (frame 13)

5.   b   (frame 19)

6.   (1) b; (2) c; (3) a   (frames 1-8)

CHAPTER TWO
Data-Processing Principles

Source documents for use in data processing are of many shapes and sizes.
They may be handwritten or typewritten. Technologies have been developed
that allow these different documents to be used directly at the input stage of
the data-processing cycle; such equipment, however, tends to be very expensive. Thus, standard formats for handling data have been developed. By far
the most common format is the Hollerith punched card. This card was origin-
ally developed in 1887 by Dr. Herman Hollerith to aid the processing of data
for the United States Census Bureau.

After completing this chapter you will be able to:

- identify the major responsibilities of the staff of a data-processing
  department;
- define the term program;
- identify the main features of the 80-column and the 96-column
  punched card;
- describe methods of reducing the size of data for recording in
  punched cards;
- describe the unit-record principle;
- design simple card layouts;
- describe how cards are punched and verified;
- define the terms master record, detail record, and summary
  record; and
- define the terms record and file.

1. Before discussing the way in which the staff of a data-processing department is organized to work with computer systems, we should remind ourselves
why we use—and need—computers. Modern life is very complex and even
small businesses are faced with processing large amounts of data. Most of
this data has to be processed quickly and accurately in order to be put in a
form useful to managers. Managers need to know, for example, how much
money has been received, how much money is owed, how much has been
spent on people and materials, how much stock is left in the warehouse, on a

regular and timely basis. This information is then used to make decisions about future activities.

Computer systems are ideally suited to provide these kinds of information. They are designed to process information in large quantities quickly and accurately. A computer system does exactly what it is told over and over again without question and without needing the coffee breaks, vacations, and three-day weekends that you and I find so desirable.

Let's now consider the people who work with computers and the way their jobs are organized. People who work with computers are more important than you might think, for while it is possible to have a very modern, fast, and efficient computer system, without a good staff to run it, you might as well switch it off.

Figure 2-1 shows the organization of a typical data-processing department. Not all departments are organized in exactly this way, but all of the functions performed by the people shown have to be performed, even if a single person performs several of them.

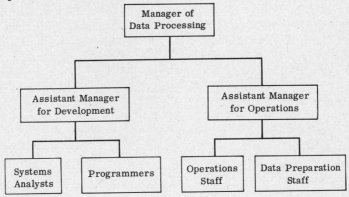

Figure 2-1. Organization of a Typical Data-Processing Department

As you can see from Figure 2-1, there is a manager of data-processing who is responsible for the entire operation. This person is knowledgeable about all aspects of data processing and usually has a good understanding of the operations and data-processing needs of the company for which he or she works.

Reporting to the manager are the assistant manager for _____ _____ and the assistant manager for _____.

- - - - - - - - - - - - - - - - - - -

development, operations

2.   The assistant manager for development is generally responsible for co-ordination of the work of two groups of people—systems analysts and programmers.

A systems analyst is a person with the skills to find out the data-processing requirements of an organization and to design more efficient ways to meet those requirements. Each step of the data-processing cycle—from data entry to output—is considered by the systems analyst when designing a new data-processing system or modifying an existing one.

To give you an example, if the manager of a personnel department thought that it would be a good idea to computerize the records in the department, she or he would work with a systems analyst to design a system to do that. Together with other staff members from the personnel department, they would spend a great deal of time discussing how the new system should operate. The systems analyst would find out what information is to be used as source data, how the data is to be prepared, what operations are to be performed on it, and what type of output reports are required.

To design a system that meets the objectives of the personnel department, the analyst combines what has been learned from talking with the personnel department with a knowledge of the specific computer to be used to process the data. The analyst will also estimate the costs involved in creating and operating the system. Chapter 10 deals with systems analysis in detail.

When the systems analyst has designed the complete data-processing system, a programmer begins work on the very specific instructions the computer requires in order to process the data accurately.

These sets of instructions, called programs, tell the computer what types of input data it will receive, exactly what calculations to perform on it—and in what order—and, finally, what type of output to produce. In Chapters 7 and 8 you will learn how programs are designed and written.

Match the following:

_____ (1) systems analyst   (a) a set of instructions for a computer

_____ (2) programmer   (b) the person who uses information from a computer

_____ (3) program   (c) the person who designs the most efficient way to process data

         (d) the person who writes detailed instructions for a computer

- - - - - - - - - - - - - - - - - - -

(1) c; (2) d; (3) a

3. The other assistant manager shown in Figure 2-1 is responsible for operations—that is, for the day-to-day running of the computer system and the equipment associated with it. For example, part of operations is data preparation. As you remember from Chapter 1, data may be punched into cards or entered directly onto magnetic tape or a magnetic disk. The assistant manager for operations is responsible for the timely preparation of data and for the smooth functioning of the computer system while it is processing data. The computer system requires operators to keep the various parts of the system running. The computer sometimes prints out error messages signaling that

something has gone wrong with the processing; it is an operator's responsibility to respond to these messages. Operators also load input data into the system and remove output.

Which of these statements is true?

_____ (a) Programmers are responsible for preparing data for entry to a computer.

_____ (b) An operator prepares the instructions used by a computer system to process data.

_____ (c) The assistant manager for operations designs the best way to produce a report.

_____ (d) none of the above

- - - - - - - - - - - - - - - - - - -

d

4.   Before looking at punched cards, we should point out that, although punched cards are still the most commonly used form of data entry, the computer business is changing rapidly. There are many computer systems in business that use punched cards very sparingly, entering data in other ways. We discuss the punched card at some length in this chapter for two main reasons. First, the punched card can be read with the human eye. This makes it easier to understand. Second, many of the principles used in the design of punched cards are used in the design of other input mediums also. In Chapters 3 and 4 we will deal with other data-entry processes in more detail.

The punched card is a standard-sized data-recording medium made of strong, durable paper. Figure 2-2 on the following page shows the most common format of the punched card. Refer to it while reading this frame and frames 5 through 11. The punched card is printed with ten rows of digits. Each digit, 0 through 9, is repeated 80 times across the card. This gives

80 _____ of digits.

- - - - - - - - - - - - - - - - - -

columns

5.   Which rows labeled in Figure 2-2 are not represented by printing on the card itself? _____

- - - - - - - - - - - - - - - - - -

rows 11 and 12

6.   Each column in a card can be used to record one <u>character</u>. A character is a digit (numbers 0 through 9), a letter of the alphabet, or a special symbol (@, #, %, or the like).

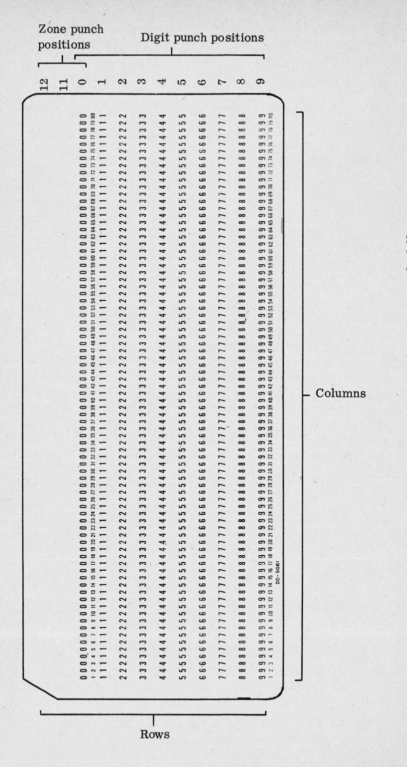

Figure 2-2. A Punched Card (approximately full size)

Which of these are characters?

_____ (a) N

_____ (b) +

_____ (c) George

_____ (d) all of the above

- - - - - - - - - - - - - - - - - -

a, b (A character is a single number, letter, or symbol, not a combination of them.)

7. Since each column of the card can record one character, how many characters can be recorded in the entire card? _____

- - - - - - - - - - - - - - - - - -

80

8. Characters are recorded by means of rectangular holes punched in the appropriate position(s) in a column. Notice that rows 0 through 9 on the card are called _____ punch positions.

- - - - - - - - - - - - - - - - - -

digit

9. You might expect that rows 0 through 9 would be used to represent

_____.

- - - - - - - - - - - - - - - - - -

digits

10. Letters of the alphabet are represented by two holes in a column, one in a digit-punch position and one in a zone-punch position. Zone punches are made in rows _____.

- - - - - - - - - - - - - - - - - -

0, 11, and 12

11. The "0" row may be regarded as either a _____ punch position or as a _____ punch position, depending on its use.

- - - - - - - - - - - - - - - - - -

zone, digit (more about this later)

12. Figure 2-3 shows a punched card (reduced in size) with the digits 0 through 9 punched into it. In addition to the rectangular holes in the card, the appropriate digit is printed at the top of the column.

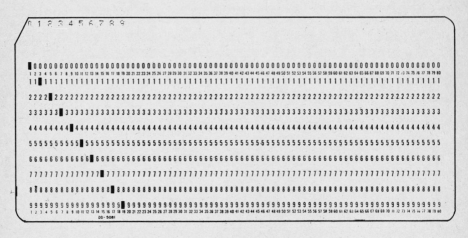

Figure 2-3. Representation of Numeric Characters
in the Punched Card

13. How many holes are needed to represent each digit? _____

- - - - - - - - - - - - - - - - - - -

one

14. Each digit is represented by punching a rectangular hole in the appropriate row. Thus, the number 4 is represented by a hole in the _____ row.

- - - - - - - - - - - - - - - - - - -

fourth (4)

15. Any digit may be punched in any column. In the example at the top of the next page, which digit is punched in which column? _____

- - - - - - - - - - - - - - - - - - -

8 in column 35

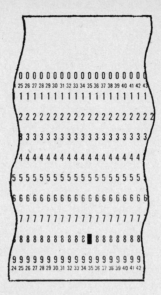

16. In the card below, what number is punched in column 53? _____

Column 62? _____

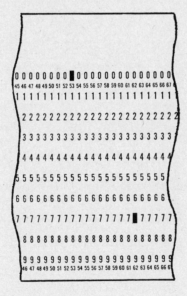

- - - - - - - - - - - - - - - - - -

0, 7

17. Notice that cards can be punched with or without the appropriate digit or character at the top of each column. The card is said to be _interpreted_ when data is both punched in it and printed on it.

Cards are interpreted on an <u>interpreter</u>, a machine that reads the holes and then prints the appropriate character at the top of each column. Interpreting is an optional operation and is for the convenience of human operators— the machines concern themselves only with the holes.

An interpreted card has data represented by:

_____ (a) characters printed above the appropriate columns.

_____ (b) a hole, or holes, punched in the appropriate columns.

_____ (c) both

_____ (d) neither

- - - - - - - - - - - - - - - - -

c

18. Figure 2-4 shows the letters of the alphabet punched and interpreted in a card. Each letter is represented by one _____ punch and one _____ punch.

- - - - - - - - - - - - - - - - -

zone, digit

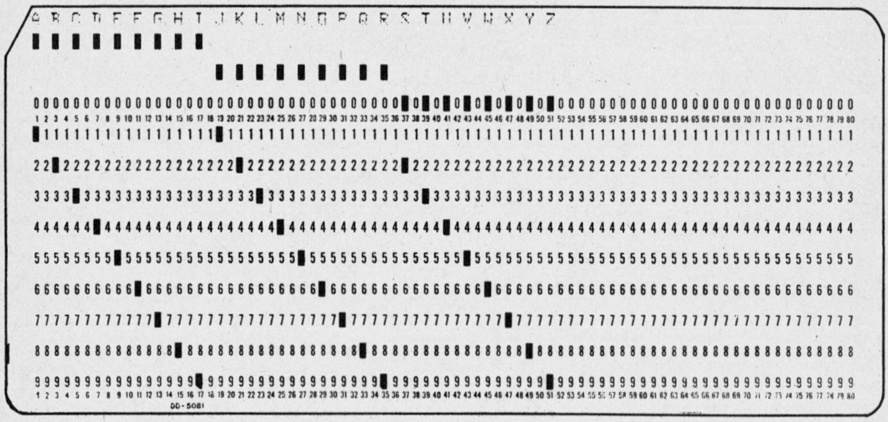

Figure 2-4. Representation of Alphabetic
Characters in the Punched Card

19. The letter "A" is represented by holes in row _____ and in row _____. (Check Figure 2-2 if you're not sure about row numbers in the zone-punch positions.)

- - - - - - - - - - - - - - - - -

12, 1

20. What letter is represented by holes in rows 11 and 8? _____

In rows 0 and 5? _____

- - - - - - - - - - - - - - - - - - -

Q, V

21. What is the word punched into columns 15 through 20 of this card?

_____ (Check Figure 2-4 if you need to.)

- - - - - - - - - - - - - - - - - - -

HARRIS

22. Normally you will not have to look at the holes in the card to figure out what is punched in it because all characters punched into a card can be

_____ on it to make it easy to read.

- - - - - - - - - - - - - - - - - -

interpreted

23. Refer to Figure 2-4. The letters A through I are represented by a zone

punch in row _____ and a _____ punch in the appropriate row.

- - - - - - - - - - - - - - - - - -

12, digit

24. Notice that A is represented by punches in rows 12 and 1, B by punches in rows 12 and 2, C by punches in rows 12 and 3, and so on. What punches is

J represented by? _____

- - - - - - - - - - - - - - - - - - -

rows 11 and 1

25. Letters J through R are represented by zone punches in row 11 and an appropriate digit punch. What letters are represented by a zone punch in

row 0 and an appropriate digit punch? _____

- - - - - - - - - - - - - - - - - - -

S through Z

26. In addition to digits and the alphabet, many special characters may also be punched into cards. These are shown in Figure 2-5.

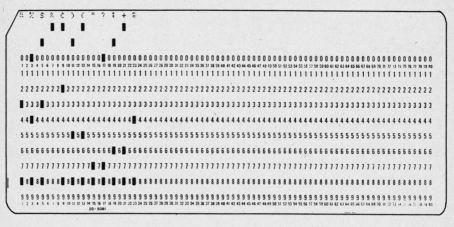

Figure 2-5. Representation of Special Characters
in the Punched Card

How many holes are punched to represent $ (the dollar sign)? _____

In which rows? _____

- - - - - - - - - - - - - - - - - -

3 holes; rows 11, 3, and 8

27. This representation of characters is called the <u>Hollerith</u> <u>code</u>, after its inventor. Figure 2-6 on the next page shows the Hollerith code.

Character	Columns Punched	Character	Columns Punched
A	12-1	0	0
B	12-2	1	1
C	12-3	2	2
D	12-4	3	3
E	12-5	4	4
F	12-6	5	5
G	12-7	6	6
H	12-8	7	7
I	12-9	8	8
J	11-1	9	9
K	11-2		
L	11-3	#	8-3
M	11-4	!	11-8-2
N	11-5	@	8-4
O	11-6	$	11-8-3
P	11-7	%	0-8-4
Q	11-8	¢	12-8-2
R	11-9	&	12
S	0-2	*	11-8-4
T	0-3	,	0-8-3
U	0-4	.	12-8-3
V	0-5		
W	0-6		
X	0-7		
Y	0-8		
Z	0-9		

Figure 2-6. The Hollerith Code

Figure 2-6 includes the Hollerith code for all digits, letters, and some commonly used special characters. (You do not need to memorize these codes.)

There is another type of punched card that is gaining in popularity. This is the 96-column card. It was designed for use with the IBM System/3 computer, introduced in 1969, but is now used by other manufacturers also. Figure 2-7 shows a typical 96-column card. Notice that the holes are round and that the data is interpreted in three rows across the top of the card.

Figure 2-7. The 96-Column Card

There is one row of interpretation for each of the three tiers in which characters are punched. Each tier has 32 columns and 6 rows in which holes can be punched.

The A and B rows make up the zone portion of a column, with the rows 1 through 4 being the digit portion. Combinations of punches in zone and digit portions of a column form characters. Figure 2-8 on the following page shows the codes for the 96-column card. This code is called a Binary-Coded Decimal (BCD) code.

The advantages of the 96-column card are its smaller size and the increased amount of data that can be stored in it.

Match the following:

_____ (1) 80-column card

_____ (2) 96-column card

(a) uses the BCD code
(b) uses the Hollerith code
(c) has a zone and a digit portion in each column

- - - - - - - - - - - - - - - - - -

(1) b, c; (2) a, c

Punch Positions			0	1	2	3	4	5	6	7	8	9
	Zone	B										
		A	A									
	Digit	8									8	8
		4					4	4	4	4		
		2			2	2			2	2		
		1		1		1		1		1		1

Numeric Characters

Punch Positions			A	B	C	D	E	F	G	H	I	J	K	L	M	N	O	P	Q	R	S	T	U	V	W	X	Y	Z
	Zone	B	B	B	B	B	B	B	B	B	B	B	B	B	B	B	B	B	B	B								
		A	A	A	A	A	A	A	A	A	A										A	A	A	A	A	A	A	A
	Digit	8								8	8							8	8								8	8
		4				4	4	4	4						4	4	4	4						4	4	4	4		
		2		2	2			2	2				2	2			2	2			2	2			2	2		
		1	1		1		1		1		1	1		1		1		1		1		1		1		1		1

Alphabetic Characters

Punch Positions			}	¢	.	<	(	+	|	¦	$	.	)	;	¬	-	/	&	,	%	_	>	?	:	#	@	'	=	"	¥
	Zone	B	B	B	B	B	B	B	B	B	B	B	B	B	B	B														
		A	A	A	A	A	A	A	A												A	A	A	A	A	A	A			
	Digit	8		8	8	8	8	8	8	8	8	8	8	8	8	8			8	8	8	8	8	8	8	8	8	8	8	8
		4				4	4	4	4					4	4	4	4					4	4	4	4				4	4	4	4
		2		2	2			2	2	2	2			2	2				2	2			2	2	2	2				2	2
		1			1		1		1		1		1		1		1		1		1		1		1		1		1

Special Characters

Figure 2-8. The Binary-Coded Decimal Character Set for the IBM System/3

28. Once data is punched into a card, it is available for processing by machine. The same data may be used for several different purposes, so its arrangement is important. To give maximum flexibility to card systems, it is customary to record details of only one transaction or event in one card. The card is then called a unit record. Punched-card data processing is sometimes referred to as unit-record processing. A record is defined as a collection of related items of data that are treated as a unit. Figure 2-9 on the following page shows how the data from a sales report might be arranged on the unit-record principle. Each item from the report is recorded on a separate card. In addition to data about the item, the card also records customer number, customer name, salesman number, and so on.

If all sales reports are treated in this way, at the end of the week or month a series of different reports can easily be prepared. To show how much each customer ordered during the period, the cards can be sorted on the basis of customer number and then processed. A report showing the performance of each salesman would call for the cards to be sorted by salesman number before processing. If the cards are sorted by catalog number, a report can be generated showing sales by catalog item.

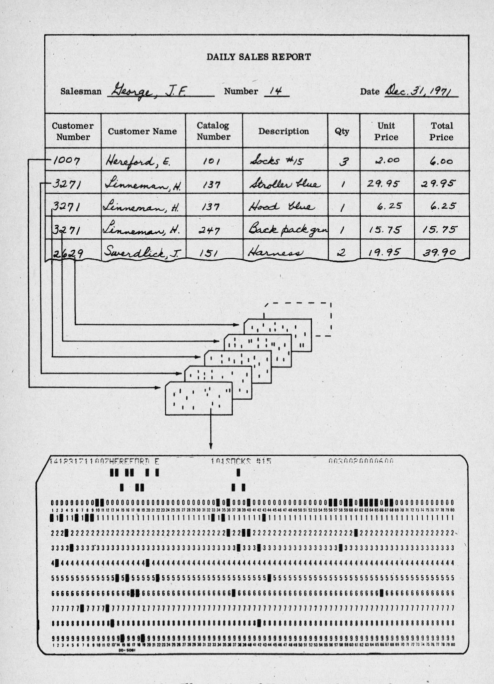

DAILY SALES REPORT

Salesman _George, J.F._   Number _14_   Date _Dec. 31, 1971_

Customer Number	Customer Name	Catalog Number	Description	Qty	Unit Price	Total Price
1007	Hereford, E.	101	Socks #15	3	2.00	6.00
3271	Linneman, H.	137	Stroller blue	1	29.95	29.95
3271	Linneman, H.	137	Hood blue	1	6.25	6.25
3271	Linneman, H.	247	Back pack grn	1	15.75	15.75
2629	Swerdlick, J.	151	Harness	2	19.95	39.90

Figure 2-9. Illustration of Unit-Record Principle

Unit-record processing refers to:

_____ (a) processing only one piece of data at a time.

_____ (b) recording only one piece of data on each card.

_____ (c) recording data for one transaction only on each card.

- - - - - - - - - - - - - - - - - -

c

29. In order that the data in the cards may be processed in a meaningful way, the location of the data in each card is important. Data like this could not be punched into a card, beginning at the left and continuing until all characters were entered. Since the catalog numbers have different numbers of digits, it would not be possible to determine where a catalog number ended and a price began.

Catalog Number	Unit Price	Description
15	37.53	Hand set
3265	1.25	Amplifier
1007	253.00	Tube
22~	150.00	Speaker

Therefore, cards are designed in such a way that the same type of data always appears in the same column of the card, like this:

The catalog number is always punched in columns 1 through 5. What is the largest number that could be punched into columns 1 through 5, if no commas were used? _____

- - - - - - - - - - - - - - - - - -

99999

30. By omitting commas, catalog numbers from 1 to 99,999 can be recorded in five card columns. If the comma were included, what is the largest number that could be recorded in five columns? _____

- - - - - - - - - - - - - - - - - - - -

9,999

31. How would the number 1 be represented in five card columns? _____

- - - - - - - - - - - - - - - - - - -

00001

32. Since a much larger number can be recorded in a given number of columns by omitting commas than by including them, commas are omitted when cards are punched, even though they may appear on the source document. Devices that print reports can be instructed to reinsert the commas on printed output as needed.

Each piece of data is recorded in a <u>field</u>. A field is the space, or number of columns, reserved for that type of data when a card is designed. Each field on a card holds a different type of data and has a different name. How many fields are there in this card? _____

- - - - - - - - - - - - - - - - - - - -

DATA-PROCESSING PRINCIPLES 29

five (The blank portion at the right-hand end of the card is not considered to be a field, since no data is to be recorded there.)

33. What is the largest number that can be punched in the field called
QUANTITY ON HAND? _____

- - - - - - - - - - - - - - - - - - - -

9999 (Remember, commas are omitted.)

34. What is the largest dollar amount that can be punched in the field called
PRICE if a dollar sign ($) and a decimal point are <u>included</u>? _____
If both of these are omitted? _____

- - - - - - - - - - - - - - - - - - - -

$99.99; 999999 ($9,999.99)

35. As with the comma, it is convenient to omit the dollar sign and the decimal point from dollar amounts when they are punched into cards, since they can be reinserted during the printing operation. Although these omissions make reading the interpreted data a little difficult, the major consideration is the saving of card columns. For example, punching $26,327,589.65 as 2632758965 saves four card columns. Remember, there are only 80 columns on a card and frequently all the data required to make up a unit record can be accomodated only by making these omissions.

When cards are designed, the size of each field is determined by considering the largest piece of data that the field will have to accomodate. If the most costly item in a catalog is $327.50, how many columns should be assigned to a field called PRICE? _____

- - - - - - - - - - - - - - - - - - - -

five (The dollar sign and decimal point are omitted.)

36. Omitting the decimal point in a dollar amount creates a problem. How should $37.50 be punched into a five-column field?

Like this?   this?   or this?

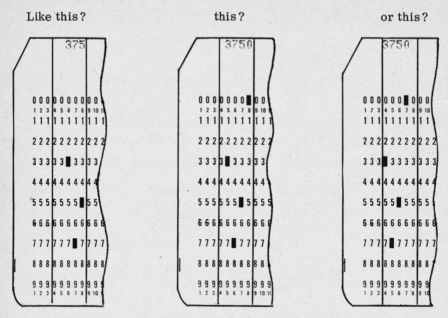

To overcome this possible confusion, a simple rule is used. All numeric data (data consisting of numbers only) is punched so that the last digit is in the right-hand column of the field. That is, it is punched so that any unused columns in the field are at the left-hand side of the field. If a dollar amount is being punched, such as $25.00, then the zeros on the dimes and cents columns must be included. Which of these shows $53.20 correctly punched into a six-column field?

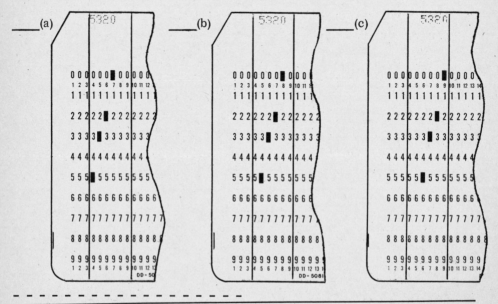

c

37. As an added precaution against numeric data being misread, the left-hand columns of the field are frequently filled with zeros. These indicate that no digits have been omitted. So $53.20 might be punched like this:

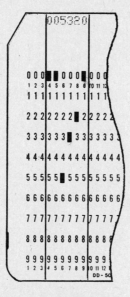

This operation is called <u>left-zero</u> <u>insertion</u>.

    Alphabetic data—names, descriptions, and the like—frequently take up a large number of columns. To reduce field sizes to a minimum, abbreviations are used wherever possible. For example, items from a catalog might be abbreviated like this: cabinet—cbnt; speaker—spkr; amplifier—amp; headset—hset; phonograph—phno. In this way all catalog descriptions can be put into a four-column field and still be recognizable. To spell them out in full would require at least ten columns. When a piece of alphabetic data does not completely fill the field in which it is punched, it is <u>left-justified</u>. That is, it is placed at the left-hand end of the field. Unused columns to the right of the data are left blank, like the punch card shown at the top of the next page.

    Although machines can be told to put decimal points and commas in numbers, it is not possible to tell them how to separate names from initials, since a name may have one, two, three, or even more initials. Apostrophes and spaces between names must also be included for the same reasons.

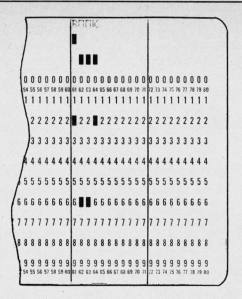

Which of the following is the best way to punch this name?

_____ (a) JACKSBASEMENTCAFE

_____ (b) JACKS BASEMENT CAFE

_____ (c) JACK'S BASEMENT CAFE

- - - - - - - - - - - - - - - - - -

c

38. Look at this partial list of sales made by a salesman.

Customer Number	Customer Name	Catalog Number	Quantity	Unit Price	Discount %
1027	Continental Cars	10030	216	15.00	5
3632	Jack's Imports Inc	572	1	376.75	10
2791	Fred's Place	1656	2	53.50	5
1100	Harris Autos	15763	50	3.75	--.
1001	Chevron Station	2	37	4.55	5

Assuming that the largest numbers and the longest name that will ever occur are shown by these four lines, write down the number of card columns that must be assigned to each field represented in the list.

_____

_____

- - - - - - - - - - - - - - - - - -

customer number, 4; customer name, 18 (JACK'S IMPORTS INC); catalog
number, 5; quantity, 3; unit price, 5; discount %, 2

39. Each transaction on the list of sales will be punched into a separate card.
This is _____ processing.

- - - - - - - - - - - - - - - - - - -

unit-record

40. The first field in the card will be the salesman number, which is never more
than 2 digits. It will be punched in columns 1 and 2. Customer number is 4 digits long. If this is to be punched immediately following the salesman number
(that is, with no blank columns between them), which card columns will it fill?

_____ (a) 3 through 7

_____ (b) 3 through 6

_____ (c) 3 through 5

- - - - - - - - - - - - - - - - - - - -

b (Four columns are needed—3, 4, 5, and 6.)

41. Again leaving no blank column, which columns will be filled by customer
name, if it follows customer number? _____

- - - - - - - - - - - - - - - - - -

7 through 24

42. To calculate the end point of a field when you know the starting point and
the length, you perform this calculation:

$$(start + length) - 1 = end point$$

In the example above we started in column 7 with a field 18 characters long.
Therefore:

$$end point = (7 + 18) - 1 = 24$$

The rest of the fields will be punched in the order in which they appear on
the sales list. Complete the table at the top of the next page. Show the card
columns that must be assigned to each field if there are to be no spaces between fields.

Field	Card Columns
Salesman number	1-2
Customer number	3-6
Customer name	7-24
Catalog number	25-____
Quantity	_____
Unit price	_____
Discount %	_____

- - - - - - - - - - - - - - - - - -

catalog number, 25-29; quantity, 30-32; unit price, 33-37; discount %, 38-39

43. When punched into a card, the first transaction looks like this:

What is the salesman's number? _____

- - - - - - - - - - - - - - - - - - -

19

CREATING A PUNCHED CARD

44. Just how do these holes get into the cards anyway? The most common way is through the use of a key-punch machine. Figure 2-10 at the top of the next page shows the IBM 029 Key Punch.

This machine allows an operator to record data from source documents in cards without handling each card individually or worrying about whether the card is lined up and ready for punching. The major concern of the operator is to hit the right keys in the right order.

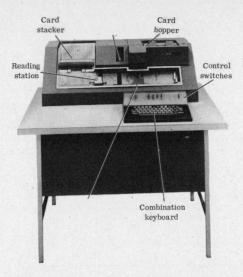

Figure 2-10. The IBM 029 Key Punch

The next photograph, Figure 2-11, shows the combination keyboard and control switches on the IBM 029. It is called a combination keyboard because it allows numeric, alphabetic, and special characters to be punched. (Another version of the IBM 029 has a keyboard with only numeric characters.)

Figure 2-11. Closeup of Combination Keyboard and
Control Switches on IBM 029 Key Punch

Although it looks much like a regular typewriter keyboard, it has some important differences. The keys that punch numeric characters are arranged at the right-hand end of the keyboard to allow an operator to punch numeric data using the right hand only. Instead of upper- and lower-case shifts, the keyboard shifts from alphabetic to numeric characters and vice versa. Most special characters and all digits are punched with the keyboard in numeric shift.

The switches above the keyboard control various functions of the machine. For example, the third switch from the right controls the printing of characters on the card as it is punched. A card may be interpreted or not, depending on the position of this switch. The switch at the right-hand end is for clearing cards from the machine when a punching job is completed.

The key-punch machine has many features designed to make the task of punching cards as easy and error-free as possible. However, since key-punch operators are human, some errors may be made. As you will recall, after data has been recorded at the input stage of the data-processing cycle,

its accuracy is _____.

- - - - - - - - - - - - - - - - -

verified

45. A machine called a verifier is used to verify the accuracy of data punched into cards. This machine is almost the same as a key punch, except that it can be set up so that no holes are punched in cards. The verifier operator feeds the punched cards through the verifier and presses the appropriate keys on the keyboard, working from the original source documents. No holes are punched, however. Instead, the verifier compares each character pressed with the character in the appropriate column of the card. If they match, the card moves one column to the left, ready for the verification of the character in the next column.

When the character punched in the card does not match that pressed by the operator, a notch is cut above the appropriate column. The operator then completes the verification of the card. Cards that have no errors are notched at the right-hand end, opposite row 1. Figure 2-12 at the top of the next page shows two cards that have been through a verifier. One is verified as being

correct. In which columns are errors indicated on the other? _____

- - - - - - - - - - - - - - - - -

57, 58, 62

46. When all the cards in a deck have been through the verifier, it is easy to pick out those that contain errors and have to be repunched. A skilled operator can feed these cards through a key punch, duplicating all columns that contain no errors and manually punching only those that have to be corrected. This eliminates the possibility of new errors being punched into a card.

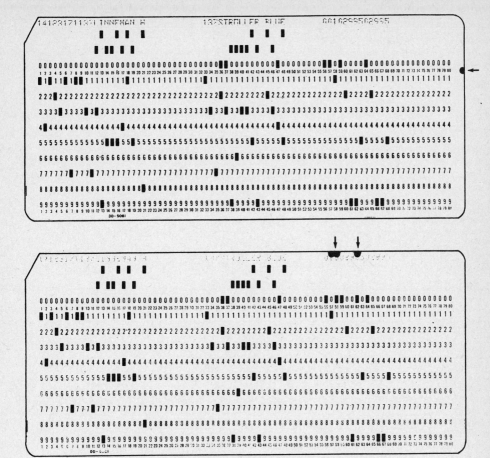

Figure 2-12. Cards Notched by a Verifier

Although it is a time-consuming task, verification of cards is essential, since the accuracy of output from a data-processing cycle depends on the accuracy of the input.

Where is the notch cut if the card is verified as correct?

- - - - - - - - - - - - - - - - - -

at the right-hand end, opposite row 1

47. Another way of recording data on punched cards is through the card punch. This is a device that is connected directly to a computer and punches cards as part of the output stage of the data-processing cycle. The card punch is illustrated in Chapter 3.

We have defined a record as a collection of data treated as a unit and generally discussed a record as the data that can be recorded in a single punched card. Records fall into three broad categories: master records, detail records, and summary records.

A <u>master record</u> contains data that is fairly constant in nature. For example, a card containing customer number, name, address, and applicable credit terms would be a master record. None of these items would change very often. The major items printed on a report are taken from master records. In the example above, a bill would include information about the customer (number, name, and the like) that is found on the master record. Information about each individual purchase would be found on detail records.

A <u>detail record</u> contains data that relates to only one transaction or event. It might contain a customer number and name and then data relating to a particular sale—catalog number, description, unit price, number ordered, and so on. Each item on an invoice would be recorded in a separate detail record.

In a payroll application, cards that contained data such as employee number, name, and number of hours worked this week would be _____ records, whereas those containing employee number, name, address, hourly wage, and number of exemptions claimed would be _____ records.

- - - - - - - - - - - - - - - - - -

detail, master

48. Match the following:

_____ (1) master record

_____ (2) detail record

    (a) contains student number, name, address, year of school

    (b) contains student number, class number, number of units, grade

    (c) contains account number, amount of this payment

- - - - - - - - - - - - - - - - - -

(1) a; (2) b, c

49. Although data in a master record is considered to be relatively permanent, the degree of this permanence depends on the application. A record containing name, address, and social-security number could remain unchanged for years. Data in a master record might, however, be changed fairly often. In an inventory-control job, a master record might contain: part number, description, location, minimum number to be maintained on hand, and current number on hand. The last piece of data will be constantly changing in the warehouse, but it may be changed in the master record only once a week when an inventory check is run. Each time an item is removed from, or placed in, the warehouse, a detail card is prepared. Each week these cards are processed, and a new master card is produced. Just one piece of data in the master record changes each week—the number on hand.

Match the following:

_____ (1) master record

_____ (2) detail record

(a) contains data that never changes
(b) contains data related to one transaction or event
(c) contains data that is relatively constant

- - - - - - - - - - - - - - - - - - -

(1) c; (2) b

50. The third basic type of record is the <u>summary record</u>. It is a summary
of a number of transactions, each of which is recorded in a separate

_____ record.

- - - - - - - - - - - - - - - - -

detail

51. The summary record could be a summary of all transactions from one
customer, or of all transactions involving the same catalog item. The summary card can be used for the production of reports that do not require the
details of each transaction to be printed. In an inventory application, a summary of the total purchases by customers might be required. An individual
customer might have purchased 50 different items, each recorded in a detail
record. Data about the customer (name, number, address, and so on) and the

total of all his or her purchases would be punched into a _____
record.

- - - - - - - - - - - - - - - - - -

summary

52. This summary record, together with many others, could then be used to
prepare a report showing the total value of purchases, arranged by customer.

To summarize, individual transactions are recorded in _____

records, whereas _____ records contain data that is fairly
permanent in nature. Summary records contain data that is generated from

processing two or more _____ records.

- - - - - - - - - - - - - - - - - -

detail, master, detail

53. A deck of related records is called a <u>file</u>. For example, all the detail records produced from invoices might be called a <u>transactions</u> <u>file</u>. Just as a record is a collection of related data, so a file is a collection of related

_____.

- - - - - - - - - - - - - - - - -

records

54. Note the similarity of the word <u>file</u> in "computer talk" and in everyday language. We talk of "having a file on so-and-so" as meaning we have a collection of records about a person arranged together in one place. You might

expect a collection of master records to be called a _____.

- - - - - - - - - - - - - - - - -

master file

55. A collection of related records is called a _____ and a

collection of related _____ is called a record.

- - - - - - - - - - - - - - - - -

file, data

OVERVIEW OF A PUNCHED-CARD
DATA-PROCESSING CYCLE

56. We will end this chapter by putting together what you have just learned with what you learned about the data-processing cycle in Chapter 1.

    Figure 2-13 shows the daily sales report we saw earlier. The report is

DAILY SALES REPORT

Salesman *George, J. F.*   Number *14*   Date *Dec. 31, 1971*

Customer Number	Customer Name	Catalog Number	Description	Qty	Unit Price	Total Price
1007	Hereford, E.	101	Socks #15	3	2.00	6.00
3271	Linneman, H.	137	Stroller blue	1	29.95	29.95
3271	Linneman, H.	137	Hood blue	1	6.25	6.25
3271	Linneman, H.	247	Back pack grn	1	15.75	15.75
2629	Swerdlick, J.	151	Harness	2	19.95	39.90

Figure 2-13. Daily Sales Report

filled out daily by each salesperson to record their business for the day. This, the first step of the data-processing cycle, is called _____.

- - - - - - - - - - - - - - - - - -

data entry

57. At the end of the week each salesperson turns in the daily reports and they are sent to be keypunched.
   Which of these statements best describes how they would be keypunched?

_____ (a) A clerk would add up the total sales for each person and punch that total onto a card.

_____ (b) Each line on the daily report would be punched onto a separate card.

_____ (c) All the information on a daily report would be punched onto one card.

_____ (d) none of the above

- - - - - - - - - - - - - - - - - -

b

58. When each line is punched onto a card, the information in each column would be punched onto a separate _____.

- - - - - - - - - - - - - - - - - -

field

59. How many columns in the card would be needed to record customer number? _____ Unit price? _____

- - - - - - - - - - - - - - - - - -

customer number—4; unit price—4

60. When all the records for one week have been punched and verified, they are all put together to make a _____.

- - - - - - - - - - - - - - - - - -

file

61. Which type of file do you think they would be?

_____ (a) master file

_____ (b) detail file

_____ (c) summary file

_____ (d) none of the above

- - - - - - - - - - - - - - - - - - - -

b

62. The detail file, consisting of one record for each transaction, would be used as <u>input</u> to the computer. What is the next step in the cycle?

_____ (a) storage

_____ (b) processing

_____ (c) output

_____ (d) none of the above

- - - - - - - - - - - - - - - - - - -

b

63. During the processing step, all the necessary calculations are performed to produce the required output. What is the set of instructions to the computer called?

_____ (a) an operator

_____ (b) an analysis

_____ (c) a program

_____ (d) all of the above

- - - - - - - - - - - - - - - - - - -

c

64. The program contains all the instructions necessary to produce the output. For example, the total weekly sales for each salesperson may be calculated by adding the totals in each detail card. If each salesperson earns a commission, the total commission earned in the week would also be calculated.

   To make the final report meaningful, it would be better to use each salesperson's name, rather than their number as punched in the detail cards. What type of record is the salesperson's name most likely to be punched in?

_____ (a) detail record

_____ (b) master record

_____ (c) summary record

_____ (d) none of the above

- - - - - - - - - - - - - - - - - - -

b

65. So in order to produce a report like that in Figure 2-14, the computer would process a detail file and a master file. Notice that the names are in alphabetical order. This sorting was also done at the processing step, after the computer had matched the detail records with the appropriate master records.

WEEKLY COMMISSION REPORT

Week Ending: December 31, 1971

Name	Sales	Commission Earned
Andrews, Hal	$1,278.00	$127.80
Fleming, Lillie	1,758.76	175.88
George, Hope	2,356.89	235.69
Harris, Andrew	529.80	52.98
Smith, James	987.10	98.71
TOTAL	$13,982.10	$1,398.21

Figure 2-14. Weekly Commission Report

If the management of this company also wanted a monthly commission report, which of these ways would be the best to produce it?

_____ (a) At the end of each month, punch all the transactions into cards and write a monthly report.

_____ (b) Put all the detail cards from the four weeks and run them as a new detail file.

_____ (c) Punch the results of the weekly report into cards and use these to produce a monthly report.

_____ (d) none of the above

- - - - - - - - - - - - - - - - - - -

c

66. Actually, any of these methods could be used, but the most efficient would be to punch the results of the weekly report into cards at the same time as the report is written. The computer would punch for each salesperson one card

that contained the salesperson's number, total sales, and commission earned. Since this record is produced from several detail records, it is called a

_____ record.

- - - - - - - - - - - - - - - - - - -

summary

The input for the monthly processing would be the few weekly summary files. This would be far fewer cards to read than if all the detail records from each week were to be reprocessed.

This is the end of Chapter 2. You should now work the Self-Test that follows.

SELF-TEST

Answer all the questions and then check against the answers that follow.

1. Label the indicated parts of this punched card.

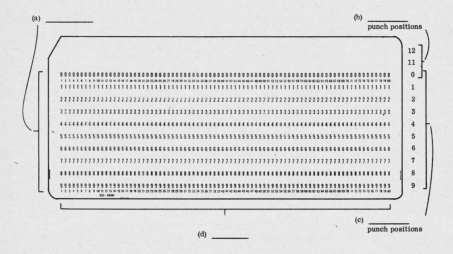

2. How many holes are used, and where are they punched, to represent numeric characters? _____
    Alphabetic characters? _____

3. What is the minimum number of columns needed to represent $1,327,456.75? _____

4. When characters are both punched into and printed on a card, it is said to be _____.

5. Punched-card data processing is sometimes called unit-record data processing because:

    _____ (a) only one character at a time is read from a card.

    _____ (b) each card records data from only one transaction.

    _____ (c) one record may be used in the production of several reports.

    _____ (d) none of the above

6. When a card is designed, each type of data is allocated to a

    _____ in which to be recorded.

7. What characters are omitted when numeric data is recorded in punched

    cards? _____

8. Using the blank card below, lay out a card design that accommodates this data in this order. (Allow 20 columns for names.)

Department number	153
Employee number	2758
Name	Rosenthal, N. J.
Social-security number	379 26 5221
Sex	M
Birth data	9.24.39
Hiring date	12.15.62
Starting wage	$2.15
Current wage	$6.78

9. Which of these statements is true of the verifier?

    _____ (a) It punches a notch over each correct column on the card.

    _____ (b) It punches a notch on the right-hand edge of each card that contains an error.

_____ (c) both

_____ (d) neither

10. Which of these statements is true?

_____ (a) A file is a collection of related records.

_____ (b) A record is a collection of related data.

_____ (c) both

_____ (d) neither

11. Match the following:

_____ (1) master record

_____ (2) detail record

_____ (3) summary record

(a) contains data about more than one transaction or event

(b) contains data that is relatively constant

(c) contains data generated by the processing of two or more records

(d) contains data related to one transaction or event

Answers to Self-Test

The numbers in parentheses refer to the frames in which the appropriate answers can be found. If you have a wrong answer or are not sure why your answer is correct, read that section of the chapter again before going on.

1. (a) rows; (b) zone; (c) digit; (d) columns (frame 4)

2. Numeric: one hole in digit-punch position (frame 7)
Alphabetic: two holes, one in zone-punch position and one in digit-punch position (frame 10)

3. Nine columns (132745675) (frame 29)

4. interpreted (frame 17)

5. b (frame 28)

6. field (frame 29)

7. $, comma, decimal point (frame 29)

8.

Dept. #	Emp. #	Name	Social Security #	Sex	Birth Date	Hiring Date	Starting Wage	Current Wage

```
0 0 0|0 0 0|0 0 0 0 0 0 0 0 0 0 0 0 0 0 0 0 0 0 0 0 0 0 0|0 0 0 0 0 0 0 0 0 0|0|0 0 0 0 0 0|0 0 0 0 0 0 0 0|0 0 0|0 0|0 0 0 0 0 0 0 0 0 0 0 0 0 0 0 0 0 0 0 0 0 0 0 0
  1 2 3 4 5 6 7 8 9 10 11 12 13 14 15 16 17 18 19 20 21 22 23 24 25 26 27 28 29 30 31 32 33 34 35 36 37 38 39 40 41 42 43 44 45 46 47 48 49 50 51 52 53 54 55 56 57 58 59 60 61 62 63 64 65 66 67 68 69 70 71 72 73 74 75 76 77 78 79 80
1 1 1|1 1 1 1|1 1 1 1 1 1 1 1 1 1 1 1 1 1 1 1 1 1 1 1 1 1|1 1 1 1 1 1 1 1 1|1 1 1 1 1 1|1 1 1 1 1 1 1|1 1 1|1 1 1|1 1 1 1 1 1 1 1 1 1 1 1 1 1 1 1 1 1 1 1 1 1 1 1 1
2 2 2|2 2 2 2|2 2 2 2 2 2 2 2 2 2 2 2 2 2 2 2 2 2 2 2 2 2|2 2 2 2 2 2 2 2 2|2|2 2 2 2 2 2|2 2 2 2 2 2 2|2 2 2|2 2 2|2 2 2 2 2 2 2 2 2 2 2 2 2 2 2 2 2 2 2 2 2 2 2 2 2
3 3 3|3 3 3 3|3 3 3 3 3 3 3 3 3 3 3 3 3 3 3 3 3 3 3 3 3 3|3 3 3 3 3 3 3 3 3|3|3 3 3 3 3 3|3 3 3 3 3 3 3|3 3 3|3 3 3|3 3 3 3 3 3 3 3 3 3 3 3 3 3 3 3 3 3 3 3 3 3 3 3 3
4 4 4|4 4 4 4|4 4 4 4 4 4 4 4 4 4 4 4 4 4 4 4 4 4 4 4 4 4|4 4 4 4 4 4 4 4 4|4|4 4 4 4 4 4|4 4 4 4 4 4 4|4 4 4|4 4 4|4 4 4 4 4 4 4 4 4 4 4 4 4 4 4 4 4 4 4 4 4 4 4 4 4
5 5 5|5 5 5 5|5 5 5 5 5 5 5 5 5 5 5 5 5 5 5 5 5 5 5 5 5 5|5 5 5 5 5 5 5 5 5|5|5 5 5 5 5 5|5 5 5 5 5 5 5|5 5 5|5 5 5|5 5 5 5 5 5 5 5 5 5 5 5 5 5 5 5 5 5 5 5 5 5 5 5 5
6 6 6|6 6 6 6|6 6 6 6 6 6 6 6 6 6 6 6 6 6 6 6 6 6 6 6 6 6|6 6 6 6 6 6 6 6 6|6|6 6 6 6 6 6|6 6 6 6 6 6 6|6 6 6|6 6 6|6 6 6 6 6 6 6 6 6 6 6 6 6 6 6 6 6 6 6 6 6 6 6 6 6
7 7 7|7 7 7 7|7 7 7 7 7 7 7 7 7 7 7 7 7 7 7 7 7 7 7 7 7 7|7 7 7 7 7 7 7 7 7|7|7 7 7 7 7 7|7 7 7 7 7 7 7|7 7 7|7 7 7|7 7 7 7 7 7 7 7 7 7 7 7 7 7 7 7 7 7 7 7 7 7 7 7 7
8 8 8|8 8 8 8|8 8 8 8 8 8 8 8 8 8 8 8 8 8 8 8 8 8 8 8 8 8|8 8 8 8 8 8 8 8 8|8|8 8 8 8 8 8|8 8 8 8 8 8 8|8 8 8|8 8 8|8 8 8 8 8 8 8 8 8 8 8 8 8 8 8 8 8 8 8 8 8 8 8 8 8
9 9 9|9 9 9 9|9 9 9 9 9 9 9 9 9 9 9 9 9 9 9 9 9 9 9 9 9 9|9 9 9 9 9 9 9 9 9|9|9 9 9 9 9 9|9 9 9 9 9 9 9|9 9 9|9 9 9|9 9 9 9 9 9 9 9 9 9 9 9 9 9 9 9 9 9 9 9 9 9 9 9 9
DD-5091
```

(frame 29)

9. b (frame 44)

10. c (frame 53)

11. (1) b; (2) d; (3) c (frame 47)

CHAPTER THREE
An Overview
of Computer Systems

This chapter is designed to give you a broad overview of computer systems. You will learn the basic components of a computer system and the relationships between them. You will also become familiar with a wide range of equipment for the input and output of data. Finally, you will study a series of typical computer systems.

After completing this chapter you will be able to:

- describe the components of the <u>central processing unit</u>;
- describe the function of the <u>storage unit</u>, the <u>control unit</u>, and the <u>arithmetic-logic unit</u>;
- identify a wide range of equipment as <u>input</u>, <u>output</u>, <u>input-output</u>, and/or <u>auxiliary-storage</u> devices;
- describe <u>sequential</u> and <u>random-access processing</u>;
  describe specialized equipment such as <u>magnetic-character reader-sorter</u>, <u>optical-character recognition</u>, and <u>computer-output-to microfilm</u> devices; and
- describe various <u>data-entry</u> devices.

1.   In Chapters 1 and 2 we have made reference to <u>computer systems</u>. A computer system consists of a wide variety of <u>devices</u>, each performing a specific, and limited, function. For example, a machine that reads punched cards is essential to most computer systems, but is not itself a computer. Similarly, a machine that prints reports is not a computer, but is an important part of most computer systems.

A typical computer system is shown in Figure 3-1 at the top of the next page. Although the individual pieces of equipment may appear to be independent of one another, they are in fact connected by electrical cables under the floor.

Figure 3-1. The IBM 370/135 Computer System

The heart of a computer system is the central processing unit, or CPU. The CPU has three basic parts, as shown in Figure 3-2 below. The control unit interprets instructions—those contained in a program for example—and issues the appropriate commands to the other two parts of the CPU as well as to other devices in the computer system.

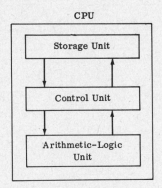

Figure 3-2. The Central Processing Unit

The storage unit holds instructions and data necessary for any particular use of the computer system. It is the common link between all parts of the system.

The arithmetic-logic unit performs all the required operations, arithmetic and logical, on data supplied to the computer system.

Match the following:

_____ (1) storage unit

_____ (2) arithmetic-logic unit

_____ (3) control unit

(a) performs required operations on data

(b) common link between all devices in a computer system

(c) interprets instructions

(d) issues commands

(1) b;   (2) a;   (3) c, d

2.   Let's now look at the functions of each part of the CPU in more detail, beginning with the storage section. You will recall that a program is a detailed set of instructions that tells a computer system exactly what kind of data it is to use for input, what operations to perform on that data, and what type of output to produce. After a programmer has written the program, it is converted into a form that the computer can understand. (How this is done will be explained in detail in Chapter 8.) When a program is in use, it is placed, or stored, in the storage unit. Also in the storage unit is a space for the input data and another space for the output data. Chapter 5 explains in detail how data is stored and how the computer knows exactly where it is stored.

Also in the storage section at all times is a special program, supplied by the computer manufacturer, called the supervisor. The supervisor contains all the instructions necessary for controlling the operation of the entire computer system, for transferring data from one device to another, and for checking that all devices are functioning correctly. The supervisor will be discussed in more detail in Chapter 9.

Which of these statements is true?

_____   (a) The storage unit controls the operation of the computer system.

_____   (b) The supervisor is a program that controls the operation of the computer system.

_____   (c) The storage unit contains the program being used by the computer system and input and output data for that program.

_____   (d) all of the above

- - - - - - - - - - - - - - - - - - -

b, c

3.   The storage unit of the CPU just stores instructions and data; it does not interpret instructions or process data. The interpretation of the instructions in a program is done by the control unit. Instructions in the program are transferred, one at a time, to the control unit, where an instruction is analyzed to see which devices and what data are needed to carry out that instruction. The control unit then sends messages that will transfer data from device to device. Or it may send messages to the arithmetic-logic unit telling what operations to perform on data.

The arithmetic-logic unit performs arithmetic operations and makes logical decisions based on data. Arithmetic operations—addition, subtraction, multiplication, and division—are performed on data according to the instructions received from the control unit. Logical decisions about the arithmetic operations to be performed can also be made. For example, "If sex is female, add one to number-of-females; otherwise add one to number-of-males" involves making a logical decision as to whether to add one to number-of-females or one to number-of-males. The control unit tells the arithmetic-logic unit what operations to perform and where it will find the necessary data.

Match the following:

_____ (1) storage unit

_____ (2) control unit

_____ (3) arithmetic-logic unit

(a) performs operations such as multiplication and addition

(b) interprets instructions in a program

(c) contains the program being processed

(d) contains the supervisor

- - - - - - - - - - - - - - - - - -

(1) c, d; (2) b; (3) a

4. Many computer programs have so many instructions and require so much data that there is not room in the CPU storage unit for them. To handle these cases, an <u>auxiliary storage</u> component is used. This auxiliary storage is separate from the central processing unit, but the control unit is able to transfer instructions and data to and from it at will.

A computer system can perform only five basic types of operation—arithmetic, logical, data transfer, data input, and data output. As we have seen, the first three are performed by the central processing unit. Data-input and data-output operations can be performed by a wide variety of devices; most of the rest of this chapter is devoted to an overview of these devices.

Figure 3-3 shows the relationships between the central processing unit, auxiliary storage, input devices, and output devices.

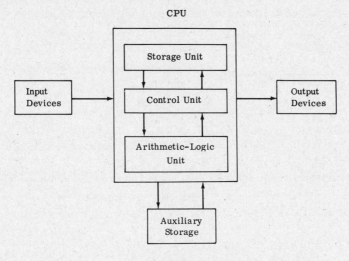

Figure 3-3. Relationships Between Components
of a Computer System

<u>Input devices</u> can take many forms and there may be many input devices connected to the CPU at one time. Whatever type of input device is being used, however, the input data is converted into electrical impulses that are

transferred to predetermined locations in storage. Input consists of two basic types—instructions to the computer on how to process data and data to be processed.

Instructions are transferred from storage to the control unit, which interprets them and then tells the other components what to do with the data or where to put data in storage. For example, if data from two fields are to be added together to create data for a third field, the control unit issues the appropriate command to the arithmetic-logic unit. This unit then transfers the proper data from storage, performs the addition, and transfers the result back into storage.

As processing is completed, the control unit issues commands to one of the many output devices that may be connected to the CPU to transfer processed data from storage and record it in whatever form is required.

Which of these statements is true?

_____ (a) Only data to be processed is placed in auxiliary storage.

_____ (b) Many input and output devices may be connected to the CPU at the same time.

_____ (c) both

_____ (d) neither

- - - - - - - - - - - - - - - - - -

b

5. Let's briefly review before we discuss input and output devices in more detail.

Instructions to the computer system are interpreted by the _____

_____ and then issued as commands to other components.

- - - - - - - - - - - - - - - - -

control unit

6. What two types of information are placed in storage by the input component? _____

- - - - - - - - - - - - - - - - -

instructions and data to be processed

7. Which of these components is usually contained in the central processing unit?

_____ (a) arithmetic-logic unit

_____ (b) output

_____ (c) auxiliary storage

_____ (d) none of the above

- - - - - - - - - - - - - - - - - -

a

8.   From which component(s) does the arithmetic-logic unit obtain data to
operate on? _____

- - - - - - - - - - - - - - - - - -

storage

9.   The storage component contains:

_____ (a) instructions.

_____ (b) data to be processed.

_____ (c) results of computations in the arithmetic-logic unit.

_____ (d) all of the above

- - - - - - - - - - - - - - - - - -

d

10. Now let's look at input and output devices in more detail. They will be
discussed together because the two functions are frequently combined into one
piece of equipment.

     As we explained in Chapter 2, the punched card still has an important role
in computer systems. Although the amount of data that can be recorded in it
is limited to 80 characters, the punched card has the advantage of being easily
punched, verified, sorted, and collated on punched-card machines. These
machines are called peripheral devices because they are not linked directly to
the CPU. Therefore they are not part of the computer system, although they
are an important part of the total operation of a data-processing department.
Refer to Appendix I for a brief overview of punched-card peripheral devices.

     The fact that punched cards can be interpreted and read by people makes
them a very versatile medium. For example, many bills are printed on
punched cards and mailed to customers. The information printed on the card
includes the amount owed by the customer and the customer number. This is
done as an output operation of the computer. The customer writes the amount
paid on the card and mails it back with a check. The amount paid is then keypunched into the card. This new data (along with the customer number) is then
used when the card serves as input to a program to produce the next month's
bill.

The versatility of the punched card also leads to serious disadvantages. Cards that have been bent, folded, or mutilated cannot be processed through a machine. Individual cards can also be lost fairly easily. Finally, after a stack of cards has been sorted into some special sequence, they can be dropped, necessitating resorting.

Data from punched cards is transferred to storage by means of a <u>card reader</u>, acting as an input device. Output from the computer may be punched into cards by a <u>card punch</u>. These two devices are frequently combined into a single unit, a card <u>read-punch</u> unit, which acts as an input-output device. Figure 3-4 shows such a unit.

This unit is capable of reading input data from one card file and punching output data into another card file at the same time. The card read-punch unit is, however, a relatively slow input-output device.

Figure 3-4. The IBM 2540 Card Read-Punch Unit

But how are punched cards read? By far, the most common method is through the use of reading brushes. Figure 3-5 at the top of the next page shows how the reading is done. In a unit that reads punched cards, there is one brush for each of the 80 card columns. Figure 3-5 shows just one brush reading one column.

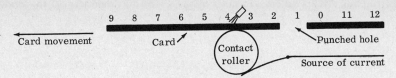

Card passing between contact roller and brush acts as an insulator so that no impulse is available at the brush.

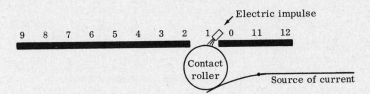

When brush makes contact with roller, a circuit is completed and an electrical impulse is available to instruct the machine to do a specific job.

Figure 3-5. Schematic of Brush Reading Numeral 1

An electrical current is supplied to the contact roller. The card moves between the brush and the roller. Where no holes have been punched in the card, the brush is kept from making contact with the roller so no current flows. However, when a hole in the card passes over the roller, the brush falls through the card and makes contact with the roller. Thus, a very brief electrical current, called an electrical impulse, will flow. As soon as the hole passes the roller, the brush and roller are again separated and no current flows.

Because the speed at which the card moves between the brush and roller is fixed, the machine knows which row has been punched. Thus, it can determine which character is punched into a column by determining how many holes there are and where they occur. Remember, all 80 columns are read at the same time. The electrical impulses that are generated flow through a control panel and are directed to appropriate locations within the machine.

The second method of reading cards uses light and photo-electric cells in place of the roller and brushes. Figure 3-6 at the top of the next page shows the light system.

In some respects this method of reading cards is similar to the operation of a photo-electric burglar alarm. When light falls on the cell, an electric current is generated. Each time a hole passes between the light source and the cell, an electrical impulse is generated, which is then used in the same way as the impulses generated in the brush reading system. There are 80 photo-electric cells in the reading unit, one for each column of the card. Light readers have the advantage of being much faster than the brush readers.

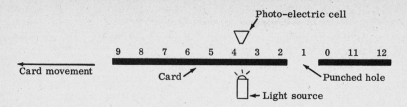

Card passing between light source and photo-electric cell prevents current from being generated in cell.

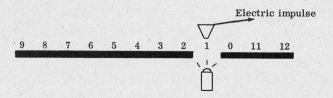

When hole comes between light source and photo-electric cell, electrical current is generated in cell.

Figure 3-6. Schematic of Light Reading Numeral 1

A card-reading unit reads:

_____ (a) all rows in the card at the same time.

_____ (b) all columns in the card at the same time.

_____ (c) both

_____ (d) neither

- - - - - - - - - - - - - - - - -

b

11. Which of these statements is true?

_____ (a) Brush card readers are faster than light readers.

_____ (b) Both types of card readers generate electrical impulses.

_____ (c) both

_____ (d) neither

- - - - - - - - - - - - - - - - -

b

12. Another common way of recording data is on a <u>magnetic tape</u>. Figure 3-7 shows a magnetic tape drive and a reel of magnetic tape.

Figure 3-7. The CDC 667 Magnetic Tape Drive
and Reel of Magnetic Tape

In some respects they are not unlike regular tape recorders. Just as you can record music on a tape recorder and then play it back again, so data can be recorded on magnetic tape. The magnetic tape drive can both record data on tape and read data off tape, although not at the same time. When data is read from the tape, the drive is acting as an input device, the data being transferred into the storage unit of the CPU. The drive acts as an output device when data is transferred from storage to the magnetic tape.

Magnetic tape has three major advantages over punched cards. First, data can be transferred to and from tape at very high speeds. Second, the individual records written on tape can be very large; the number of characters per record being determined by the characteristics of the computer system in use rather than by the characteristics of magnetic tape. Third, since tapes are typically 2,400 to 3,600 feet long, millions of characters can be stored on them. A single magnetic tape could record the equivalent of over 100,000 punched cards.

Characters are represented on magnetic tape by tiny magnetized spots, each alphabetic and numeric character having its own unique arrangement of magnetic spots. Because the spots can be placed very close together, magnetic tapes can record from 500 to 3,000 characters per inch.

The operator can remove a reel of magnetic tape from the tape drive and replace it with another reel. This means that a tape containing data that has to be used only once a week can be stored out of the system when not in use. When the data is required, the operator replaces the tape on the drive unit.

Magnetic tapes do have three major disadvantages, however. First, the data on a tape may only be processed sequentially. That is, the records on a tape have to be read in the order in which they are written on the tape. Assume we have a tape containing one record for each of 1,000 employees, arranged by employee number. To read the record for employee number 789, we would have to read all the records for employees 1 through 788 first. There is no convenient way for the CPU to instruct the tape drive to skip to record number

789. So unless most of the records on a tape are needed for processing each time the tape is used, the use of tapes can be quite inefficient.

Second, although a tape may be used for both input and output operations, it cannot be used for both at the same time. Therefore, if we need to add records to a file that is stored on tape, we must read all the records from the tape and write them onto another tape, inserting the new records at the appropriate places.

Third, identification of tapes is difficult. Since the data stored on them cannot be read by the human eye, quite elaborate labeling systems must be used. This is especially important because some computer installations have thousands of tapes to keep track of. In addition to putting labels on the outside of the tape, the first part of the data in a file stored on tape is usually for identification. Before reading the data from a tape, a program often instructs the computer system to check the identification on the beginning of the tape. Despite these precautions, even in well-run computer departments, mistakes are made and data is written onto tapes that should have been saved for further use.

Which of the following is true?

_____ (a) The card read-punch is frequently used as an auxiliary storage device.

_____ (b) The magnetic tape drive is a relatively slow input-output device.

_____ (c) both

_____ (d) neither

- - - - - - - - - - - - - - - - - - -

d

13. Which of these is a disadvantage of magnetic tape?

_____ (a) Only a small amount of data can be stored on a tape.

_____ (b) Tapes cannot be used as output devices.

_____ (c) Tapes are difficult to identify.

_____ (d) all of the above

- - - - - - - - - - - - - - - - - - -

c

14. The use of tapes is quite efficient when:

_____ (a) only a few records on the tape are to be processed.

_____ (b) most of the records on the tape are to be processed.

_____ (c) large amounts of data that are not constantly in use are to be stored.

_____ (d) none of the above

- - - - - - - - - - - - - - - - - -

b, c

15. Another very useful input-output device is shown in Figure 3-8.

Figure 3-8.   The IBM 3278 Keyboard Terminal

This keyboard terminal, often called a typewriter terminal, can be linked to
a computer system by means of a regular telephone line, making it an extremely useful device. A branch office hundreds of miles from the headquar-
ter's computer system can send input data and receive output by way of the
keyboard terminal.

The operator uses specified codes to "talk" to the computer, giving data
and asking for output. Both the operator's input and the computer's output are
printed on paper that is automatically fed through the terminal.

The display terminal is similar to the keyboard terminal, the main difference being that data is displayed on a screen and not printed out. The display terminal (shown in Figure 3-9 on the next page) can also be linked by
telephone line to a computer system.

Figure 3-9. The CDC 751-10 Display Terminal

Communication with the computer system is through the keyboard, and all input and output data is displayed on the screen. If suitable instructions are stored in the computer, the display station can show diagrams and graphs, which obviously is very useful in science and engineering. Airline-reservation systems often display a seating plan of the airplane, showing which seats have already been booked for a particular flight.

Terminals provide a quick and easy method of updating data files that are stored in a computer system. Operators who know the program for the computer system may have access to individual records within a file and may change them at will. This procedure eliminates the need to punch data into cards and, using a card reader, to update records in a file.

In the next chapter we will discuss terminals in more depth and describe more elaborate terminal systems.

Which of the following statements describes a keyboard terminal?

_____ (a) It may be used only as an input device.

_____ (b) It may be connected to a computer system by a telephone line.

_____ (c) both

_____ (d) neither

- - - - - - - - - - - - - - - - - - - -

b

16. Match the following:

_____ (1) card read-punch

_____ (2) display terminal

_____ (3) magnetic tape device

(a) can be used as auxiliary storage

(b) shows input and output data on a screen

(c) is a relatively slow input-output device

(d) operates only as an output device

- - - - - - - - - - - - - - - - - - -

(1) c; (2) b; (3) a (If you said that the display terminal is a relatively slow device, you're really thinking! It is only as fast as the fastest typist when used as an input device! And in computer terms, that's not very fast.)

17. Another important input-output medium is the magnetic disk pack, shown in Figure 3-10. The magnetic disk pack also serves as auxiliary storage and is one of the most useful and flexible data-storage mediums.

Figure 3-10. A Magnetic Disk Pack

A disk pack is made up of a series of metal disks stacked one above the other with a space between each. Data is recorded on each side of the disks by means of read-write heads which move in and out between them. These heads can read and write data at the same time. Data is recorded on the disks in the form of tiny magnetic spots, each character being represented by a unique combination of spots. As with magnetic tape, these spots can be placed very close together and a typical disk pack might hold 10 million characters— the equivalent of approximately 100,000 punched cards.

Although the storage capacity of a typical disk pack may not be greater than that of a typical magnetic tape, it has one major advantage over tapes.

Each record in a file stored on magnetic disk is located at a known <u>address</u>, or location. The read-write heads can be moved directly to any address on the disk, making it possible to have access to data in a particular record very rapidly. Similarly, new data may be written into a record very rapidly. Of course, if necessary, it is possible to read or write records in sequence.

This procedure is called <u>random access</u>. Random access allows the computer to go directly to a specific record in a file without reading all the preceding records. Thus, using the earlier example of sequential processing with tapes, if the employee file were stored on a magnetic disk, we could read the record for employee number 789 without reading most of the records for employees 1 through 788.

When in use, disk packs are mounted on <u>magnetic disk drives</u>, similar to the one shown in Figure 3-11. When the data on a particular disk pack is not required for processing, the disk pack can be removed from the drive and stored.

Figure 3-11. The CDC 844 Magnetic Disk Drive
and Controller

Which of these statements is true?

_____ (a) Although disk packs can store a large amount of data, they are relatively slow input-output devices.

_____ (b) Data may be recorded on only one side of a disk.

_____ (c) In order to find a needed piece of data, the disk must be searched from the beginning.

_____ (d) none of the above

- -

d

18. Figure 3-12 compares the characteristics of punched cards, magnetic tapes, and magnetic disk packs.

	Punched Cards	Magnetic Tape	Magnetic Disk
Record length	80 characters	Essentially unlimited	Essentially unlimited
Typical storage capacity (characters)	80	10 million	10 million
Type of processing	Sequential only	Sequential only	Sequential and random access
Speed of input-output operation	Slow	Fast	Very fast
Disadvantages	Easily damaged	Data not visible to naked eye, difficult to label	Data not visible to naked eye, relatively expensive

Figure 3-12. Comparison of Characteristics of Punched Cards, Magnetic Tapes, and Magnetic Disks

Another auxiliary storage device that has random-access capability is the magnetic drum. This is a large metal cylinder that rotates at high speed past fixed read-write heads. As with magnetic disks, data is stored on the surface of the drum in the form of magnetic spots. Figure 3-13 at the top of the next page shows a typical magnetic-drum storage unit.

Magnetic drums can store more data and read and write it much faster than is possible with magnetic disks. They are, however, considerably more expensive.

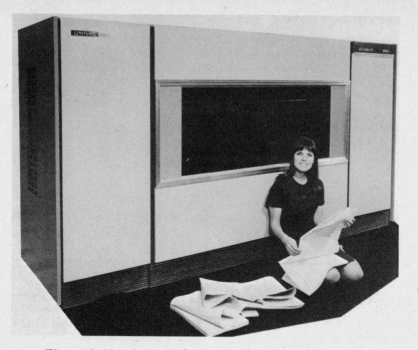

Figure 3-13.   A Typical Magnetic-Drum Storage Unit

Which of these statements is true?

_____ (a) In a magnetic disk drive the read-write heads are stationary.

_____ (b) Magnetic drums can store more data than magnetic disks.

_____ (c) Data can be read from magnetic disks faster than from magnetic drums.

_____ (d) none of the above

- - - - - - - - - - - - - - - - - - - -

b

19. Another input-output device that also serves as auxiliary storage is the data cell. This device is used in situations where very large amounts of data have to be readily accessible for processing at all times, as for example, in large insurance companies or banks having millions of accounts. The data cell combines both magnetic tape and magnetic disk technology.

Each data cell contains a strip of tape on which data can be recorded. When the data on a particular strip is needed for processing, the cell is moved mechanically to a read-write station. There the tape is unwound and can be accessed randomly for the required data. Once the data has been read and/or new data written, the tape is rewound onto the cell and the cell is moved back to its storage location.

Figure 3-14 shows data cells and the mechanism for moving them.

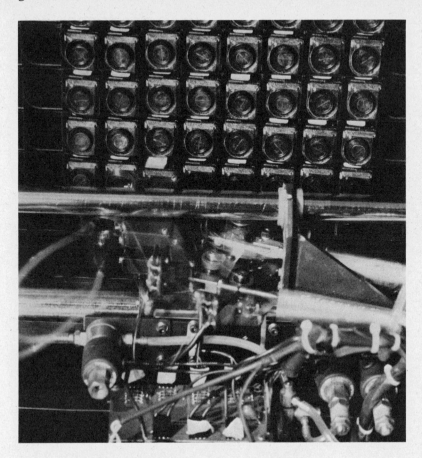

Figure 3-14. Data-Cell Storage System

A mass-storage unit in which data cells are stored is shown in Figure 3-15 at the top of the next page. This particular unit can hold 2,000 data cells, has up to four read-write stations, and can store up to 16 _billion_ characters. Because there is a mechanical process involved in moving data cells, access to data in this system is relatively slow, with access times being higher than for magnetic disks but lower than for magnetic tape drives.

Match the following:

_____ (1) fastest access time

_____ (2) slowest access time

  (a) magnetic disk
  (b) magnetic drum
  (c) magnetic tape
  (d) data cell

- - - - - - - - - - - - - - - - - -

(1) b; (2) c

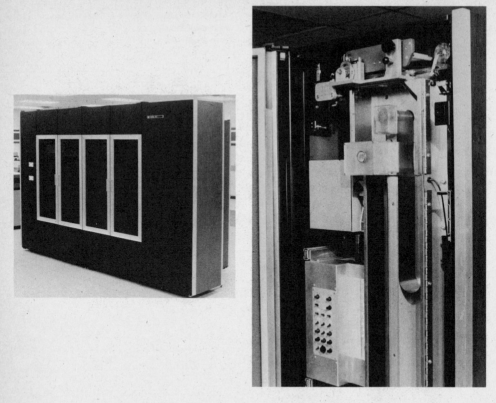

Figure 3-15. Control Data 38500 Mass Storage System

20. Now we will look at devices that are used for output only. By far the most common output device used in business is the line printer, which comes in many different sizes and versions, one of which is shown in Figure 3-16.

Figure 3-16. The IBM 3211 Line Printer

Printers operate in different ways, but all produce output that can be read by the human eye.

High-speed line printers can produce up to 15,000 lines of output <u>per min-ute</u>, although speeds of 1,000-3,000 lines per minute are more common. The characters are produced on the paper in much the same way as in a typewriter. Metal characters impact on a carbon ribbon that marks the character on the paper. Line printers, as their name suggests, print a whole line of text at one time, a line having up to 132 characters. The paper, a long, continuous sheet approximately 12 inches wide, is fed through the printer on sprockets. Perfor-ated at 11-inch intervals, it can be torn to produce sheets approximately 12 inches wide and 11 inches long. This is standard-sized computer-output paper. When a large number of sheets have been printed in a report, the resulting stack of paper is placed in a burster that mechanically "bursts" the sheets apart at the perforations, leaving a stack of single sheets.

Multiple copies of reports can be produced on a line printer by using mul-tiple layers of paper with carbon paper between them. When a report has been printed, the layers of paper are run through a decollator and separated into the appropriate number of individual copies. These individual copies are then separated into individual sheets in the burster.

Another popular type of line printer is called the <u>dot-matrix printer</u>. Rather than having sets of characters, a dot-matrix printer uses sets of 35 tiny wires to form the required character. Signals from the computer cause the appropriate wires to be extended from the holder and to impact a carbon ribbon, causing the character to be printed as a series of dots. Figure 3-17 shows the pattern that would be formed if all 35 wires were extended and how 14 of them are used to form character "4."

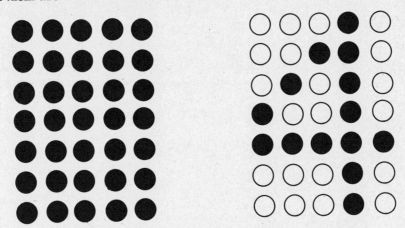

Figure 3-17. Dot-Matrix Character Representation

Both the line and dot-matrix printers are called <u>impact printers</u>, because characters are created on paper through impact on carbon ribbon. In other types of printers, called <u>nonimpact printers</u>, characters are created by heat, electrostatic energy, or laser beams.

Heat, or thermal, nonimpact printers frequently use a wire matrix similar to the dot-matrix impact printer. The wires needed to form a character are heated and brought into contact with heat-sensitive paper, burning a series of dots to represent each character. A typical portable printer that uses the thermal, nonimpact process is shown in Figure 4-8, page 94.

The electrostatic printer also uses a wire matrix to form characters by placing a series of invisible dots on special paper. The dots are formed by electrostatic impulses and become visible after a toner, or developer, is automatically applied to the paper.

Thermal and electrostatic nonimpact printers have the advantage of being very quiet when operating, but the disadvantages of being relatively slow and producing only one copy at a time.

One of the newest types of printers available is the laser printer. This printer uses a laser beam to burn characters on regular paper. It is the fastest type of printer available, capable of printing 20,000 lines of output per minute. It is very expensive, but becomes cost-effective in computer systems that produce a very large volume of printed output. Although the laser printer can make only one copy at a time, its speed makes it economical to produce multiple copies by rewriting the entire output more than once. A typical laser printer is shown in Figure 3-18.

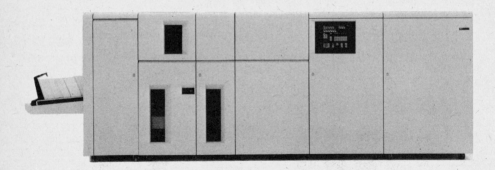

Figure 3-18. The IBM 3800 Laser Printer

Match the following:

_____ (1) impact printers

_____ (2) nonimpact printers

(a) all require special paper
(b) are very quiet
(c) can produce multiple copies without reprinting output
(d) require a carbon ribbon in order to produce characters on paper

- - - - - - - - - - - - - - - - - - -

(1) c, d; (2) b

21. Which of these statements is true?

_____ (a) Line impact printers are faster than thermal nonimpact printers.

_____ (b) The wire dot matrix is used only in electrostatic printers.

_____ (c) The laser printer is the fastest printer available.

_____ (d) all of the above

- - - - - - - - - - - - - - - - - -

a, c

22. Match the following:

_____ (1) impact printer(s)   (a) thermal printer
                                     (b) line printer
_____ (2) nonimpact printer(s)   (c) electrostatic printer
                                     (d) laser printer

- - - - - - - - - - - - - - - - - -

(1) b; (2) a, c, d

23. In the last few pages we have discussed a large number of different devices that may be included in a computer system. Figure 3-19 shows how they might be combined in a computer system. Of course, not all these devices are necessarily found in the same computer system—in the diagram they are included primarily as a review. The numbers refer to the figure in which each device is illustrated.

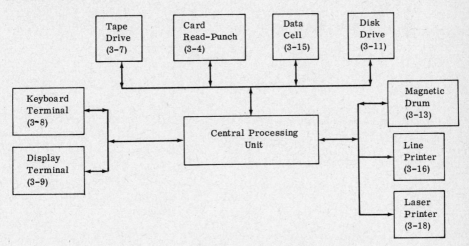

Figure 3-19. Devices in a Computer System

    The next few frames are designed as a review of all devices in a computer system.

Match the following:

_____ (1) input device only	(a) line printer
_____ (2) input–output device	(b) card reader
	(c) data cell
_____ (3) output device only	(d) magnetic tape
	(e) central processing unit

- - - - - - - - - - - - - - - - - - -

(1) b; (2) c, d; (3) a

24. Which of these devices can be used for auxiliary storage?

_____ (a) data cell

_____ (b) magnetic drum

_____ (c) magnetic disk

_____ (d) all of the above

- - - - - - - - - - - - - - - - - - -

d

25. Instructions to the computer system are interpreted by the:

_____ (a) arithmetic–logic unit.

_____ (b) control unit.

_____ (c) storage unit.

_____ (d) none of the above

- - - - - - - - - - - - - - - - - -

b

26. When a program is being processed, the storage unit contains the:

_____ (a) instructions to be processed.

_____ (b) input data.

_____ (c) output data.

_____ (d) all of the above

- - - - - - - - - - - - - - - - - - -

d

27. On which device can needed data be found without searching all the data from the beginning?

_____ (a) magnetic drum

_____ (b) magnetic tape

_____ (c) card reader

_____ (d) none of the above

- - - - - - - - - - - - - - - - - -

a

28. Match the following:

_____ (1) random-access
processing

_____ (2) sequential-access
processing

(a) the ability to go directly to the
needed record in a file

(b) the processing of records in a file
by taking them in order from beginning to end

(c) the ability to store large amounts of
data for later processing

- - - - - - - - - - - - - - - - - -

(1) a; (2) b

SPECIALIZED EQUIPMENT

29. So far we have discussed types of devices that can be found in most computer systems. That is, all systems have a CPU, input and output devices,
and some form of auxiliary storage device. We will now look at three devices
that have somewhat specialized applications but nevertheless have a big impact
on all our lives.

Figure 3-20 shows a major imput device used in banking: the magnetic-
character reader-sorter.

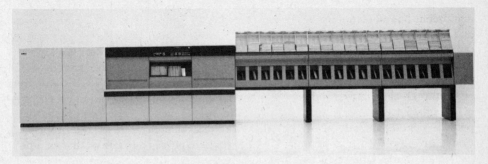

Figure 3-20. The IBM 3890 Magnetic-Character Reader-Sorter

This device can read the symbols at the bottom of a check and convert them into electrical impulses which are then transmitted to storage. It can also sort checks by bank number or account number before transmitting the data.

Part of the processing of a check includes typing the amount of the check on the lower right corner, as shown in the sample check below. The numbers on the lower left side are preprinted and show the bank number and customer account number. It is these numbers at the bottom of the check that the machine reads.

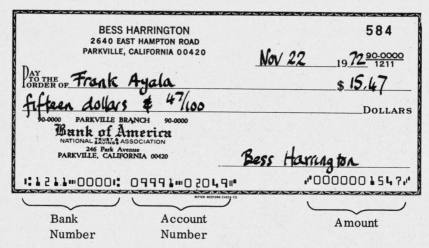

The machine uses <u>magnetic-ink</u> <u>character</u> <u>recognition</u> (MICR) in its operation. The ink used to print the numbers is magnetized, and special reading heads decode the magnetic fields created. The numbers have to be a specified shape and size in order for the reader to recognize them. They have the obvious advantage of being readable with the human eye. However, one disadvantage of MICR is that only numbers can be used. There is no provision for letters or special characters. Although this is not too much of a problem in banking applications, where bank and customer identification can be easily made using only numbers, it does create a problem in other areas.

To overcome this problem, <u>optical-character</u> <u>recognition</u> (OCR) equipment has been developed. Whereas most data to be entered into a computer is recorded first on a source document that may be typed or handwritten, OCR equipment has been designed so that it can read typewritten data, both letters and numbers, and convert them directly into electrical impulses. These impulses can then be recorded directly onto magnetic tape or disks. No keypunching is required, not only saving time but also reducing the chances of errors. Figure 3-21 at the top of the next page shows a typical OCR machine.

Optical-character readers have been developed that will read and recognize <u>handwritten</u> letters and numbers. No special ink is required, so ballpoint pens or pencils may be used to prepare the data that is to be used as input. There are certain limitations to the size and shape of characters that can be read, but this development is likely to greatly speed up many business data-processing applications. As yet, however, there are serious problems with the reliability of this type of OCR machine.

Figure 3-21.   The IBM 3886 Optical-Character Reader

OCR equipment is relatively expensive, requiring a steady flow of 10,000 to 15,000 documents a day to justify its use.

A major application of OCR is the processing of gasoline credit-card charges. When a charge card is used in a gas station, customer-identification information from the card is imprinted on the charge slip together with a gas-station identification number and the total sales amount. The slip is then passed through an optical-character reader and the pertinent information read directly off it. The handwritten information on the slip is ignored.

Which of these statements is true?

_____ (a) MICR equipment can read both typed and handwritten characters.

_____ (b) OCR equipment requires the use of a special magnetic ink.

_____ (c) both

_____ (d) neither

- - - - - - - - - - - - - - - - - - -

d

30. In an attempt to overcome the storage problems associated with the thou-sands of pages of printed output produced by some computer applications, de-vices have been developed that record output data directly on microfilm. As it is produced, data is displayed on a screen (like a television screen) and photographed by a high-speed camera. Using this system, output data can be recorded on film at approximately the same speed as it can be recorded on magnetic tape. The film is then processed and can be read on a microfilm

reader. A few feet of microfilm can store output that would require thousands of printed pages.

Data can also be recorded directly onto <u>microfiche</u>, a 4- by 6-inch piece of film that can hold up to 200 full pages of information. Machines that perform this function are called <u>computer-output-to-microfilm</u> (COM) devices.

An alternative COM method is to first record the output data on magnetic tape and then record it onto microfiche or microfilm. Figure 3-22 shows such a COM device.

Figure 3-22. The Kodak Komstar 300 Microimage Processor

Microfiche and microfilm can be read using special readers that project the desired page onto a screen. Readers are available that will automatically find the desired page of data and project it on the screen, allowing an operator to select one page from thousands in a matter of seconds.

COM techniques are especially useful when large volumes of computer output have to be easily accessible. For example, if copies of bills charged on credit are placed on microfilm or microfiche, when a customer calls with a query, a copy of the bill in question can be retrieved and displayed very rapidly. The customer-service person can then help the customer without the delay of making a manual search through files.

It is also possible to use microfilm as an input medium using a <u>computer-input-from-microfilm</u> (CIM) technique. Data that has been put on microfilm is put through a CIM device and then used as input. Also, data that has been prepared manually and then microfilmed can be read into the computer using CIM.

Write down the meaning of each of these:

MICR   _____

OCR   _____

COM   _____

CIM   _____

- - - - - - - - - - - - - - - - - - -

MICR, magnetic-ink character reader; OCR, optical-character recognition; COM, computer-output-to-microfilm; CIM, computer-input-from-microfilm

Data-Entry Devices

31. In Chapter 2 we discussed the card punch at some length. Historically, this has been the most common device to prepare data for entry into the computer. You will recall that the card-punch operator reads the source documents and punches the data from them into predetermined fields in a punched card. The punched card is then read by the card reader, thus making the data available for processing by the computer system.

We also mentioned in Chapter 2 that punched cards are being used less and less as the need for faster methods of processing data increases. The two other mediums being used are magnetic tape and magnetic disk.

Key-to-tape data-entry devices allow data to be recorded directly on tape. The data is typed from source documents through a keyboard and onto magnetic tape. When all the data has been entered, it is verified by entering it again. This time the device compares what is being typed with what is on the tape. If there is an error, the operator can erase the incorrect character on the tape and enter the correct one. Figure 3-23 at the top of the next page shows a typical key-to-tape data-entry device.

Data may be recorded either on regular magnetic tape or on cassettes, similar to those used in sound tape recorders.

The key-to-disk data-entry device is very similar, the primary difference being that it records data on a disk rather than on tape. Figure 3-24 is the second photograph on the next page. It shows a typical key-to-disk encoder. Note that the disk is about the size of a 45-rpm record. Some of these small disks are flexible. That is, they can be bent without being damaged and are sometimes called "floppy" disks.

These devices have the advantage of being relatively small and of being independent of a CPU for their operation. Thus they can be used at the place most convenient for the recording of data. For example, in many large organizations it would be more convenient to record data on goods shipped and goods received in individual warehouses rather than to send all the source documents to one central location for processing.

Figure 3-23. An IBM 050 Magnetic-Data Transcriber

Figure 3-24. The IBM 3741 Data-Entry Unit

Which of these statements is true?

_____ (a) Key-to-tape data-entry devices have to be connected to the CPU in order to operate.

_____ (b) Punched cards are being replaced by key-to-disk and key-to-tape data-entry devices.

_____ (c) Key-to-disk devices have the disadvantage that data entered on them cannot be verified.

_____ (d) none of the above

- - - - - - - - - - - - - - - - - - -

b

TYPICAL COMPUTER SYSTEMS

32. To close this chapter we will look at some typical computer systems and classify them by size and general uses.

Computer systems are designed, built, and marketed by many companies, some of which are Control Data Corporation, Digital Equipment Corporation, Honeywell Inc., International Business Machines, Inc. (IBM), National Cash Register, Texas Instruments, UNIVAC (Sperry Rand Corporation), Ohio Scientific, and Westinghouse Electric Corporation. Some of these companies are very large, some small. Some companies offer a full range of business and scientific computers, others specialize in certain types of computer systems.

The size of a computer is determined generally by the amount of data that can be stored in the CPU. The measure used is number of bytes of storage, where one byte is the space needed to store one character, such as "A", "9", or "=". The storage capacity of computers ranges from about 2,000 bytes to over 2,000,000 bytes. Because these numbers have lots of zeros, CPU storage is usually described in terms of 1,000s of bytes, with the letter "K" used to denote 1,000s. For example, a CPU capable of storing 2,000 bytes would be described as having 2K of storage. One with 2,000,000 storage bytes would be described as having 2,000K of storage.

Which of these statements is true?

_____ (a) 64K means 64,000 bytes of storage.

_____ (b) 1,000,000 bytes of storage is described as 10K.

_____ (c) 128K of storage can hold 128,000 characters.

_____ (d) none of the above

- - - - - - - - - - - - - - - - - - -

a, c (1,000,000 bytes is 1,000K)

33. Computers can be classified into four broad categories, as shown in Figure 3-25 at the top of the next page. A word of warning, however. These categories are very general, and there is no firm dividing line between each.

For example, some medium-sized computers, based on CPU storage capacity, are called minicomputers because they are <u>physically</u> very small.

Category	CPU Storage Capacity
Micro	Less than 16K
Mini	16K – 64K
Small	64K – 256K
Medium	256K – 1,000K
Large	More than 1,000K

Figure 3-25. Broad Categories for Describing Computer Size

Match the following:

_____ (1) micro

_____ (2) small

_____ (3) medium

(a) 256K – 1,000K
(b) 16K – 64K
(c) 64K – 256K
(d) less than 16K

- - - - - - - - - - - - - - - - - -

(1) d; (2) c; (3) a

34. A typical microcomputer is shown in Figure 3-26.

Figure 3-26. The Radio Shack TRS-80 Microcomputer

This computer has, in its basic form, a 4K storage capacity. It sells for $599 and is the cheapest fully assembled microcomputer currently available for home use. It has a keyboard terminal for input and a display screen for output. Data and programs can be stored on cassette tapes and read into memory as required through a <u>cassette</u> <u>tape</u> <u>unit</u>. Also available are a 16K memory, two kinds of printer, and a disk drive.

Figure 3-27 shows a typical minicomputer, the Lockheed System III. It has 16K storage capacity, keyboard, display terminal, disk drive, and line printer. Designed for small companies, it can be used for a variety of business applications.

Figure 3-27. The Lockheed System III Minicomputer

The IBM System/3, shown in Figure 3-28 at the top of the next page, is a typical small-business computer. It is designed for small businesses moving from punched-card processing systems to computers. Since the System/3 was designed primarily for use with the 96-column punched card, it has a <u>multi-function</u> <u>card</u> <u>unit</u>. This card unit, in addition to reading and punching cards, can collate, sort, and print cards. (These operations are briefly described in Appendix I.)

The basic system includes, in addition to the card unit, a printer and a keyboard terminal. A more flexible version of this system uses a magnetic disk unit for auxiliary storage.

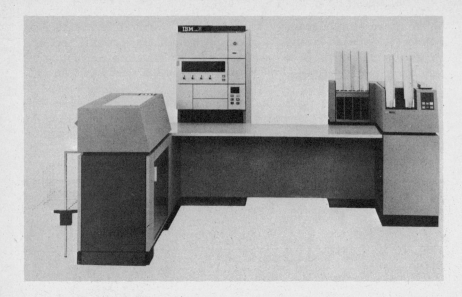

Figure 3-28. The IBM System/3 Model 10

A medium-sized computer, the UNIVAC 90/80, is shown in Figure 3-29 at the top of the next page. This is a very flexible system that can use a wide range of input-output devices—card readers, card punches, printers, magnetic tape drives, magnetic disk drives as well as remote terminal devices.

Figure 3-29.   The UNIVAC 90/80

Large computer systems are frequently used by service companies that specialize in selling computer time and services to companies that have no, or limited, computer facilities.   The Cyber 176 is shown in Figure 3-30 on the next page.   It expands on the company's Cyber 170 series and is one of the largest commercially available systems.

Figure 3-30. Control Data Cyber 176

Appendix II shows characteristics of selected computer systems. The list is not exhaustive, but is intended to illustrate the broad range of computer systems available. Some of the technical information shown is discussed in more detail in later chapters.

This is the end of Chapter 3. You should now work the Self-Test that follows.

SELF-TEST

Answer all the questions and then check the answers that follow.

1. The central processing unit of a computer system usually contains the:

    _____ (a) storage unit.

    _____ (b) arithmetic-logic unit.

    _____ (c) input devices.

    _____ (d) all of the above

2. Match the following:

    _____ (1) control unit   (a) magnetic tape drive

    _____ (2) arithmetic-logic unit   (b) performs calculations on data

                                       (c) magnetic-character sorter-reader

    _____ (3) input-output device   (d) interprets instructions and issues commands

3. Which of these devices may be used for auxiliary storage?

_____ (a) card- read-punch

_____ (b) display terminal

_____ (c) magnetic disk drive

_____ (d) all of the above

4. Match the following:

_____ (1) card read-punch

_____ (2) magnetic disk drive

(a) can read magnetized characters on checks

(b) relatively slow device

(c) each record can be stored at a known address

(d) input–output device

5. Which of these statements is true?

_____ (a) Brush card readers are slower than light card readers.

_____ (b) A card reader reads all columns in a card at the same time.

_____ (c) both

_____ (d) neither

6. Which of these statements is true?

_____ (a) Random access to records is very easy on magnetic tape.

_____ (b) In order to read a record on magnetic disk, all records before it have to be read.

_____ (c) The magnetic drum has random-access capability.

_____ (d) none of the above

7. Match the following:

_____ (1) input-only device

_____ (2) input-output device

_____ (3) output-only device

(a) optical-character reader

(b) data cell

(c) line printer

(d) display terminal

(e) card reader

8. Which of the following statements is true?

_____ (a) Line impact printers are faster than thermal nonimpact printers.

_____ (b) Nonimpact printers can produce multiple copies without re-printing output.

_____ (c) Printed output may be produced on magnetic-character recognition equipment.

_____ (d) all of the above

Answers to Self-Test

The numbers in parentheses after each answer refer to the frames in which the appropriate answers can be found. If you have a wrong answer or are not sure why your answer is correct, read that section of the chapter again before you go on to the next chapter.

1.   a, b (frame 1)

2.   (1) d; (2) b; (3) a (frame 2)

3.   c (frame 17)

4.   (1) b, d; (2) c, d (frames 10, 17)

5.   c (frame 10)

6.   c (frames 12, 17, 18)

7.   (1) a, e; (2) b, d; (3) c (frames 10, 15, 19, 20, 29)

8.   a (frame 20)

CHAPTER FOUR
Telecommunications

The devices discussed in the last chapter were primarily those found in the "computer room." That is, they are located close to the central processing unit and operated by the staff of the data-processing department. In this chapter we will discuss equipment and systems that can be used at almost any distance from a computer and that can be operated by almost anyone, without extensive training in data processing.

After completing this chapter you will be able to:

- define telecommunications;
- define batch processing and on-line processing;
- define real-time data processing and time sharing;
- describe the use of the light pen and audio-response devices;
- define an intelligent terminal and a point-of-sale terminal; and
- describe remote job entry.

1.   The use of keyboard terminals and display terminals at great distances from the main computer system is made possible by telecommunications. Telecommunications refers to the exchange of data between terminals and computers. Although data is usually sent over telephone lines, it may also be sent over microwaves via satellites.

Telecommunications requires the use of some equipment that we have not yet discussed. Figure 4-1 shows the basic telecommunications system.

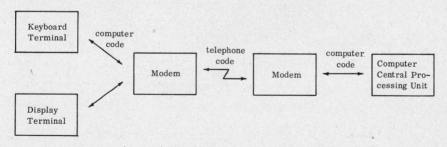

Figure 4-1.   Basic Telecommunications System

When the keys on a keyboard terminal are struck, the appropriate computer code is generated and passed into a <u>modem</u>, which converts it into a code that can be sent over telephone lines to the computer. At the computer end is another modem. As you might expect, this modem will convert the telephone code into _____ code.

- - - - - - - - - - - - - - - - - - -

computer

2. The computer code is then used as input to the central processing unit. When the required output is generated, it is in the form of _____ code, so it has to be converted into _____ code.

- - - - - - - - - - - - - - - - - - -

computer, telephone

3. At the keyboard end of the line, the opposite conversion takes place and the computer code causes the output to be printed on the terminal.

In Figure 4-1 the modem is shown as a device that stands on its own. Often, however, the modem is built into the terminal device, which is then plugged directly into a telephone.

To reach your friendly computer, you simply pick up the phone and dial the computer's number. A certain tone tells you that you are connected and can begin sending data. Then you press a switch on the terminal, hang up the phone, and begin typing. Such a terminal is shown in Figure 4-2.

Figure 4-2. The Teletype Model 43 Teleprinter

Telecommunications has had the effect of making anyone with a little bit of training and with access to a terminal device and a telephone, a user of a computer system. Before telecommunications, all use of a computer was limited to the computer room. If a manager wanted a report, for example, it had to be requested some time in advance and when delivered, it was always somewhat out of date. As we shall see shortly, this has changed.

Here is a real-life example of the power of telecommunications. As a fire truck rolls to a fire in a small town in Sweden, the dispatcher enters the address of the fire into a terminal. Within a couple of minutes a list of known hazards at that address is being printed and the dispatcher is relaying it to the fire truck. Not very impressive, you might think. Maybe not—except that the computer to which the dispatcher "talked" is in Cincinnati, Ohio!

Which of these statements is true?

_____ (a) A modem converts telephone code into computer code and vice versa.

_____ (b) Telecommunications is the exchange of data between terminals and computers.

_____ (c) both

_____ (d) neither

- - - - - - - - - - - - - - - - - - - -

c

4.   There are two basically different methods of processing data we will discuss. One example is the processing of payroll checks.

Assume that each employee completes a time card each week and hands it to a supervisor. The employee doesn't expect to get a pay check immediatly—in fact, he or she knows checks are only written every other Friday. Thus each time card does not have to be processed immediately, but can be filed away until the time comes to prepare payroll checks for everyone.

Now consider going to an airline office or a large travel agent to book a flight from San Francisco to New York. You tell the clerk the day and approximate time you want to fly; you expect to leave with a confirmation that you have a seat on a particular flight (if not the ticket). Clearly, the clerk can't take your order and keep it until the end of the day or week before sending it in to be processed with many others. So a different processing method is needed to solve this problem.

Most data-processing requirements fall into one of two types—data that can be stored until a predetermined processing time and data that must be processed as soon as it is generated.

Batch processing is the name given to the first type. Batch processing is used with large quantities of data that do not have to be processed as soon as generated, but can be put together and processed at a given time, as in the payroll example. Another example of batch processing is the processing of charges made on a credit card. A merchant holds all charge slips until the end of the day or week and then sends them to the credit-card company for

_____ processing.

- - - - - - - - - - - - - - - - - - -

batch

5.   When data requires some form of immediate processing, a technique called <u>on-line</u> <u>data</u> <u>processing</u> is used with remote terminals. This term means that the terminal user is "on the (telephone) line" while the data submitted to the computer as input is being processed.

For example, many large, prepaid medical-insurance schemes maintain computerized medical records for their members. When a member is admitted to an emergency room, a nurse enters the member number through a terminal to the main computer. While the nurse waits, the computer searches the files for the patient's records and then prints the pertinent parts of it at the terminal. Thus medical information about the member can be made available to the emergency-room staff almost immediately. In serious cases, this rapid retrieval of data from the computer can mean the difference between life and death.

For a less dramatic example of on-line processing, consider a scientist with a small amount of data to be analyzed. The analysis may be very complicated and may take hours to do by hand. So the scientist enters the data and a few instructions to the computer through a terminal. Within a few seconds or minutes the computer completes the analysis and prints the results at the terminal. The scientist is thus relieved of the problem of having the data punched into cards for entry to the computer and has the analysis within minutes instead of, at best with punched cards, hours.

Which of these statements is true?

_____ (a) Batch data processing refers to the gathering of large quantities of data for processing at a given time.

_____ (b) On-line data processing refers to the processing of data as soon as it is submitted as input from a terminal.

_____ (c) both

_____ (d) neither

- - - - - - - - - - - - - - - - - - -

c

6.   Figure 4-3 at the top of the next page shows a typical telecommunications system that might be used by a large manufacturing company to process orders and maintain its inventory.

At predetermined times during the day, each order point submits all the necessary information about the orders it has received through a terminal to the home-office computer. There the data is edited and stored on magnetic tape or disk. The editing ensures that the data stored is as accurate as possible and that, for example, the terminal operator hasn't ordered a part that doesn't exist.

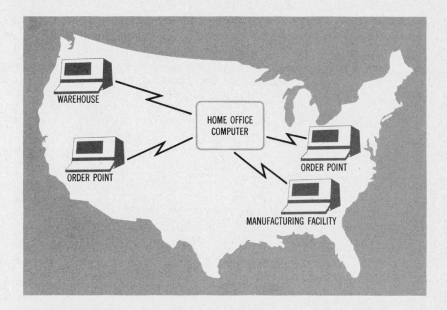

Figure 4-3. A Typical Telecommunications System

At the end of the day, the data that has been stored is used as an input file for a batch-processing operation that will write shipping instructions for the warehouse, update the inventory file, and back-order items not currently in stock. The shipping instructions are relayed over the telecommunications system and printed at the warehouse, while information about items that are out of stock can be printed at the manufacturing plant.

This type of operation is a combination of on-line and batch processing. Its main advantage is in getting data to be processed to the computer quickly and getting output to the appropriate users in a timely fashion.

For many applications, however, even these time savings are not great enough. In situations where a decision made at, say, 10:45 will have an effect on all decisions made after 10:45, a much faster method of recording decisions is needed.

Consider the use of credit cards and the way in which merchants have to check to see if customers may make purchases over, say, $100. Or imagine a customer with a new credit card and a credit limit of $750. That is, the customer cannot owe the credit-card company more than $750 at any time. The customer goes to a store and purchases a stereo unit for $625 and charges it. The merchant calls the credit-card company for authorization to accept the charge and an operator uses a terminal to check the customer's balance. Since it is less than $750, the charge is authorized, and the operator immediately enters the $625 against the customer's account. If 15 minutes later the customer attempts to charge \$215 in another store, that merchant will be told by the company operator that the charge may not be accepted, since the combined charges (\$625 plus \$215) exceed the customer's \$750 credit limit.

In this example it is essential that every new piece of data about a customer be entered and available to make further decisions about the customer immediately. Computer systems that have this characteristic—that data entered into the system is immediately available for use in future decisions—are called <u>real-time</u> <u>data-processing</u> <u>systems</u>. Real-time systems are always on-line also, since it is essential to get data to and from the computer as quickly as possible.

Which of these statements is true?

_____ (a) All on-line systems use telecommunications.

_____ (b) All real-time systems are also on-line.

_____ (c) All batch-processing applications require on-line terminals.

_____ (d) all of the above

- - - - - - - - - - - - - - - - - - -

a, b

7. Airline-reservation systems require real-time, on-line processing. When a travel agent receives a request for a seat on a particular flight, the information about the date and flight number is entered through a terminal. The computer then sends as output to the terminal information about the availability of seats. If a display terminal is being used, a plan of the plane may be displayed showing which seats are available, the location of nonsmoking seats, and so on. When the customer selects a seat, that information is sent to the computer and the master record for that flight is altered to show the seat as booked. The master record is kept constantly up to date and the chance of overbooking a flight is very small. (Some airlines <u>deliberately</u> overbook flights, but that's another story!)

The development of telecommunications, along with the development of computer systems themselves, has led to the practice of <u>time</u> <u>sharing</u>. The time-sharing industry has had a very rapid growth since it makes possible relatively cheap access to computer systems. A company will buy a computer system and rent its processing time to other companies. The computer is programmed to accept requests for processing from remote locations and to "share out" the available processing time among the various users. Thus, while the system is producing output for me, it may be performing some calculations for you. Then, while outputting the results of those calculations for you, it may be inputting some data of mine. In this way, the system can "juggle" many jobs at the same time. Customers are charged a fee that is determined primarily by the amount of computer time they use. We will have more to say about time sharing in Chapter 9.

Which of these statements is true?

_____ (a) Real-time data processing enables data entered in the computer to be immediately available for decision making.

_____ (b) Time sharing is the process of gathering large amounts of data together for processing at the same time.

_____ (c) Random access refers to the use of terminals placed a long way from the main computer.

_____ (d) none of the above

- - - - - - - - - - - - - - - - - -

a

8. We will now look at some of the equipment that is used in telecommunications systems and that is bringing the computer into all our lives.

Figure 4-4 shows a display terminal. It is similar to the one in Figure 3-9 (page 60) but has one additional feature. The operator is using a light pen to communicate directly with the computer. On the screen is a summary report, and by touching one of the items in it with the light pen, the operator signals the computer to display a detailed breakdown of that item. This is a very fast and efficient way of retrieving information.

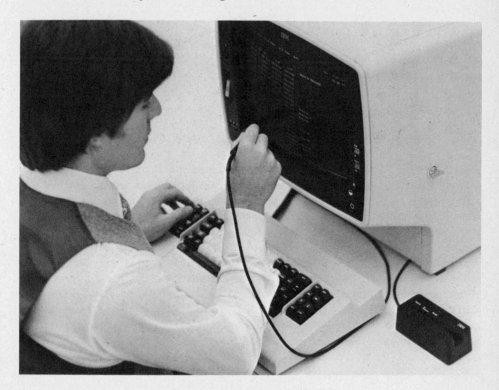

Figure 4-4. IBM 3270 Display Terminal with Light Pen

Telecommunications systems are increasingly making use of <u>intelligent</u> <u>terminals</u>. An intelligent terminal is one that can perform certain editing and data-checking functions through logic circuits built into the terminal. Figure 4-5 shows a typical intelligent terminal that has a printer as well as a display. It can be programmed to check certain aspects of data as it is entered and before it is transferred to the main computer. This method of data editing is very economical, since it frees the main computer to do more complex work.

Figure 4-5. The Teletype Model 40/4 Intelligent Terminal

The difference between intelligent terminals and microcomputers is not always distinct, and microcomputers are often used as intelligent terminals. For example, a researcher in an animal research center may use a microcomputer to collect and edit data and to perform some fairly straightfoward analyses. For more complex analyses, however, the microcomputer is linked to a large computer and in effect becomes a terminal for that large computer.

A specialized type of intelligent terminal is shown in Figure 4-6 at the top of the next page. <u>Graphics</u> <u>terminals</u> are designed specifically for the display of complex charts and diagrams. For example, an architect could enter detailed plans for a building into a graphics terminal and project a front view of the building onto the display screen. By using the appropriate commands, the architect can make the image rotate on the screen, showing what the building would look like from almost any angle. The same general technique is also used in the design of automobiles. Although the programs necessary to do this type of thing are very expensive to develop, the process is useful because in a matter of minutes designers can see views of a car that would otherwise take hours or days to draw.

Figure 4-6. The Tektronix 4051 Graphics Terminal

Many graphics terminals also have the capability to project data and charts charts in color, greatly adding to the ease of interpreting complex information. Which of these statements is true?

_____ (a) An intelligent terminal can perform some operations on data before it is transmitted to the main computer.

_____ (b) A graphics terminal is specifically designed for the display of charts and diagrams.

_____ (c) Microcomputers may be used as intelligent terminals for larger computers.

_____ (d) all of the above

- - - - - - - - - - - - - - - - - - - -

d

9. Not all terminal devices are large. For example, the terminal in Figure 4-7 at the top of the next page is the size of a regular briefcase and weighs less than 20 pounds. The telephone fits into the modem on the right-hand side. The use of this terminal truly makes the computer as close as the nearest telephone (provided there is an electrical outlet close to the telephone).

Figure 4-7. Texas Instrument Silent Portable
Data Terminal, Model 700

Such a terminal has almost unlimited uses. For example, a freelance programmer can carry it around and have access to a computer from a client's
office, a motel room, or home.
  The device shown in Figure 4-8 does not even require an electrical outlet.

Figure 4-8. The IBM 2721 Portable Audio-Response Terminal

It is an audio-response unit that fits into a briefcase and weighs about 10 pounds. Using synthesized speech, the computer sends signals to the audio-response unit which are then converted into audible words through a speaker. The person using the unit makes contact with the computer by dialing the appropriate number, and the computer may respond with "Good morning, please type in your name." The person's name could then be incorporated into any other messages the computer might send. The computer is usually programmed to prompt the user entering data. For example, the computer might say "Now enter customer number." When the user has done that, the computer might repeat the number so that the user can verify that the correct number was typed. A system like this leaves very little room for error in data entry.

Audio-response units have limited vocabularies, ranging from about 50 words to as many as 2,000. Although the equipment and programs needed at the main computer are very complex and expensive, the units themselves are cheap and reliable. Their application is practically unlimited, and very little training is required for users.

Many banks use audio-response to enable tellers to check customers' balances. These systems often use just a telephone, the customer account number being entered into the computer using the buttons on the telephone itself. This system is fast and private—only the teller is able to hear the computer responses. Another advantage is that, when not being used to communicate with the computer, the telephone can be used as a regular telephone.

Retail stores are using telecommunications systems in ever-increasing numbers. The heart of a retail computer system is the point-of-sale terminal, the terminal at the cashier's counter. Point-of-sale systems vary widely in the specific way in which they operate, but all are intended to combine the production of a customer bill with the recording of information about all the sales made at that point. Some terminals record data on magnetic tape for later processing while others are connected directly to a central computer and operate on-line.

Figure 4-9 at the top of the next page shows a typical point-of-sale terminal that is an intelligent terminal. It can calculate the total price of multiple items, total a bill, calculate sales tax due, and print an itemized bill. The pertinent information needed by the central computer for accounting and inventory control is relayed directly by the terminal.

Increasingly, point-of-sale terminals are being used to remove the need for clerks to enter prices through a keyboard. Such terminals use the universal product code that is found on nearly all merchandise. Each item has its own code, often called the "zebra code" after the stripes used to record it. Using a light wand, such as that shown in Figure 4-10, the second photograph on the next page, the clerk reads the zebra code directly into the terminal, where it is converted into the universal product code number for that item. Each product has its own number. The terminal looks in a file to find the cost of the item, displays the cost on the terminal and adds it to the customer's bill. This system is generally faster than having the clerk enter the price through the keyboard and greatly reduces the chance of errors on bills.

Figure 4-9. The NCR 2151 Point-of-Sale Terminal

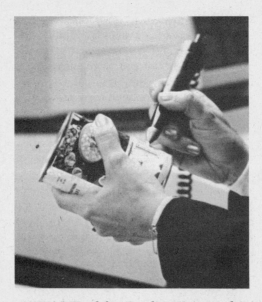

Figure 4-10. A Light Wand for Reading Universal Product Codes

Another version of this system uses light readers built into the check stand. These are even faster, since all the clerk has to do is slide the item, zebra stripes down, over the light reader.

Which of these statements is true?

_____ (a) Audio-response units are expensive and difficult to use.

_____ (b) The universal product code can be read directly by computer devices.

_____ (c) Point-of-sale terminals can increase the speed and accuracy of salesclerks.

_____ (d) all of the above

- - - - - - - - - - - - - - - - - -

b, c

10. Figure 4-11 shows a remote-batch terminal that is used to submit large quantities of data to a main computer and to print the output when processing is complete. It consists of a printer, card reader, and minicomputer.

Figure 4-11. A Remote-Batch Terminal

This type of equipment might be used in each warehouse of a large distribution company. Punched cards are used to record each day's activities. Some processing of the data in these cards is done using the minicomputer, but the data is transmitted to a large central computer for most batch processing. The output is stored on magnetic disk or magnetic drum at the central computer until the remote unit is ready to receive and print it.

This type of system is useful because it allows batch processing of large quantities of data generated at many locations to be done on one large computer, rather than on medium-sized computers at each location.

Batch processing on a central computer can be initiated at many devices. For example, a keyboard terminal can be used to instruct the main computer to process a particular data file using a particular program, both of which are already stored on magnetic disk at the main computer site. The output can then be printed directly back to the terminal, printed immediately at the main computer, or stored on disk for printing at the terminal or main computer at some later time.

The use of a telecommunications system in this way is called <u>remote job entry</u>. That is, the request for a batch-processing job to be performed, and perhaps the data and the program required, can be submitted from a remote location via a terminal device.

The last device we will discuss is essential to any large telecommunications system. It is called a <u>communications controller</u> and is placed between the remote terminals and the main computer. As its name implies, its job is to control the flow of data in the system. It prevents data from different terminals getting mixed up and ensures that input and output flow to and from the central processing unit in the most efficient way.

The communications controller is a minicomputer that can be programmed to perform a variety of tasks such as keeping track of how many terminals are in use, which parts of the computer system the terminals are using, and the assignment of priorities to certain users so that they can be given access to the system when it is busy.

Which of these statements is true?

_____ (a) Remote job entry refers to the submission of jobs for batch processing via a telecommunications system.

_____ (b) The flow of data in and out of the central processing unit is controlled by an intelligent terminal.

_____ (c) both

_____ (d) neither

- - - - - - - - - - - - - - - - - - - -

a

11. The telecommunications systems described in this chapter are revolutionizing the use of computers. While the main computer and its operation have become very complex and expensive, access to computers for a wide variety of routine tasks has become simpler and cheaper. A single large computer may be connected to 100 or more terminal devices at the same time. In addition, it may also be running batch-processing jobs. With a good overall control system for the computer, each user may think that he or she has the computer to themselves.

Figure 4-12 at the top of the next page shows how all the equipment described in this chapter and all of that described in Chapter 3 might be connected to the same central processing unit. The numbers refer to the figure in which each device is illustrated.

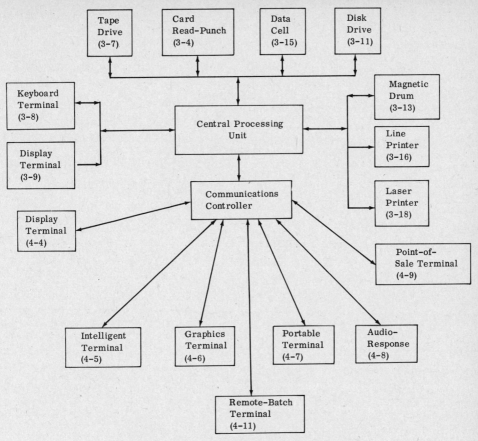

Figure 4-12. A Large Computer System
with a Telecommunications Capability

This is the end of Chapter 4. You should now work the Self-Test that follows.

SELF-TEST

Answer all the questions and then check against the answers that follow.

1. Telecommunications:

_____ (a) is the exchange of data between terminals and computers.

_____ (b) uses telephone lines.

_____ (c) can use microwaves via satellites.

_____ (d) all of the above

2. A modem:

_____ (a) is a small portable terminal.

_____ (b) converts computer code to telephone code.

_____ (c) converts telephone code to computer code.

_____ (d) all of the above

3. Which of these statements is true?

_____ (a) Batch processing refers to the processing of data as soon as it is submitted as input from a terminal.

_____ (b) On-line data processing refers to the gathering of large quantities of data for processing at a given time.

_____ (c) both

_____ (d) neither

4. Real-time data-processing systems:

_____ (a) are always on-line.

_____ (b) make input data immediately available for decision making.

_____ (c) both

_____ (d) neither

5. Which of these statements is true?

_____ (a) Intelligent terminals do not require operators.

_____ (b) Microcomputers can be used as intelligent terminals for remote central computers.

_____ (c) Graphics terminals are designed specifically for displaying charts and diagrams.

_____ (d) all of the above

6. Audio-response systems:

_____ (a) are very simple to use.

_____ (b) use synthesized speech to allow the computer to talk to operators.

_____ (c) can be used through any telephone.

_____ (d) all of the above

7. Point-of-sale terminals:

_____ (a) combine the production of customer bills with the collection of sales information.

_____ (b) can replace clerks at the checkout stand.

_____ (c) can be used only with the universal product code.

_____ (d) none of the above

8. Which of these statements is true?

_____ (a) The universal product code can be read by a light wand.

_____ (b) Remote-batch entry refers to the use of batch processing to control a large number of remote terminals.

_____ (c) A communications controller ensures the efficient flow of data between remote terminals and the central processing unit.

_____ (d) all of the above

Answers to Self-Test

The numbers in parentheses refer to the frames in which the appropriate answers can be found. If you have a wrong answer or are not sure why your answer is correct, read that section of the chapter again before you go on.

1. d (frame 1)

2. b, c (frame 2)

3. d (frame 3)

4. c (frame 6)

5. b, c (frame 8)

6. d (frame 9)

7. a (frame 9)

8. a, c (frame 9)

CHAPTER FIVE

Data Representation and Storage

In this chapter we will discuss the way data is stored and represented in electronic computer systems. You will learn about two new numbering systems, the binary and the hexadecimal. The importance of these two numbering systems for computers and the physical layout of storage devices will be explained. An optional appendix to this chapter shows you how to perform basic arithmetic operations with binary numbers.

After completing this chapter you will be able to:

- convert numbers from binary to decimal and vice versa;
- convert numbers from hexadecimal to decimal and vice versa;
- describe the advantages of using binary numbers in computers;
- define the terms bit and byte;
- explain the purpose of parity bits;
- identify the extended binary-coded decimal interchange code (EBCDIC);
- describe the semiconductor memory chip; and
- describe how data is represented on magnetic tape and magnetic disk.

1.   The underlying principles of data representation in electronic computers are fairly simple, although the technical problems involved in actually storing and retrieving data are extremely complex. Data is represented in terms of an electric current flowing or not flowing or of a magnet being magnetized in one direction or the other. Think of an electric light bulb: It is either on or off—it can't be both at the same time. So a single light could be used to represent the numbers 0 and 1. If the light is off, it represents 0. If it is on, it represents 1. Look at the illustration at the top of the next page.

But how does this help with numbers greater than 1? Here is where the binary numbering system is used. The binary system uses only two digits (bi means two), 0 and 1, to represent numbers. The decimal numbering system, the one we're most familiar with, uses ten digits (0, 1, 2, 3, . . . , 9) to represent numbers.

1

ON

0

OFF

Both the decimal and binary number systems are positional numbering systems. That is, a digit takes on different values according to the column it is in. The decimal system goes like this:

Thousands	Hundreds	Tens	Ones
7	3	0	1

The number represented by 7,301 is _____

_____ .

- - - - - - - - - - - - - - - - - -

seven thousand three hundred and one.

2.   In the binary system columns have these values:

Sixteen	Eight	Four	Two	One
1	0	1	0	1

Only the digits 0 and 1 can be used in the binary system. To find out what the binary number 10101 equals in decimal numbers, we must add together the values of the columns containing a 1. Thus, binary 10101 = 16 + 4 + 1 = 21 in decimal numbers.

Notice that for each column in binary a 1 is worth <u>twice as much</u> as a 1 in the column to the right of it. What number would be represented by a 1 in the

<u>sixth</u> column from the right in a binary number? _____

- - - - - - - - - - - - - - - - - -

32 (2 × 16, the value of a 1 in the fifth column)

3.   The binary system is based on <u>powers of two</u>, as illustrated at the top of the next page.

Sixteen	Eight	Four	Two	One
2^4	2^3	2^2	2^1	2^0
2×2×2×2	2×2×2	2×2	2	1 (by definition)

Notice that as we move from right to left, each column is twice the column to its right.

What decimal number do you think is represented by binary 1000000?

_____

- - - - - - - - - - - - - - - - - -

64 (2×32)

4. Here is a table to show the conversion of the first ten decimal numbers to binary numbers. The first five conversions have been made. Try to complete the table.

Decimal	Binary			
	8	4	2	1
1				1
2			1	0
3			1	1
4		1	0	0
5		1	0	1
6				
7				
8				
9				
10				

- - - - - - - - - - - - - - - - - - - -

110, 111, 1000, 1001, 1010

5. Now let's practice changing binary numbers to decimal numbers. Look at the column headings again. They are shown in the chart at the top of the next page.

128	64	32	16	8	4	2	1	
	1	0	1	0	1	0	0	(line 1)
1	1	0	0	0	0	1	1	(line 2)

Remember, to convert a binary number to a decimal number we have to decide what each column in the binary number represents in decimal and then add them all together, like this:

binary number   1   0   1   1
decimal number   8 + 0 + 2 + 1   =   11

Here's another example:

binary number   1   0   1   1   1
decimal number   16 + 0 + 4 + 2 + 1   =   23

What is the decimal number represented by the binary number on line 1 in the chart above? _____

- - - - - - - - - - - - - - - - - -

84   (64 + 0 + 16 + 0 + 4 + 0 + 0 = 84)

6.   What is the decimal number represented by the binary number on line 2 in the chart above? _____

- - - - - - - - - - - - - - - - - -

195   (128 + 64 + 2 + 1 = 195)

7.   What decimal number does this binary number represent: 10110101?

_____

- - - - - - - - - - - - - - - - - -

181

8.   This method of converting from binary to decimal works, but there is a quicker and easier method. It is called the double-and-add method. Here's how it works with 1011.

We start at the left-hand end of the binary number
and write down 1.

    1   0   1   1

    1

Then we double it (the 1) and add the next binary
digit, in this case 0.

    1   0   1   1

    1   2
      2+0

Then we double this number and add the next binary
digit.

    1   0   1   1

    1   2   5
        4+1

Then we double this number and add the next binary
digit.

    1   0   1   1

    1   2   5   11
           10+1

The last number we write down is the decimal equivalent of the binary number.

Complete this conversion from binary to decimal.

    1   0   1   0   0   1

    1   2   5
      2+0   4+1

- - - - - - - - - - - - - - - - - -

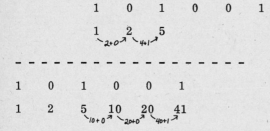

1   0   1   0   0   1

1   2   5   10   20   41
        10+0   20+0   40+1

9. Use the double-and-add method to convert 10000000 to a decimal number.

- - - - - - - - - - - - - - - - - -

1   0   0   0   0   0   0   0
1   2   4   8   16   32   64   128

10. What is the decimal equivalent of 10101010? _____

- - - - - - - - - - - - - - - - - -

170

11. What is the decimal equivalent of 11111111? _____

- - - - - - - - - - - - - - - - - -

255

12. What is the decimal equivalent of 101010101010? _____

- - - - - - - - - - - - - - - - - -

2730

13. As you can see, the double-and-add method is quicker and easier to use because it does not require memorizing the decimal equivalent of each column in binary number.

How do we convert decimal numbers to binary numbers? The simplest method is to divide repeatedly by 2, making a note of the remainders as we go along. Convert 27 to a binary number like this:

```
2 ) 27
2 ) 13      1    1st remainder
2 )  6      1    2nd remainder
2 )  3      0    3rd remainder
2 )  1      1    4th remainder
     0      1    5th remainder
         ←──── last quotient
```

Now, take the last quotient (the answer to the last division) and write it down as the first digit of the binary number. Then write down the remainders in the reverse order to which they were found, like this:

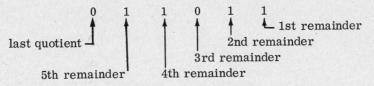

Here's another example. Convert 47 to binary.

```
2 ) 47
2 ) 23    1
2 ) 11    1
2 )  5    1
2 )  2    1
     1    0
```

What is the binary number that is equivalent to 47?

_____ (a) 101111

_____ (b) 11101

_____ (c) 1111

_____ (d) none of the above

- - - - - - - - - - - - - - - - - - -

a

14. The first digit in the number is the last quotient, and the other digits are the remainders in the reverse order to which they were found. What binary number represents 79?

- - - - - - - - - - - - - - - - - - -

1001111

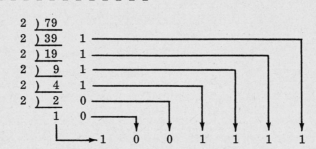

15. Here's another for you to try. Convert 158 to binary.

- - - - - - - - - - - - - - - - - - -

10011110

16. This one is a little more tricky. Convert the decimal number 101 to binary.

1100101

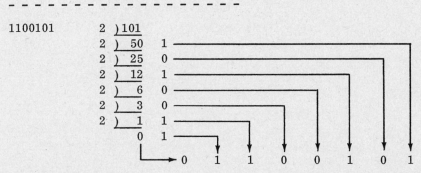

Notice that the last step has a remainder of zero, so it need not be written as part of the binary number.

17. If we were to represent binary numbers with electric light bulbs, we would arrange them in a row like this:

Notice that each bulb is marked with the decimal number that it represents. If this pattern of lights were on, what decimal number would be represented? (Remember, on represents 1 and off represents 0.)

----

18. It is possible to do addition, subtraction, multiplication, and division with binary numbers. We will demonstrate addition and subtraction in the appendix to this chapter. Most computers perform all mathematical operations in binary arithmetic since these can be performed very quickly. However, it is not easy for human beings to communicate with computers in binary, since large numbers are difficult to read and write. For example, the decimal number 532,976 is equivalent to 10000100000111110000 in binary. Even much smaller numbers (3,726 = 111110001110) are cumbersome to use. In order to reduce the error involved in converting to binary from decimal and back again, other systems have been developed to aid communication between computers and human beings. The simplest is called <u>Binary-Coded Decimal</u> (BCD for short). Figure 5-1 shows light bulbs representing one cell of a binary-coded decimal system.

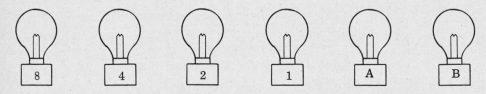

Figure 5-1. One Cell of a Binary-Coded Decimal System

In the BCD system each cell can represent only one character—that is, one letter, number, or special character. Each section of the cell, in this case each light bulb, is called a <u>bit</u>, a shorthand for <u>bi</u>nary dig<u>it</u>. Numbers are represented by the four bits on the left. The two on the right, marked A and B, are used to represent letters and special characters. (See Figure 2-8, page 25.) For now, we are only concerned with the representation of numbers in BCD. The number represented by the cell is the sum of the individual bits that are on. If a bit is on, it represents the number assigned to it. If it is off, it represents zero (0). What number is represented by this cell? (For convenience we will leave the A and B bits off these diagrams.)

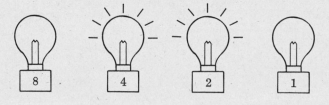

- - - - - - - - - - - - - - - - -

6 (The 4 and 2 bits are on. So the number represented by the cell is 4 + 2 = 6.)

19. What number is represented by the cell shown at the top of the next page?

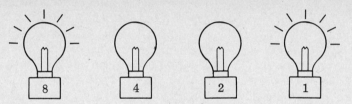

_____ (a) 8001

_____ (b) 9

_____ (c) 42

_____ (d) 6

- - - - - - - - - - - - - - - - - - - -

b

20. Which of these statements is true?

_____ (a) The number represented by a BCD bit is the sum of the individual cells that are off.

_____ (b) The number represented by a BCD cell is the sum of the individual cells that are on.

_____ (c) A BCD cell is made up of six bits.

_____ (d) none of the above

- - - - - - - - - - - - - - - - - - -

b, c

21. On this diagram, mark the bits that would be on if the cell were representing the number 7.

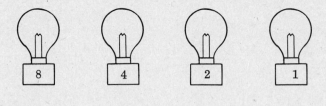

- - - - - - - - - - - - - - - - - -

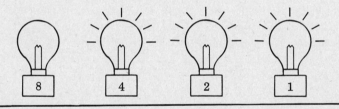

22. If these bits are on, what number is represented?

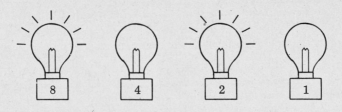

- - - - - - - - - - - - - - - - - - -

0

23. That was a tricky question. Remember, each cell can represent only <u>one</u> digit from 0 to 9. Since 8 + 2 = 0, the zero (0) is represented by bits 8 and 2. To represent the number 10, the 1 would be stored in another cell like this:

What number do you think the following cell represents?

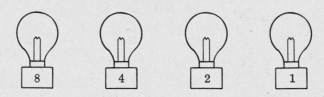

_____ (a) 10

_____ (b) 0

_____ (c) blank (or nothing)

_____ (d) none of the above

- - - - - - - - - - - - - - - - - - -

c

24. If no bits are on, then the cell represents a blank, or nothing. This is important to remember, otherwise we might have blanks where we wanted zeros and zeros where we wanted blanks.

What is the largest number that could be represented by two cells in the

BCD system? _____

- - - - - - - - - - - - - - - - - - -

99

25. How could the system be extended to include numbers up to 9,999?

- - - - - - - - - - - - - - - - - - - -

By adding two more cells to the left, one for hundreds and one for thousands.

26. Four cells would be needed to represent numbers up to 9,999, as shown here. What number is represented by the bits that are on in this diagram?

- -

4,379

27. By putting a 1 in the bits that would be on and a 0 in those that would be off, show how 2,056 would be represented in the BCD system.

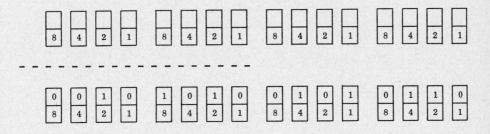

28. In a computer, the cells are normally arranged vertically. The number 2,056 is also represented in the figure shown at the top of the next page.

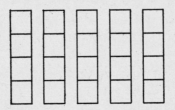

How would 46,371 be represented in these cells? (You should ignore the comma.)

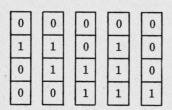

- - - - - - - - - - - - - - - - -

29. So far we have not discussed the actual physical layout of the cells in a computer. This will be left until various methods of representing data have been discussed.

The binary-coded decimal system was used extensively in older computer systems. Most modern systems, however, use a more flexible coding system: the Extended Binary-Coded Decimal Interchange Code. Remember that as EBCDIC. In the EBCDIC system each cell has eight bits and is called a byte.

Which of these statements is true?

_____ (a) In the BCD system, a cell contains eight bits.

_____ (b) A byte contains eight bits.

_____ (c) A cell in the EBCDIC system is called a byte.

_____ (d) none of the above

- - - - - - - - - - - - - - - - -

b, c

30. The greater size of the EBCDIC system has a major advantage. It can be used to represent more characters—256 to be exact. This means that it is

possible to store both upper- and lower-case letters (that is, capitals and small letters) and many special characters and still have plenty of code combinations left over for other purposes.

The EBCDIC byte is divided into two parts, as shown in this diagram.

Zone Portion				Digit Portion			
0 (8)	1 (4)	2 (2)	3 (1)	4 (8)	5 (4)	6 (2)	7 (1)

The top row of numbers identifies each bit, while the numbers written in parentheses show what each bit represents when it is on.

As you remember, the Hollerith code used in punched cards also has a zone and digit portion. These parts of the EBCDIC byte serve a similar purpose. Different entries in the zone portion combine with the same entry in the digit portion to represent different characters. For example, 1100 0001 represents the letter A, whereas 1101 0001 represents the letter J. Figure 5-2 shows the meaning of various combinations of entries in the zone portion of the EBCDIC byte.

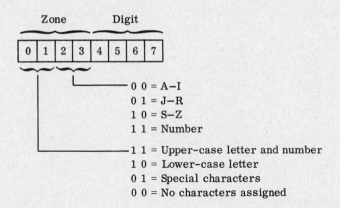

Figure 5-2. Meaning of Entries in Zone Portion of EBCDIC Byte

As before, a 1 indicates that the bit is on, a 0 that it is off. What would be the entry in the zone portion for the upper-case letter S?

_____ (a) 10

_____ (b) 11

_____ (c) 1110

_____ (d) 1011

- - - - - - - - - - - - - - - - -

c (11 indicates that it is upper case, 10 that it is a letter in the series S-Z.)

31. What would 1001 in the zone portion mean?

_____ (a) That the character in the digit portion was a special character.

_____ (b) That the character in the digit portion was a capital letter in the series J-R.

_____ (c) That the character in the digit portion was a small letter in the series J-R.

- - - - - - - - - - - - - - - - - -

c

32. A 1111 in the zone portion would mean that the character in the digit portion was a _____.

- - - - - - - - - - - - - - - - - -

number

33. Figure 5-3 shows the EBCDIC code for the ten numbers and the letters of the alphabet. Notice how the digit portions are arranged in repeating patterns, each series of patterns having a different zone arrangement.

0	1111	0000		I	1100	1001
1	1111	0001		J	1101	0001
2	1111	0010		K	1101	0010
3	1111	0011		L	1101	0011
4	1111	0100		M	1101	0100
5	1111	0101		N	1101	0101
6	1111	0110		O	1101	0110
7	1111	0111		P	1101	0111
8	1111	1000		Q	1101	1000
9	1111	1001		R	1101	1001
A	1100	0001		S	1110	0010
B	1100	0010		T	1110	0011
C	1100	0011		U	1110	0100
D	1100	0100		V	1110	0101
E	1100	0101		W	1110	0110
F	1100	0110		X	1110	0111
G	1100	0111		Y	1110	1000
H	1100	1000		Z	1110	1001

Figure 5-3. Representation of Numbers and Letters in EBCDIC

Data is transferred, in the form of bits and bytes, back and forth between various parts of the computer system at very high speeds. This means that there is a possibility that a bit might be "lost" during the transfer. To guard against this possibility, each EBCDIC byte has a <u>parity</u> bit associated with it. Some computers operate on an <u>odd-parity</u> system. That is, an odd number of bits in any byte must be on. The parity is, in effect, a ninth bit as shown here:

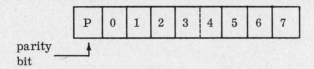

parity
bit

The parity bit is either on or off. Its condition is such as to make the total number of bits in the byte that are on an <u>odd</u> number, like this:

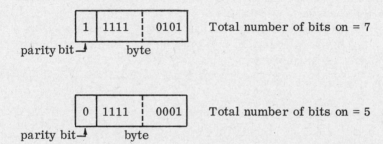

The condition of the parity bit is determined by the computer system when it first receives the input data. Whenever the byte is transferred, its parity bit goes along. When it reaches its destination, the computer system counts up the number of bits that are on, and if it is not an odd number, then a bit must have been lost on the way. If this is the case, the system will probably try to make the transfer again.

Which of these bytes have odd parity?

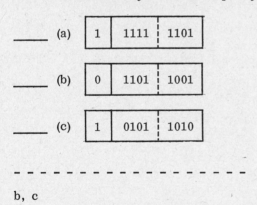

- - - - - - - - - - - - - - - - - - -

b, c

34. Of course, if two bits were lost, there would still be odd parity and the computer would not be aware of its error. However, the loss of one bit is very rare, and the loss of two nearly impossible. Some computer systems operate with <u>even</u> parity, meaning that an even number of bits must be on in each byte.

Which of these statements is true?

_____ (a) Odd parity means that an odd number of bits must be off.

_____ (b) The parity bit is always on.

_____ (c) Parity bits are always in the zone portion of the byte.

_____ (d) none of the above

— — — — — — — — — — — — — — — — — —

d

35. Most computers use the EBCDIC system to represent data in storage. There are many times when a programmer or a person performing maintenance on a computer needs to know exactly what characters are in a particular part of storage. Using a special program it is possible to instruct the computer to print out the part of storage of interest, byte by byte.

A listing of storage that just showed whether each bit was on or off might look like this:

    1110:0011   1011:0111   1111:0010   1001:1001

This is quite difficult to read, however, as the reader has to remember what each of the 256 combinations of 1's and 0's means. So as the computer writes out the contents of memory, it converts each byte into a number in the hexa-decimal numbering system, which uses 16 basic characters to represent num-bers. These are shown in figure 5-4.

Decimal	Hexadecimal	Decimal	Hexadecimal
0	0	8	8
1	1	9	9
2	2	10	A
3	3	11	B
4	4	12	C
5	5	13	D
6	6	14	E
7	7	15	F

Figure 5-4. Hexadecimal Numbers

What is 12 in hexadecimal? _____

— — — — — — — — — — — — — — — — — —

C

36. What is the decimal number equal to F in hexadecimal? _____

— — — — — — — — — — — — — — — — — —

15

37. Numbers up to 15 are represented by a single hexadecimal number. 16 is represented by 10_{hex}. (The "hex" is used to avoid confusion with decimal numbers.) So a "1" in the second column from the right represents 16. What do you think 20_{hex} represents?

_____ (a) 17

_____ (b) 32

_____ (c) 20

_____ (d) none of the above

- - - - - - - - - - - - - - - - - -

b $[20_{hex} = (2 \times 16) + 0 = 32]$

38. The second column from the right tells us how many 16's there are in the hexadecimal number. What do you think 11_{hex} represents?

_____ (a) 17

_____ (b) 33

_____ (c) neither

- - - - - - - - - - - - - - - - - - -

a $[11_{hex} = (1 \times 16) + 1 = 17]$

39. What does 15_{hex} represent? _____

- - - - - - - - - - - - - - - - - - -

21 $[(1 \times 16) + 5 = 21]$

40. What does $1E_{hex}$ represent? (Use Figure 5-4.) _____

- - - - - - - - - - - - - - - - - -

30 $[(1 \times 16) + 14 = 30]$

41. What does $4F_{hex}$ represent? _____

- - - - - - - - - - - - - - - - - - -

79 $[(4 \times 16) + 15 = 64 + 15 = 79]$

42. How about $B6_{hex}$? What does it represent? _____

- - - - - - - - - - - - - - - - - -

43. That was a more tricky conversion because you have to do several things.

$$B6_{hex} = (B \times 16) + 6$$
$$= (11 \times 16) + 6$$
$$= 176 + 6$$
$$= 182$$

Lastly, what does CC_{hex} represent? _____

- - - - - - - - - - - - - - - - - -

204   $[(C \times 16) + C = (12 \times 16) + 12 = 192 + 12 = 204]$

44. How do we convert from decimal to hexadecimal? We can use the same general system as used for converting from decimal to binary, except that this time we divide by 16. For example, convert 137 to hexadecimal.

$$16 \,) \, \underline{137} \quad (8 \text{ rem } 9$$
$$\underline{128}$$
$$9$$

Sixteen divides into 137 8 times with a remainder of 9. How then should we write 137 as a hexadecimal?

_____   (a) 89_{hex}

_____   (b) 98_{hex}

_____   (c)   neither

- - - - - - - - - - - - - - - - - -

a $[137 = (8 \times 16) + 9]$

45. Here's another example. Convert 125 to hexadecimal.

$$16 \,) \, \underline{125} \quad (7 \text{ rem } 13$$
$$\underline{112}$$
$$13$$

But we can't use the remainder as it is, so we must convert it to hexadecimal.

What is 13 in hexadecimal? _____   What is 125 in hexadecimal? _____

- - - - - - - - - - - - - - - - - -

D, $7D_{hex}$

46. If we divide by 16 and get an answer (quotient) larger than 10, then we have to convert it to hexadecimal, using the table in Figure 5-4. For example, converting 162 to hexadecimal we have:

$$16 \,) \, \underline{162} \quad (10 \text{ rem } 2$$
$$\underline{160}$$
$$2$$

But the 10 must be converted to hexadecimal, so we will have

$$16 \,) \, \underline{162} \quad (\text{A rem } 2$$
$$\underline{160}$$
$$2$$

which gives $162 = A2_{hex}$.

It is not essential to fully understand the hexadecimal system to complete this book. But if you want to learn more about it, an excellent source is another Self-Teaching Guide: Ruth Ashley's Background Math for a Computer World.

The following diagram shows how the contents of each byte in storage may be converted to a hexadecimal number.

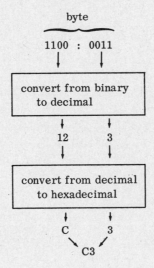

So the part of memory that we listed in frame 35 (page 118) might be converted to hexadecimal like this.

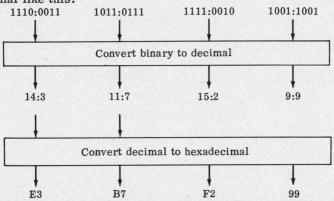

47. So much for number systems and codes. But how are they used to represent data in storage. What does storage look like?

The most common form of internal storage for computers is <u>magnetic core storage</u>. Figure 5-5 on the next page shows a portion of magnetic code storage. Each core is very small indeed, about the size of a pinhead. In the picture the

cores look rather like little metal bars, but in fact they are shaped like dough-
nuts, as Figure 5-6 shows. Each core has three thin wires passing through it.

Figure 5-5. Magnetic Core Storage

Figure 5-6. Arrangement of Core and Grid Wires

Each core is made of <u>ferrite</u>, a form of iron that is very easy to magnetize.
It can be magnetized in a clockwise or a counterclockwise direction, depending
on the direction of the electrical impulses flowing through the wires X and Y,
as shown in Figure 5-7 at the top of the next page.

If the core is magnetized in a clockwise direction, it is said to be ON. If
magnetized in a counterclockwise direction, it is OFF. Thus each core operates in a binary fashion, just like the light bulbs discussed earlier.

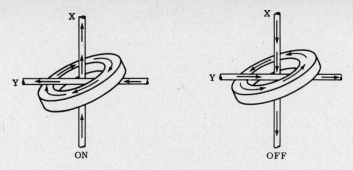

ON   OFF

Figure 5-7. Magnetization of Cores

The thin wire in Figure 5-6 is called the sense wire and is used to "read" the direction of the magnetization in the core. This reading is then transmitted wherever it is needed. (Just how this is done is beyond the scope of this book.)
Each core operates in a binary fashion; it can be either ON or OFF. This means that each core can be used as a single _____ in the EBCDIC code.

- - - - - - - - - - - - - - - - - -

bit

48. How many magnetic cores would be needed to represent one byte (excluding the parity bit)? _____

- - - - - - - - - - - - - - - - - -

8

49. Which of these statements is true?

_____ (a) Magnetic cores are doughnut-shaped and made of ferrite.

_____ (b) Magnetic cores act as binary bits.

_____ (c) both

_____ (d) neither

- - - - - - - - - - - - - - - - - -

c

50. As seen in Figure 5-5, large numbers of magnetic cores are arranged together in a grid. Each grid is called a <u>core plane</u> and the full storage section is made up by stacking core planes together, either horizontally or vertically. Figure 5-8 at the top of the next page shows core planes arranged vertically.

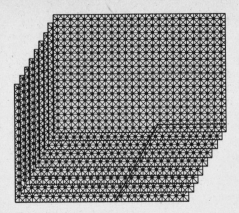

Figure 5-8. Vertically Stacked Core Planes

Figure 5-9 shows how the cores are used to represent data. Nine cores in each vertical column represent one byte in the EBCDIC code plus a parity bit. Each column also has an address, shown by the numbers 1001, 1002, and so on. (There is nothing magical about having 10 columns in the diagram. In reality there are many more, but this is just a convenient section from Figure 5-8.)

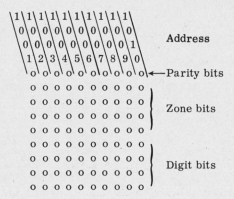

Figure 5-9. Representation of EBCDIC Code
and Parity Bit in Core Storage

Each byte has an address so that the computer can readily locate any piece of data in storage. The addresses in storage are similar to the numbers on mailboxes in the post office. To find a letter, the user goes to the appropriate box—say, number 1007—and retrieves the letter to read it. Similarly, the computer can go directly to any address in storage and read what is there. There is an important difference between mailboxes and storage, however. In order to read a letter in a mailbox, we first have to remove it from the box, leaving the box empty. When a computer reads the contents of an address in storage, however, the contents are not removed—they remain there. In fact, they remain there until something else is written into that storage address.

For example, if the letter "A" is stored at address 1003 and the computer is instructed to read the contents of address 1003, after the reading operation the letter "A" remains at address 1003. If the computer is later instructed to write the number "9" at address 1003, it first erases the "A" and then writes "9."

Which of these statements is true?

_____ (a) Each byte in storage has an address.

_____ (b) The contents of an address is not removed when the computer reads it.

_____ (c) Before writing a new character at an address, the computer first erases the character already there.

_____ (d) all of the above

– – – – – – – – – – – – – – – – – – – –

d

51. In these diagrams a black dot will represent 1 (the ON condition), and a circle (o) will represent a 0 (the OFF condition). What character is stored at address 1001 (that is, in column 1001) in this diagram? You may want to refer to the EBCDIC codes shown in Figure 5-3 (page 116). _____

– – – – – – – – – – – – – – – – – – –

9 (The zone portion shows that the character is a number, and the digit portion shows which number. Remember, the parity bit is not considered part of the EBCDIC code.)

52. What character is stored at address 1002 in the diagram shown at the top of the next page? _____

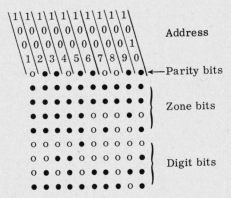

7

53. This diagram shows the number 13579 stored at addresses 1001 through 1005, and the word CLASP stored at addresses 1006 through 1010.

As you remember from Chapter 2, a field is a number of columns in a punched card that is reserved for data of the same type. The same word can be used for core storage. A certain number of bytes, each with its own address, is reserved for data of a particular type.

When it is reading data from storage, how does the computer know where one field begins and another ends? To read 13579 from the piece of core shown on the diagram above, the computer would be instructed to "read the characters at address 1001 and the next 4 bytes."

What instructions would you give the computer if you wanted it to read the

word CLASP? _____

- - - - - - - - - - - - - - - - -

Read the characters at address 1006 and the next 4 bytes.

54. Look at this piece of core storage. What would you read if you were instructed to "read the characters at addresses 1003 and the next 4 bytes"?

(You will need Figure 5-3 again.) _____

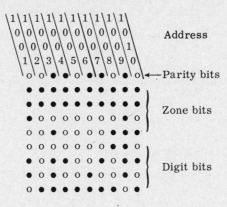

PEACE

55. Another commonly used storage device is the <u>magnetic thin-film memory plane</u>, shown in Figure 5-10. This works in much the same way as magnetic core storage. However, all the components are mounted on thin sheets of glass or plastic. Instead of doughnut-shaped pieces of ferrite, thin wafers of nickel-iron alloy are stuck on the glass and connected by thin wires, also stuck to the glass. These sheets of glass are then arranged in the same way as the magnetic core planes.

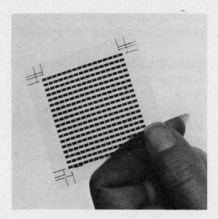

Figure 5-10. Magnetic Thin-Film Memory Planes

Thin-film memory planes have the advantage of being smaller in size and faster in operation than magnetic core planes.

Thin-film memory planes:

_____ (a) have components stuck on sheets of glass or plastic.

_____ (b) are slower in operation than magnetic core planes.

_____ (c) are arranged in the same way as magnetic core planes.

_____ (d) none of the above

- - - - - - - - - - - - - - - - - -

a, c

56. The location of a field of data in the core plane is identified by:

_____ (a) giving the address of each byte in the field.

_____ (b) giving the number of bytes to be read and the address of the last one.

_____ (c) giving the address of the first byte to be read and the number of additional bytes to be read.

_____ (d) none of the above

- - - - - - - - - - - - - - - - - -

c

57. In recent years the <u>semiconductor chip</u> has revolutionized the computer industry. The chip is made up of <u>transistors</u> that act as <u>gates</u>, allowing an electric current to flow or not to flow. Each gate represents a bit that is ON when current flows through it and OFF when current cannot flow. The bits are arranged in bytes, each byte having an address, allowing the chip to act as a storage device. Figure 5-11 at the top of the next page shows a chip compared to a paper clip. This particular chip can store about 1,000 bytes of information.

The obvious advantage of the chip is its small size (without which the pocket calculator and the microcomputer would not be possible). In addition to their use as storage devices, chips can be built which contain complete central processing units—the "computer on a chip." Such chips, called <u>microprocessors</u>, are being used in a wide variety of ways. They can control street lighting, carburation and ignition timing in automobiles, and cooking times and temperatures in microwave ovens. Their impact on our everyday lives will be enormous.

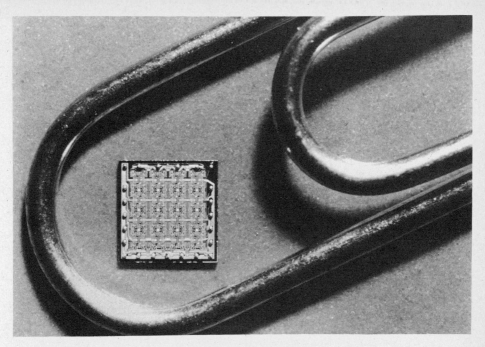

Figure 5-11. A Semiconductor Memory Chip
Compared to a Paper Clip

Two other recent developments have great implications for reducing the
cost of mass storage and for increasing the amount of storage that can be
readily accessed by computer. One is the magnetic-bubble memory. The
magnetic bubbles are tiny negatively magnetized spots on a positively magnetized plastic film. Magnetic fields can make the bubbles form into patterns
that represent data. The other development is the use of lasers to record
data on a photographic sheet embedded in a heat-sensitive plastic. Some ex-
perimental laser memories can store 13 million bytes per square inch, which
is about 1,000 times more than a standard magnetic tape.

58. The methods of storing data described above can be used for both main
and auxiliary storage. However, as you remember, there are other types of
auxiliary storage. We will now look at data storage and representation in two
of them.

Figure 5-12 shows how data is recorded on magnetic tape using the EBCDIC
code. Each black bar (|) represents a magnetized spot on the tape. That is,
a bit that is on. The arrangement of the code on the tape differs from that in
normal use. Notice that the parity bit (P) is close to the center of the tape.

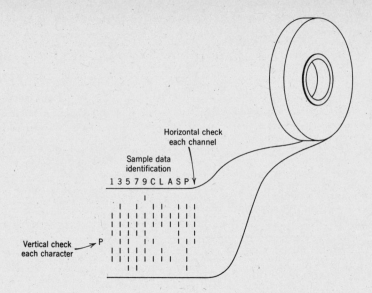

Figure 5-12.   Representation of Data on Magnetic Tape

The EBCDIC code is rearranged on tape in such a way as to put the least-used bits in the code on the outside of the tape, where the chances of damage or loss are greatest.

Two types of parity check are performed on magnetic tape coding. One is the regular parity check of each byte. The other is a parity check along each channel for one record. The check ensures that each channel of a record also has odd parity. In Figure 5-12 the horizontal parity check bits are those at the right-hand of each channel. The parity bits are automatically assigned to each byte and channel as the data is recorded on the tape.

Data recorded on magnetic tape:

_____ (a) uses a rearranged EBCDIC code.

_____ (b) has a vertical and a horizontal parity check.

_____ (c) both

_____ (d) neither

- - - - - - - - - - - - - - - - - - -

c

59. The EBCDIC code is rearranged on magnetic tape so that:

_____ (a) a horizontal parity check can be performed.

_____ (b) the least-used bits are on the outside.

_____ (c) both

_____ (d) neither

- - - - - - - - - - - - - - - - - - - -

b

60. The EBCDIC code is also used to record data on a magnetic disk. The bytes are arranged horizontally, one after the other, as shown in Figure 5-14.

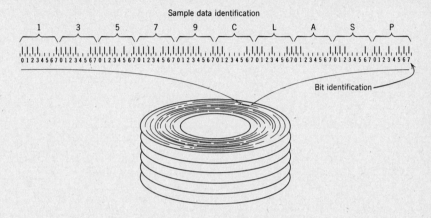

Figure 5-13. Representation of Data on Magnetic Disk

There are no parity bits on magnetic disks, since more complex methods of checking accuracy are used.

This is the end of Chapter 5. You should now work the Self-Test that follows. After the Self-Test, you will find an appendix to Chapter 5, which discusses the binary number system. You are not required to do the appendix; it is an optional exercise.

SELF-TEST

Answer all the questions and then check against the answers that follow.

1. Convert 987 to binary.

2. Convert 10010101 to decimal.

3. Convert 239 to hexadecimal.

4. Convert CB_{hex} to decimal.

5. Give two reasons for using binary numbers with computers. _____

    _____

    _____

6. Match the following:

    _____ (1) bit   (a) the eight bits that make up an EBCDIC cell
    _____ (2) byte   (b) the eight bytes that make up an EBCDIC cell
                             (c) the individual parts of a code that may be ON
                                  or OFF

7. A parity bit is:

    _____ (a) the eighth bit in an EBCDIC byte.

    _____ (b) used to indicate where a new field begins.

    _____ (c) used only on magnetic disks.

    _____ (d) none of the above

8. In magnetic core storage:

    _____ (a) each bit is a small doughnut-shaped piece of ferrite.

    _____ (b) each bit is stuck to a sheet of glass.

    _____ (c) the direction of magnetization of a core determines if it is ON
                    or OFF.
    _____ (d) none of the above

9. Which of the following statements is true?

    _____ (a) A byte is composed of eight bits.

    _____ (b) A bit is composed of eight bytes.

_____ (c) Each character in EBCDIC is represented by six bits.

_____ (d) none of the above

10. Match the following:

_____ (1) magnetic tape

_____ (2) magnetic disk

(a) has a vertical parity check bit
(b) has a horizontal parity check bit
(c) has no parity check bit

11. Which of the following statements is true?

_____ (a) A chip consists of small magnetic rings stuck on glass.

_____ (b) Laser mass-storage systems are used in microcomputers.

_____ (c) both

_____ (d) neither

12. Which of these statements is true?

_____ (a) Each byte in storage has its own address.

_____ (b) When data is read from an address in storage, the data remains there.

_____ (c) Before new data is written at an address, the data already there is erased.

_____ (d) all of the above

Answers to Self-Test

The numbers in parentheses after each answer refer to the frames in which the appropriate answers can be found. If you had a wrong answer or are not sure why your answer is correct, read that section of the chapter again before going to the next chapter.

1. 1111011011 (frame 1)

2. 149 (frame 7)

3. EF_{hex} (frame 43)

4. 203 (frame 34)

5. Because they can be represented by components that are either ON or OFF, and because mathematical operations can be performed very quickly with binary numbers. (frame 27)

6. (1) c; (2) a (frames 18 and 29)

7. d (frame 32)

8. a, c (frame 47)

9.   a (frames 30, 31)

10. (1) a, b; (2) c (frame 58)

11. d (frame 57)

12. d (frame 50)

The appendix to Chapter 5 follows.   If you wish to bypass the appendix, turn to Chapter 6.

APPENDIX TO CHAPTER 5

Binary Arithmetic

1. The purpose of this appendix is to show you how to perform addition and subtraction with binary numbers. You will also see how these two operations are used to solve multiplication and division problems.

  There are four basic facts to learn about binary addition, as shown in Figure 5-14.

$$0 + 0 = 0$$
$$0 + 1 = 1$$
$$1 + 0 = 1$$
$$1 + 1 = 1 \quad \text{and carry 1 to the}$$
$$\text{next column}$$

Figure 5-14. Binary Addition Facts

Here's a very simple addition:

$$
\begin{array}{r}
1\ 0 \\
+\ \ \ 1 \\
\hline
1\ 1
\end{array}
$$

What is the result of this addition?

$$
\begin{array}{r}
1\ 0\ 1 \\
1\ 0 \\
\hline
\end{array}
$$

- - - - - - - - - - - - - -

111

2. Here's an example that requires the carrying of a 1 to the next column.

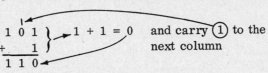

    $1 + 1 = 0$ and carry ① to the
            next column

What is the result of this addition?

$$
\begin{array}{r}
1\ 0\ 1\ 0 \\
+\ \ \ \ 1\ 1 \\
\hline
\end{array}
$$

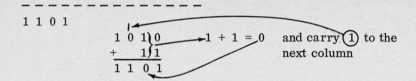

1 1 0 1

```
   1 0 1 0      1 + 1 = 0    and carry ① to the
 +     1 1                   next column
   1 1 0 1
```

3. Complete this addition.

```
      1 0 0 1
    +     1 1
```

- - - - - - - - - - - - - -

1 1 0 0   (Notice that two "carries" are necessary)

```
      1 0 0 1
    +     1 1
      1 1 0 0
```

4. Complete this addition.

```
      1 0 1 1
    +     1 1
```

- - - - - - - - - - - - - -

1 1 1 0

```
      1 0 1 1
    +     1 1
      1 1 1 0
```

5. Complete this addition.

```
      1 0 1 1
    +   1 0 1
```

- - - - - - - - - - - - - -

1 0 0 0 0

6. Here's one more for practice.

```
      1 1 1 1
    +   1 1 1
```

- - - - - - - - - - - - - -

7. The most difficult thing about adding two binary numbers together is remembering to carry over 1's and to then add them in the next column. Addition in binary can get rather more complicated, however, if we have to add three or more numbers together, because there may be several carried over 1's in each column. So the best way to handle additions with more than two numbers is just the way a computer would do it, add only two numbers at a time. For example, the best way to do this addition

```
      1 0 1 1 0
        1 0 1 1
        1 1 0 0
    + 1 0 1 0 1
```

is like this (the carried over 1's are omitted):

```
      1 0 1 1 0
    +   1 0 1 1    add the first two numbers
    1 0 0 0 0 1
    +   1 1 0 0    add the third number to the result
    1 0 1 1 0 1
    + 1 0 1 0 1    add the fourth number to the result
  1 0 0 0 0 1 0
```

Add these binary numbers: 1 0 0 1 0 + 1 1 1 0 0 + 1 0 1 0 1 1

– – – – – – – – – – – – – – –

1 0 1 1 0 0 1

8. Subtraction with binary numbers is just about as easy. There are four subtraction facts to be learned, as shown in Figure 5-15.

$$0 - 0 = 0$$
$$1 - 1 = 0$$
$$1 - 0 = 1$$
$$0 - 1 = 1 \quad \text{and borrow 1 from the}$$
next column

Figure 5-15. Binary Subtraction Facts

Here's a simple example.

```
  1 1 1 0
-     1 0
---------
  1 1 0 0
```

Complete this subtraction.

```
  1 0 1 1
- 1 0 0 1
```

- - - - - - - - - - - - - -

1 0

9. Borrowing from the next column is done like this.

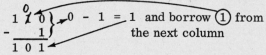

Borrowing 1 from the next column means that we must subtract 1 from the next column of the top number.
Complete this subtraction.

```
  1 1 0 1
-     1 1
```

- - - - - - - - - - - - - -

1 0 1 0

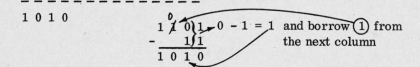

10. What happens if we try to borrow 1 from the next column and find a 0 there? As in this example.

$$1\;0\;0 \qquad 0 - 1 = 1 \text{ and borrow } 1 \text{ from}$$
$$-\underline{1} \qquad\qquad\qquad \text{the next column}$$
$$1$$

Borrowing 1 is the same as subtracting 1 from the next column of the top number. But 0 - 1 = 1 and borrow 1 from the next column. We do that, and the completed subtraction looks like this:

$$\begin{array}{r} 0\;1 \\ 1\;0\;0 \\ -\;\underline{1} \\ 1\;1 \end{array}$$

Complete this subtraction.

$$\begin{array}{r} 1\;0\;0 \\ -\;\underline{1\;1} \\ \end{array}$$

- - - - - - - - - - - - - -

$$\begin{array}{r} 1 \\ 0\;1 \\ 1\;0\;0 \\ -\;\underline{1\;1} \\ 1 \end{array}$$

11. Subtracting binary numbers in this way tends to become very tricky, as repeated borrowing from column to column can become necessary. Thus, another method is used, called subtraction by the 1's complement method. Although it looks rather complicated at first, it is actually much faster for a computer to do subtraction this way than in the way shown above.

Here's how we would use the 1's complement method for this subtraction: 100 - 11

Step 1.   Make the two numbers the same length by adding 0's to the left-hand end of the number to be subtracted.

Before	After
1 0 0	1 0 0
1 1	0 1 1

Step 2.   Complement the number to be subtracted by changing each 0 to a 1 and 1 to a 0.

Before	After
1 0 0	1 0 0
0 1 1	1 0 0

Step 3. <u>Add</u> the two numbers.

```
  1 0 0
+1 0 0
1 0 0 0
```

Step 4. Take the 1 that was carried over at the left-hand end
of the result and add it to the right-hand column of the
result of step 3.

```
    1 0 0
  +1 0 0
 ①0 0 0
+      1
       1 ◄── answer to 100 - 11
```

This looks like a long and complicated procedure, but it is much
more efficient for a computer to do subtractions this way because
once the number to be subtracted has been complemented, the rest
of the operation is addition. So really the computer needs only one
set of rules in order to do both addition and subtraction.

Here are the first two steps for this subtraction:

1 0 0 0 - 1 0 1

Step 1. Make the two numbers the same length by adding 0's
to the left-hand end of the number to be subtracted.

Before	After
1 0 0 0	1 0 0 0
1 0 1	0 1 0 1

Step 2. Complement the number to be subtracted.

Before	After
1 0 0 0	1 0 0 0
0 1 0 1	1 0 1 0

Now you complete the next two steps.

Step 3. Add the two numbers.

Step 4. Take the 1 that was carried over and add it to the result of step 3.

- - - - - - - - - - - - -

Step 3.   1 0 0 0
           + 1 0 1 0
          1 0 0 1 0

Step 4.   1 0 0 0
           + 1 0 1 0
         ①0 0 1 0
           +   ➛1
              1 1 ◄—answer to 1 0 0 0 - 1 0 1

12. Work each of the four steps to solve this subtraction:

$$1 0 1 0 0 - 1 1 1$$

Step 1. Make the two numbers the same length.

            Before   After

Step 2. Complement the number to be subtracted.

            Before   After

Step 3. Add

Step 4. Add the carried over 1.

— — — — — — — — — — — — —

Step 1.   Before   After

1 0 1 0 0   1 0 1 0 0
   1 1 1   0 0 1 1 1

Step 2.   Before   After

1 0 1 0 0   1 0 1 0 0
0 0 1 1 1   1 1 0 0 0

Step 3.   1 0 1 0 0
            + 1 1 0 0 0
            1 0 1 1 0 0

Step 4.   1 0 1 0 0
            1 1 0 0 0
        ①0 1 1 0 0
        +   1
        1 1 0 1 ← answer to 1 0 1 0 0 - 1 1 1

13. Now try this subtraction, looking back at the four steps if you need to.

$$1 0 0 1 0 1 \ - \ 1 1 0 1 1$$

— — — — — — — — — — — — —

Here are the main parts of the process.

After complementing:
    1 0 0 1 0 1
    1 0 0 1 0 0

After adding: 1 0 0 1 0 0 1

After adding carried 1:   1 0 1 0   answer to 100101 - 11011

14. Here's one more for you to try.

    10010110 - 101101

- - - - - - - - - - - - - -

1101001

15. Multiplication is a form of repeated addition. For example,

    101101 x 11

is this addition:

```
        101101    (101101 x 1)
      + 101101    (101101 x 10)
      10000111
```

We multiply by each digit in turn, moving the result one column to the left each time (as in regular multiplication with decimal numbers). This multiplication:

    101101 x 101

looks like this as an addition:

```
        101101    (101101 x 1)
        000000    (101101 x 00)
      + 101101    (101101 x 100)
      11100001
```

In that example it was easy to add three binary numbers together, since one of them was all zeros. However, in this example, we will add the results of multiplication two at a time.

$$1100101 \times 111$$

1100101	(1100101 x 1)
+ 1100101	(1100101 x 10)
100101111	add the two results
+ 1100101	(1100101 x 100)
1011000011	(the answer to 1100101 x 111)

Although it looks rather complicated it is actually quite simple. See if you can complete this multiplication.

$$11011 \times 111$$

11011	(11011 x 1)
+ _____	(11011 x 10)
	add the two results
+ _____	(11011 x 100)
	(the answer to 11011 x 111)

- - - - - - - - - - - - - -

10111101

11011
+ 11011
1010001
+ 11011
10111101

16. However many digits there are in the numbers, we use the same method. Try this multiplication:

$$101010 \times 11101$$

– – – – – – – – – – – – – –

10011000010

```
            101010     (x  1)
            000000     (x  00)
        +  101010      (x  100)
           11010010
        + 101010       (x  1000)
          1000100010
        + 101010       (x  10000)
         10011000010   (the answer!)
```

17. Division in binary is a process of repreated subtraction and is done very much like "long division" with decimals. Here's an example:

$$110 \div 11$$

```
          1 0
   1 1 | 1 1 0
      1 1 ← subtraction possible, put ① in quotient
       0 0 ← remainder plus next digit from number being divided
       1 1 ← subtraction not possible and no more digits in number
             being divided, so put ⓪ in quotient and stop
```

Thus, $110 \div 11 = 10$.

Complete this division.

```
             1 0
    1 1 | 1 1 1 1 0
         1 1
          0 1
          1 1
          0 1 1
```

So, $11110 \div 11 = $ _____.

– – – – – – – – – – – – – –

1010

```
          1010
    11 | 11110
         11
         01
         11
         011
          11
          00
          11
```

18. Of course, the subtractions used in this form of division often require the 1's complement method and a computer will always do them that way. To simplify the working, however, the next two examples can be done without complementing, as no "borrowing" is required.

    Try this division in binary: $1010101 \div 101$

```
                 _ _ _ _ _ _ _ _ _ _ _ _
10001
                    10001
           101 ⌐ 1010101
                  101
                    00
                  101
                    01
                  101
                    10
                  101
                   101
                   101
                     0
```

19. Here's one more for you to try: $10111110 \div 101$.

- - - - - - - - - - - - -
100110

```
              100110
        101 ⌐10111110
              101
               01
              101
               011
              101
              111
              101
              101
              101
               00
```

20. We have, of course, taken only a very brief look at binary arith-
    metic. If you would like to learn more about binary arithmetic,
    and computer math in general, a good book is Ruth Ashley's
    Background Math for a Computer World, another Self-Teaching
    Guide.

You should now proceed to Chapter 6.

CHAPTER SIX

Development of
Computer Programs

Computers can perform large numbers of operations at very high speeds with very little human involvement. However, a computer has to be told <u>exactly</u> what operations to perform and in what order to perform them. As you know, these sets of instructions are called <u>computer programs</u> and are prepared by programmers. A program is a series of instructions written in a coded form that the computer is able to translate into its own language. In this chapter, the process of preparing programs is discussed in general terms, the specifics being covered in Chapters 7 and 8.

After completing this chapter you will be able to:

- define <u>absolute machine language</u> and <u>symbolic programming language</u>;
- identify the purpose of <u>input-output</u> instructions, <u>move</u> instructions, <u>arithmetic</u> instructions, <u>transfer-of-control</u> instructions, and <u>editing</u> instructions;
- list the six basic steps in program development;
- define <u>source program</u>, <u>compiler</u> or <u>assembler</u>, and <u>object program</u>, and describe their relationship;
- identify the uses of <u>compilation-time</u> and <u>execution-time</u> <u>diagnostics</u>;
- explain <u>debugging</u>;
- identify advantages of <u>stored programs</u>; and
- describe the basic uses of <u>COBOL</u>, <u>FORTRAN</u>, <u>BASIC</u>, and <u>PL/1</u>.

1. As you will recall, a computer program is a detailed set of instructions that tells a computer what types of input data it will receive, exactly what calculations to perform on it and in what order, and, finally, what type of output to produce.

Of course, a program has to be understood by a computer as well as by people. The only language a computer can understand is <u>absolute machine language</u>, and each computer has its own. That is, a program that is understood by an IBM 370 would not be understood by a CDC 7600, and vice versa. Programs for both machines can be understood by people, however.

Absolute machine language has two basic components. First, it has a set of codes—one for each operation that the computer can perform. For example, the code 14 might mean "add" and the code 9J might mean "divide." Second, there is an address for each code to tell the computer where the data to be operated on can be found, and an address for the data resulting from the operations.

For example, the instruction 14 2071 3001 might mean "add the data at address 2071 to the data at 3001 and put the result at address 3001."

Writing programs in absolute machine language has two major disadvantages. First, the list of codes to be memorized by a programmer is long and the codes themselves give no clue as to what they mean. Second, keeping track of the addresses at which instructions and data are stored is very tedious and time consuming. An error in writing an address—say 3010 instead of 3001—will cause the program to fail and also be very hard to find in a long program.

Which of these statements is true?

_____ (a) Absolute machine language is the same for all computers.

_____ (b) Absolute machine language cannot be understood by people.

_____ (c) An instruction in absolute machine language is made up of a code and one or more addresses.

_____ (d) none of the above

- - - - - - - - - - - - - - - - - - -

c

2.   To overcome the problems with using absolute machine language for writing programs, symbolic programming languages have been developed. Symbolic programming languages are easier to use since operations are described using either English words such as ADD, SUBTRACT, EQUALS, or the mathematical symbols that represent the operations (such as +, -, =).

For example, the machine-language instruction in frame 1 might be written as ADD COST TO TOTAL in a symbolic language if the data at address 2071 were the cost field and the data at address 3001 were the total field. A statement like this is clearly easier to understand.

In symbolic language that is similar to mathematics, the area of a rectangle (length × width) might be calculated by a statement like this:

a = 1 * w

where a represents the area, 1 the length, w the width, and $*$ represents multiplication.

It is important to understand that a computer cannot understand instructions written in a symbolic language. Therefore it is necessary to translate a symbolic-language program into absolute machine language. This is done by the computer itself, using special translation programs. We will describe the translation process and several symbolic languages later in this chapter and look at how one symbolic language is used in Chapter 8.

Match the following:

_____ (1) absolute machine
         language
_____ (2) symbolic programming
         language

(a) can be understood by a computer
(b) can be understood by a person
(c) must be translated before the com-
    puter can understand it

- - - - - - - - - - - - - - - - - -

(1) a, b; (2) b, c

3.   When a new computer system is installed, or an existing one modified, a
systems analysis is performed. This analysis determines the types of data
processing that are required, how and where data should be recorded, the
types of reports that are to be produced, and the types of equipment that are
best suited to the particular application. Systems analysis is described in
more detail in Chapter 10.

Once the decisions have been made on what will be done with data, a programmer is given the responsibility for writing the program for the computer.
The programmer follows a series of steps in preparing the program, all of
which are described later in this chapter.

Five basic types of instructions can be used in a computer program.
These are:

(a) input-output,
(b) move,
(c) arithmetic,
(d) transfer of control, and
(e) editing.

The number of individual instructions available depends on the system—the bigger the system, the more instructions there are.

Input-output instructions are, of course, concerned with controlling input
and output operations. An instruction might be "read the next record in the
card reader. " The computer system will then do whatever is necessary to
read the data from the next card. An output instruction might be "print the
next line of output on the printer using the format already described. " The
computer will do just that.

Move instructions are used when data must frequently be moved to prevent
it from being destroyed, as new data is read into its address. If part of the
data in an input record is a customer's name, and this is to be printed on a report, then that field has to be moved from the input area to the output area before a new record is read. No calculations are performed on it, of course, so
it is a direct move, and might be expressed as "move the data at address 1008
to address 5006. " This move is necessary because another card may be read
before the name is used as output.

Another reason for moving data from one storage location to another is to
rearrange it. If records on a magnetic tape are not in sequence, they can be
sorted into ascending order. Records are read and moved to various storage

locations from where they can be moved to an output device in correct sequence. (Sorting from tapes is much more complex than this, of course.)

Match the following:

_____ (1) input-output instruction

_____ (2) move instruction

(a) transfer data from address 1385 to address 1435

(b) read the next record

(c) go to address 1292 for next instruction

- - - - - - - - - - - - - - - - - -

(1) b; (2) a

4.   The third type of instructions are <u>arithmetic</u>. These are the instructions that tell the computer to add, subtract, multiply, and divide.

Which of these is an arithmetic instruction?

_____ (a) Multiply data at address 1386 by 27.

_____ (b) Divide data at address 5329 by data at address 1027.

_____ (c) Transfer data at address 5329 to address 1027.

_____ (d) all of the above

- - - - - - - - - - - - - - - - - -

a, b

5.   The instructions prepared by the programmer are, after translation, stored in sequence in storage. The computer moves through them one at a time, performing one and then moving on to the next. Sometimes, however, different sets of instructions should be followed by different types of data. For example, a discount of 5 percent may be allowed on all orders of $500 or more. So the total value of each order must be tested to see if it is less than $500. If it is, no discount is to be allowed, and the normal processing should continue. However, if the order is for $500 or more, the system has to switch to a set of instructions that will calculate the discount and subtract it from the value of the order. Then the normal set of instructions can be returned to. Figure 6-1 at the top of the next page shows how these instructions are arranged.

The test instruction and the "go to B" instruction are together called a <u>transfer-of-control</u> instruction. They say: if VALUE is not less than $500, instruction B will control the next step in the processing; if value is less than $500, the next instruction in sequence, instruction A, will control the processing. This type of transfer of control is also referred to as a <u>conditional</u> <u>branch</u>. That is, the processing <u>branches</u> to instruction A or instruction B depending on the <u>condition</u> of VALUE, here its size.

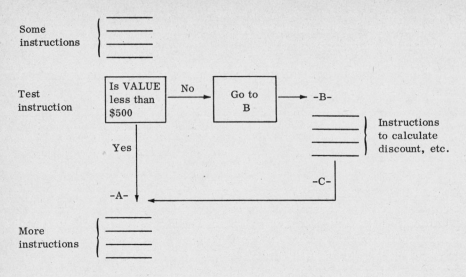

Figure 6-1. Example of Test and Branch Instructions

What do you think instruction C does? _____

_____

– – – – – – – – – – – – – – – – – – –

It branches the processing to instruction A.

6. Instruction C branches the processing to instruction A when the instructions relating to the discount are completed. This is called an <u>unconditional branch</u> because it is made irrespective of the condition of any data.

A conditional-branch instruction essentially says "when you get to here, if such-and-such is true, go there, otherwise go somewhere else." An unconditional branch says, "when you get to here, go to there."

A conditional branch:

_____ (a) is a transfer of control instruction.

_____ (b) always has a test associated with it.

_____ (c) transfers control of processing to one of two possible instructions.

_____ (d) all of the above

– – – – – – – – – – – – – – – – – – –

d

7. Match the two lists shown at the top of the next page.

_____ (1) move instruction

_____ (2) unconditional-branch
           instruction

_____ (3) conditional-branch
           instruction

(a) go to instruction at address 3270

(b) add data at address 4732 to data at
     address 1565

(c) if data at address 2370 is less than
     0, go to instruction 5222, otherwise
     go to instruction 4982

(d) transfer the data from address 1555
     to address 2400

- - - - - - - - - - - - - - - - - - -

(1) d; (2) a; (3) c

8.   Transfer of control and branching will be discussed in more detail in Chapters 7 and 8.
     The fifth type of instruction is that of editing. As you recall from Chapter
2, when numerical data is punched into cards, all commas and decimal points
are left out in order to save space. However, when data is to be printed in the
form of a report, these symbols are needed. Editing instructions are used to
do this; they add commas, decimal points, or dollar signs ($) as required when
data is moved from main storage to be printed.
     Editing also removes unnecessary zeros from the left of the number as
well as inserting the appropriate punctuation. Editing instructions also tell the
computer how many decimal places to print and if a minus (-) or credit (CR)
sign should be printed.
     If these digits were in storage, 0120376, and if they represented an amount
of money, how should they be edited for printing?

_____ (a) $01,203.76

_____ (b) $1,203.76

_____ (c) 1203.76$

- - - - - - - - - - - - - - - - - - -

b

9.   Match the following:

_____ (1) move instruction

_____ (2) arithmetic instruction

_____ (3) editing instruction

(a) insert decimal point three places
     from left-hand end of field

(b) go to instruction at address 1327

(c) add contents of 1009 to contents of
     3265

(d) copy data at address 1327 into ad-
     dress 1676

- - - - - - - - - - - - - - - - - - -

(1) d; (2) c; (3) a

10. Match the following:

_____ (1) transfer-of-control instruction
_____ (2) input-output instruction

(a) read next record
(b) go to instruction at address 1327
(c) print next line
(d) if HOURS WORKED is zero, go to instruction 1020

- - - - - - - - - - - - - - - - - -

(1) b, d; (2) a, c

11. Those are the basic instructions a programmer has to give to a computer system so that it can process data according to an original plan. But how does the programmer go about writing the program and introducing it to the computer system?

There are six basic steps in the development of a program, each of which will be discussed in turn:

(a) analysis of the problem,
(b) development of flowcharts describing the solution,
(c) writing the program in some coded form,
(d) compiling the object program,
(e) debugging the program, and
(f) documenting the program.

When asked to prepare a program to solve a particular data-processing problem, the programmer is usually told what the output should be like and what input data is available. These things will have been decided during systems analysis.

In analyzing the input the programmer must know what input medium is to be used—cards, tape, or the like. The order in which the data fields are arranged in the records and their size must also be determined.

The process component of the program describes what operations are to be performed on the data. Here the programmer decides the order in which to arrange these operations and the points at which logical decisions (branches) have to be made.

Finally, the programmer analyzes the output requirements. Is it to be punched into cards, written on magnetic tape, or printed as a report? If it is to be printed, what are the headings for the report, and where should each output field be placed?

It is essential that all these questions be asked, and answered, before proceeding with the next step. In obtaining the answers, the programmer will talk with the people who designed the system as well as with the people who will be using the output. He or she will talk to the latter primarily about what the output data should look like in order to be most useful to the user.

The programmer analyzes the problem to determine:

_____ (a) what type of equipment to purchase for the system.

_____ (b) the format of input and output data.

_____ (c) what calculations are necessary.

_____ (d) all of the above

- - - - - - - - - - - - - - - - - - - -

b, c

12. Once the programmer has the information needed about the program, a flowchart is drawn. Figure 6-2 shows a simple flowchart.

A flowchart is a "picture" of the program and how it operates. Notice that there are different-shaped boxes, each representing a particular type of operation. You will learn how to draw flowcharts in Chapter 7. Flowcharts are useful because they show, in order, the operations to be performed on data as well as the tests and conditional and unconditional branches that will be part of the program.

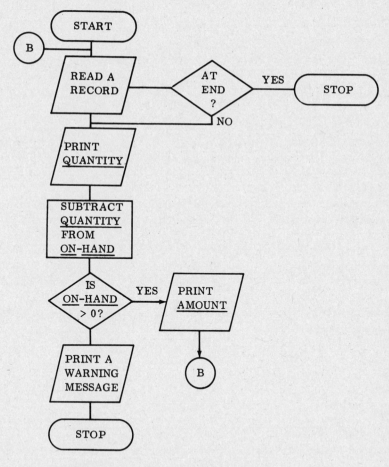

Figure 6-2. A Simple Flowchart

When the flowchart is drawn, the general accuracy of the proposed program can be checked. The programmer can take some sample data and pretend to be the computer system. Working step by step, the programmer does to the data exactly what the flowchart says to do. The final output should be exactly that expected. If it isn't, and assuming a careless mistake wasn't made along the way, the flowchart contains some wrong instructions and should be changed. Getting the correct output doesn't guarantee that the finished program will be perfect, since there are many things yet to be done, but this simple check will show any logical flaws in the planning.

Flowcharts:

_____ (a) can be used to check the basic operation of a program.

_____ (b) are made up of different-shaped boxes, each representing a particular type of operation.

_____ (c) show the operations to be performed on data during processing.

_____ (d) all of the above

- - - - - - - - - - - - - - - - - -

d

13. After the flowchart is completed, a series of detailed instructions has to be written from it. These instructions are called the source program and are usually written in a symbolic language. The particular symbolic language chosen for the source program will depend on many factors—two main considerations being the type of job being programmed and the type of computer being used.

When the source program has been written, it is punched into cards, or stored on magnetic tape or magnetic disks. In this way it becomes available for use when needed.

A _____ program is written by a programmer

using a _____ language.

- - - - - - - - - - - - - - - - - -

source, symbolic

14. Indicate the order in which these steps are performed:

_____ developing a flowchart

_____ writing the program in coded form

_____ analyzing the problem

- - - - - - - - - - - - - - - - - -

2 developing a flowchart
3 writing the program in coded form
1 analyzing the problem

15. The symbolic language used by the programmer cannot be understood directly by the computer system. It must first be translated into absolute machine language. This translation is done by the <u>compiler</u>, or <u>assembler</u>.

The compiler or assembler is a special program that does only translations from symbolic language to machine language. The translated program is called an <u>object program</u> and may be placed directly into storage or punched into cards. Just how the object program is stored depends on the computer system being used and the number of times the program will be run.

Match the following:

_____ (1) object program

_____ (2) compiler

_____ (3) source program

(a) program designed to translate an object program into a source program
(b) written by a programmer in symbolic language
(c) generated by the compiler in machine language
(d) program designed to translate a source program into an object program

- - - - - - - - - - - - - - - - - -

(1) c; (2) d; (3) b

16. A(n) _____ program is converted into a(n)

_____ program through the use of a(n)

_____.

- - - - - - - - - - - - - - - - - -

source, object, compiler or assembler

17. Match the following:

_____ (1) source program

_____ (2) object program

(a) written in machine language
(b) written in English
(c) written in a symbolic language

- - - - - - - - - - - - - - - - - -

(1) c; (2) a

18. When the source program is translated, or <u>compiled</u>, into machine language, another important thing happens. Since the source program may have some errors in it, the compiler also produces a printed listing of the source program and a list of the errors in it. These error messages are used by the programmer at the next step in the process, when <u>debugging</u> the program (that is, when finding and removing the errors in the program).

Error messages may indicate places where the programmer broke some rules of the language used. For example, the English sentence "To the other side of the room go" is not correct according to the rules of English grammar. A teacher might point out the error by saying "the verb is in the wrong place." (The teacher, of course, can decide what the sentence means, but a computer cannot second-guess an instruction.)

The source program may also contain a spelling error or typo such as IF ACE IS GREATER THAN 39 GO TO STEP 50. And because the computer will not recognize the misspelled word, it may respond with something like this:

```
UNIDENTIFIED OPERAND ACE
```

The errors detected by the compiler are called compilation-time diagnostics. They indicate the instruction in which an error occurs and the type of error. All the errors indicated by the compilation-time diagnostics must be corrected before the system can process data.

When all the compilation-time errors have been corrected, the object program must be tested for logic errors with some real data. That is necessary because, although the source program may not break any of the rules of the symbolic language in which it is written, some of the instructions may be incorrect. For example, the statement IF AGE IS GREATER THAN 39 GO TO STEP 50 may be perfectly acceptable in some symbolic language, and the computer would compile it without finding an error. However, if the program is supposed to branch to step 825 if age is greater than 39, then the output for all people over 39 will be incorrect. Errors such as these are called logic errors and the computer will not detect them when compiling a source program. The only way logic errors can be detected is through careful testing with real data.

As the computer executes the program—that is, works through it instruction by instruction—it may find an error that will cause it to stop executing and print an error message. Such an error message is called an execution-time diagnostic message.

For example, an input device might be instructed to read the employee number field in a record. If instead of finding numeric data in that field the computer found alphabetic data, the program would stop executing and print an execution-time diagnostic message to the effect that it had found "bad" data. (A good programmer would anticipate this type of error in input data and include instructions as to what to do when it arose, thereby avoiding having the computer stop executing.)

Another execution-time error can be caused by faulty transfer-of-control instructions. It is possible to put the system into an infinite loop. That is, it will continue executing the same sequence, over and over again, because the last instruction sends the system back to the first instruction in the sequence. This means that, in theory, the computer would continue to execute those instructions forever. In practice, however, some time limit is placed on the execution of the program, and if it is not finished before time is up, the system automatically stops the execution and prints a diagnostic message saying why it stopped. Beginning programmers often write infinite loops into their programs.

Which of these statements is true?

_____ (a) Compilation-time diagnostics indicate errors that occur when the object program is executing data.

_____ (b) Execution-time diagnostics indicate where the programmer broke rules of the symbolic language used.

_____ (c) Logic errors can be detected only during compilation.

_____ (d) none of the above

- - - - - - - - - - - - - - - - - -

d

19. Errors in input data will be indicated by the _____ time diagnostics.

- - - - - - - - - - - - - - - - - -

execution

20. Beginning programmers spend a lot of time debugging their programs, but even experienced programmers rarely get anything other than a very simple program to run correctly the first time.

An error in the input data would be listed in the _____ time diagnostics, while a grammatical error in the source program would be

listed in the _____ time diagnostics.

- - - - - - - - - - - - - - - - -

execution, compilation

21. Indicate the order in which these steps are performed:

_____ compiling the source program

_____ analyzing the problem

_____ debugging the program

_____ writing the program in coded form

_____ developing the flowchart

- - - - - - - - - - - - - - - -

<u>4</u> compiling the source program
<u>1</u> analyzing the problem
<u>5</u> debugging the program
<u>3</u> writing the program in coded form
<u>2</u> developing the flowchart

22. Once the source program has been fully debugged and has been tested to see that it does indeed process the data as the programmer desires, it is stored in auxiliary storage. It may be stored in a deck of cards, but is more likely to be stored on magnetic tape or magnetic disk as we discussed in Chapter 5. It is then readily available for use when required. When the stored source program is to be run with data, it is taken from auxiliary storage, compiled, and placed in the main storage in the central processing unit as a machine-language object program.

Many computer systems store source programs because they take up less auxiliary storage space than object programs. Remember, each source-language statement compiles into many statements in absolute machine language. When the source programs are stored, they are compiled to produce object programs as they are needed. On some large systems, however, it is more efficient to use the extra auxiliary storage space needed for the object program than to use the processing time required to compile the source program each time it is needed, so the machine-language object program is stored.

Stored programs have the advantage that:

_____ (a) they need to be written only once.

_____ (b) they are always available when needed.

_____ (c) both

_____ (d) neither

- - - - - - - - - - - - - - - - - -

c

23. On which of these devices may a program be stored?

_____ (a) card reader

_____ (b) magnetic disk

_____ (c) magnetic tape

_____ (d) all of the above

- - - - - - - - - - - - - - - - - -

b, c

24. The final step in the preparation of the program comes after it is stored and free of errors; the program is then documented. Program documentation refers to the gathering in one place of all relevant information used in the preparation of the program. All job descriptions, flowcharts, the written symbolic code, and so on are gathered in one place. If the program develops an error at a later date or has to be modified in some way, this documentation makes it easy for another programmer to see what has been done and why.

A run manual is also prepared. It contains all the instructions that the computer operator requires in order to run the program—what input files may have to be loaded, what type of output is being prepared, and so forth.

Which of these statements is true?

_____ (a) The source program is always placed in storage and compiled when needed.

_____ (b) The run manual shows all the information necessary for another programmer to modify the program.

_____ (c) Debugging of programs means removing the errors.

_____ (d) all of the above

- - - - - - - - - - - - - - - - - - - -

c

25. To close this chapter we will look briefly at four symbolic programming languages that are in widespread use.

Common Business-Oriented Language (COBOL) is the most widely used language in business data processing. COBOL is particularly well suited to solving business problems because it is designed to perform relatively simple operations on large quantities of data from many input files.

COBOL has three major advantages for business applications. First, it is a universal language, meaning that a program written in COBOL can be used on different manufacturers' computers with a minimum of change. Second, its English-like characteristics make it easy to learn and easier for programmers and nonprogrammers to talk about exactly what the program is doing. Third, the description of input and output data and its format is fairly simple, making complex output reports quite easy to program.

Here are three statements written in COBOL. They really need no explaination.*

```
MULTIPLY SALES BY .05 GIVING COMMISSION
ADD SALARY, COMMISSION GIVING TOTAL-EARNINGS
SUBTRACT INSURANCE, TAX, RETIREMENT FROM TOTAL-EARNINGS
  GIVING NET-EARNINGS
```

Another symbolic language that is universal in nature is FORTRAN. Its name stands for FORmula TRANslator and it is primarily used for programming scientific problems. FORTRAN was designed to perform a large number of complex mathematical operations on a relatively small amount of data. As its name implies, it is used to translate mathematical formulae into a language a computer can understand. FORTRAN is a relatively straightforward language to learn and is quite easily read and understood by mathematicians

---

*To learn more about COBOL programming, see Ruth Ashley, ANS COBOL, a Wiley Self-Teaching Guide. For more information on FORTRAN, see FORTRAN IV by Friedmann, Greenberg, and Hoffberg, also a Wiley Self-Teaching Guide.

and scientists who may not be programmers. Here are the preceding instructions written in FORTRAN (the * represents "multiply"):

```
COMMIS = SALES * .05
TOTEAR = SALARY + COMMIS
NETEAR = TOTEAR - (INSUR + TAX + RETIRE)
```

Match the following:

_____ (1) COBOL

_____ (2) FORTRAN

   (a) best suited to scientific applications
   (b) best suited to business applications
   (c) written in English-like statements
   (d) written in mathematical notation

- - - - - - - - - - - - - - - - - -

(1) b, c; (2) a, d

26. Beginners All-purpose Symbolic Instruction Code, BASIC, is a language similar to FORTRAN. It is designed primarily to solve mathematical problems and looks very similar to FORTRAN. Its major advantage, however, is that it is a "conversational" language for use in time-sharing situations. By conversational we mean that the programmer can talk to the computer through BASIC. The computer responds to each sentence the programmer writes, either by accepting it and asking for another or by pointing out some error in it. The programmer can run the program directly from a terminal and can include all the necessary data as part of the program, thereby avoiding the use of input files altogether.

BASIC is the simplest programming language and for that reason is very popular in introductory computer courses. In Chapter 8 you will learn how to write simple programs in BASIC.*

Here are the statements you have seen in COBOL and FORTRAN written in BASIC:

```
C = S * .05
T = S + C
N + T - (I + TA + R)
```

Programming Language One, called PL/1, was developed to combine the large-scale data-handling characteristics of COBOL with the mathematical characteristics of FORTRAN. It is therefore suited to use for both business and scientific data processing. Although it is more difficult to learn than either FORTRAN or COBOL, its efficiency at problem solving is making it

---

*To learn more about BASIC programming, see Albrecht, BASIC, Second edition, a Wiley Self-Teaching Guide.

increasingly popular for use on large computer systems. Here are the three statements we have written, this time in PL/1:

```
COMMISSION = SALES * .05
TOTAL-EARNINGS = SALARY + COMMISSION
NET-EARNINGS = TOTAL-EARNINGS - (INSURANCE + TAX + RETIREMENT)
```

Notice that in PL/1 the names are those from COBOL, the mathematical symbols from FORTRAN.

Match the following:

_____ (1) BASIC

_____ (2) PL/1

(a) well suited to business applications
(b) well suited to mathematical applications
(c) used in time-sharing situations

- - - - - - - - - - - - - - - - - -

(1) b, c; (2) a, b

This is the end of Chapter 6. You should now work the Self-Test that follows.

SELF-TEST

Answer all the questions then check against the answers that follow.

1. Which of these statements is true?

_____ (a) An instruction in absolute machine language is written using English words or mathematical statements.
_____ (b) Each computer system has its own absolute machine language.
_____ (c) An instruction in a symbolic language contains an operation code and one or more addresses.
_____ (d) none of the above

2. Match the following:

_____ (1) input-output instruction
_____ (2) move instruction
_____ (3) arithmetic instruction

(a) multiply data at address 1589 by 14.62
(b) go to instruction at address 1492
(c) transfer data in adder to address 3030
(d) write data at address 3030 on tape

3. Match the following:

_____ (1) transfer-of-control
_____ (2) editing instruction

(a) insert decimal point two places from the left-hand end of the field
(b) transfer data in address 1552 to adder
(c) go to instruction at address 1492
(d) if data at address 3100 is greater than .75, go to instruction at address 1092; otherwise go to instruction at address 1066

4.   An unconditional transfer-of-control instruction:

_____ (a) includes a test of data.

_____ (b) is made irrespective of the condition of data.

_____ (c) tells the computer system where to find its next instruction.

_____ (d) none of the above

5.   Indicate the order in which the steps taken in preparing a program are performed.

_____ developing the flowcharts

_____ documenting the program

_____ debugging the program

_____ compiling the source program

_____ analysis of the problem

_____ writing program in some coded form

6.   Which of these statements is true?

_____ (a) The source program is used with the object program to produce the compiler.

_____ (b) The compiler translates the source program into the object program.

_____ (c) A source program is written in machine language and the object program is in symbolic language.

_____ (d) none of the above

7.   Match the following:

_____ (1) compilation-time diagnostics   (a) indicate grammatical errors in symbolic language

_____ (2) execution-time diagnostics   (b) indicate errors that occur when data is run

                                                  (c) indicate grammatical errors in the machine language

8.   Debugging is the process of:

_____ (a) finding and correcting errors in a program.

_____ (b) writing a description of the program and its components.

_____ (c) both

_____ (d) neither

9.   A stored program is always:

_____ (a) available for use.

_____ (b) in main storage.

_____ (c) both

_____ (d) neither

10. List three places where a source program may be stored when not actually being used to process a job. _____

_____

11. The run manual contains all the information about a program that:

_____ (a) another programmer might need in order to modify it.

_____ (b) an operator needs to use the program on a computer system.

_____ (c) both

_____ (d) neither

12. Match the following:

_____ (1) BASIC

_____ (2) COBOL

_____ (3) FORTRAN

_____ (4) PL/1

    (a) a conversational language
    (b) well suited to business applications
    (c) well suited to scientific applications
    (d) uses English-like statements
    (e) uses mathematical statements

Answers to Self-Test

The numbers in parentheses refer to the frames in which the appropriate answers can be found. If you have a wrong answer or are not sure why your answer is correct, read that section again before you go on to the next chapter.

1. b (frame 1)

2. (1) d; (2) c; (3) a (frame 3)

3. (1) c, d; (2) a (frame 6)

4. b, c (frame 6)

5. __2__ developing the flowcharts
    __6__ documenting the program
    __5__ debugging the program
    __4__ compiling the source program
    __1__ analysis of the problem
    __3__ writing the program in some coded form (frame 11)

6. b (frame 13)

7. (1) a; (2) b (frame 17)

8. a (frame 17)

9. a (frame 21)

10. on cards, magnetic tape, magnetic disk (frame 21)

11. b (frame 24)

12. (1) a, c, e; (2) b, d; (3) c, e; (4) b, c, d, e (frame 24)

CHAPTER SEVEN
Flowcharting

As we saw in Chapter 6, an important step in the development of a computer program is the drawing of a <u>flowchart</u>. This chapter will teach you how to develop and draw a flowchart. If you would like to learn more about flow-charting, refer to FLOWCHARTING, by Nancy Stern (a Self-Teaching Guide).

After completing this chapter you will be able to:

- identify the <u>six</u> <u>basic</u> <u>symbols</u> used in flowcharting;
- <u>write</u> <u>a</u> <u>description</u> <u>of</u> <u>the</u> <u>procedures</u> a simple flowchart represents;
- <u>draw</u> <u>a</u> <u>flowchart</u> that represents the description of a simple procedure; and
- draw and interpret simple <u>logical</u> <u>procedures</u>.

1. Once the programmer has the information needed about the program, a <u>flowchart</u> is drawn. A flowchart is a "picture" of the program and how it operates. It shows, in order, all the operations to be performed on the data and all the conditional and unconditional branches that will be part of the program.

Figure 7-1 shows a flowchart template. It has symbols that are part of an international standard set of symbols used for drawing flowcharts of computer systems and computer flowcharts.

Figure 7-2 shows the <u>six</u> <u>basic</u> <u>flowcharting</u> <u>symbols</u> that we will be using in this chapter and describes their use.

Figure 7-1. Programmer with a Flowchart Template

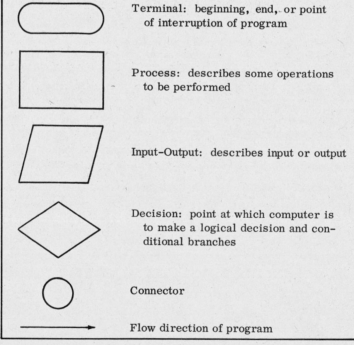

Terminal: beginning, end, or point of interruption of program

Process: describes some operations to be performed

Input-Output: describes input or output

Decision: point at which computer is to make a logical decision and conditional branches

Connector

Flow direction of program

Figure 7-2. Six Basic Flowchart Symbols

When a flowchart is <u>drawn</u>, a brief statement is written inside each block, or symbol, to describe what is to be done at that step. For example:

The flowchart contains logic information to be used by the programmer to write a source program in symbolic language. Each box is usually represented by one instruction in the source program, although sometimes more may be required as we will see later.

Which of these flowchart symobls matches the statement written inside it?

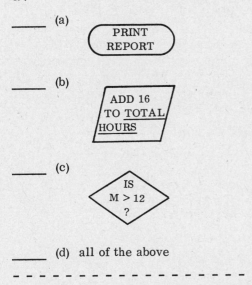

_____ (a)

_____ (b)

_____ (c)

_____ (d) all of the above

- - - - - - - - - - - - - - - - - -

c (Choice <u>a</u> is a terminal—beginning or ending; choice <u>b</u> is an input-output symbol.)

2. The arrow symbol indicates the order in which to move through the flow-chart. Flowcharts are normally drawn so that they are read from top to bottom and from left to right.

Match the flowcharting symbols you will find on the next page to the proper words.

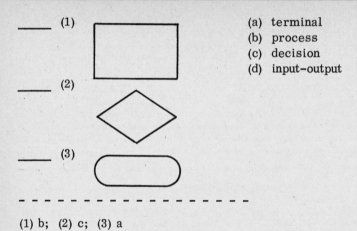

_____ (1)

_____ (2)

_____ (3)

(a) terminal
(b) process
(c) decision
(d) input–output

- -

(1) b; (2) c; (3) a

3.   Because most flowcharts of real jobs contain a large number of steps, each step is normally numbered. Also, it is often impossible, following a conditional branch, to show both sequences of instructions together. For this reason, the connector symbol is used. It shows the number of the block in the flowchart that is next in the sequence. For example:

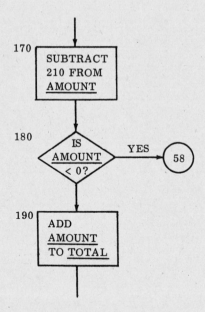

Notice that the word AMOUNT is underlined in these symbols. In this chapter we will underline all words that refer to data stored at some known address. The computer, of course, uses its normal addressing system. The underlined word is a convenient name for that data. As you will see in Chapter 8, names are assigned to all pieces of data used in writing a program in symbolic language. So "ADD 210 TO AMOUNT" means "add 210 to the data stored at the address I have called AMOUNT. "

In this example, which instruction will be executed if the contents of the address called NUMBER equal 9999? _____

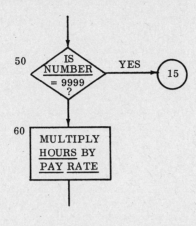

- - - - - - - - - - - - - - - - - - - -

instruction 15

4.   Notice that only the YES answer to a decision question is labeled. If one is YES, the other has to be NO. This reduces the amount of writing on the flowchart.

Here is the outline of a simple program:

    (a) Start.
    (b) Read a record.
    (c) If it is the last record, print TOTAL and then stop.
    (d) If it is not the last record, add AMOUNT to TOTAL.
    (e) Print AMOUNT.
    (f) Read another record.

All input files, whether they be in punched cards, on magnetic tape, or on magnetic disk, use a standard method to signal the computer that the end of the file has been reached. After the last record with data in it, a record is added that is blank except for a /* (slash and asterisk) in columns 1 and 2. All programs have a method of detecting this last record and telling the computer what to do when it is read.

Thus the answer to the question "Is it the last record?" is determined by examining the first two columns of each record. If they contain a /*, then the end of the file has been reached.

Draw the first symbol that is needed for the program and label it.

- - - - - - - - - - - - - - - - - - - -

START

5. Now we have started. Which block will come next?

_____ (a)

_____ (b)

_____ (c)

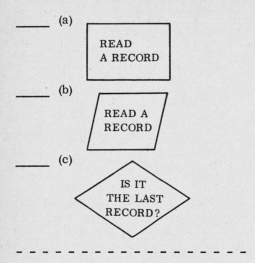

- - - - - - - - - - - - - - - - - -

b (We have to read a record before deciding if it is the last record or not.)

6. After reading a record, the question "Is it the last record?" has to be answered, so the flowchart will look like this:

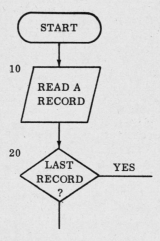

As we mentioned above, each block in a flowchart is numbered. The numbering is usually done by 10's (that is, 10, 20, 30, ...) so that if a step is forgotten it is easy to put it in the correct sequence by using numbers between the steps that go on either side of it.

If it is the last record, then the computer will print <u>TOTAL</u> (that is, the data at an address we have called <u>TOTAL</u>) and then stop. Which of the blocks at the top of the next page should follow the YES answer to the question?

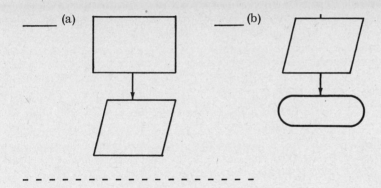

_____ (a)   _____ (b)

- - - - - - - - - - - - - - - - - -

b

7. The flowchart now looks like this:

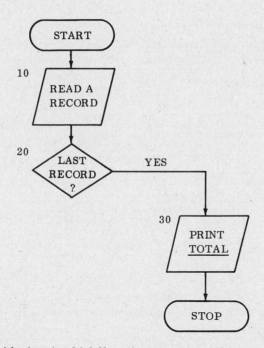

Which two blocks should follow the NO answer from the decision block?

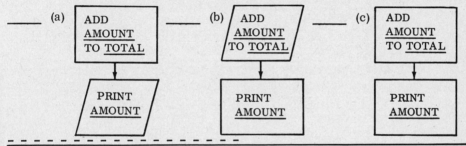

_____ (a)   _____ (b)   _____ (c)

a (☐ is a process; ▱ is input-output.)

8.   The flowchart now looks like this:

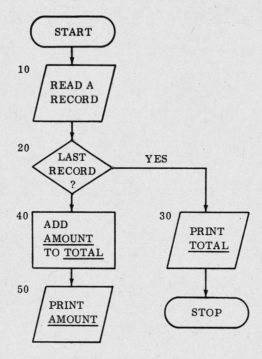

What is the last step of the program described in frame 4 in this chapter?

_____

- - - - - - - - - - - - - - - - - -

Read another record.

9.   The flowchart we have drawn so far shows how to process one record.
To show that another record must be read (and processed), what should we do?

_____ (a) Repeat the flowchart for each record to be processed.

_____ (b) Add an instruction that sends the computer back to the "read a record" instruction.

_____ (c) Nothing, because the computer will automatically go back to the
"read a record" instruction.

- - - - - - - - - - - - - - - - - -

b

10. To redraw the flowchart for every record to be processed would be a very
inefficient procedure. We don't always know how many records will have to
be processed. Each time the program is run there may be a different number,
so the connector symbol is used to instruct the computer to return to read
another record.

Here is the completed flowchart and the original instructions:

(a) Start.
(b) Read a record.
(c) If it is last record,
     print <u>TOTAL</u> and stop.
(d) If it is not last record,
     add <u>AMOUNT</u> to <u>TOTAL</u>.
(e) Print <u>AMOUNT</u>.
(f) Read another record.

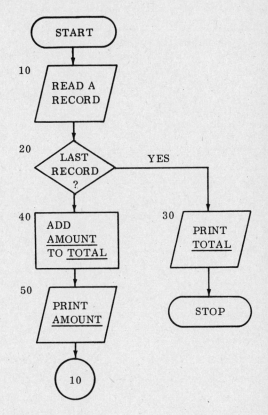

Here is another set of simple instructions. See if you can draw a flowchart for it on a separate piece of paper.

(a) Start.
(b) Read a record.
(c) If it is the last record, go to end-of-job sequence.
(d) Print <u>QUANTITY</u>.
(e) Subtract <u>QUANTITY</u> from <u>ON-HAND</u>.
(f) If <u>ON-HAND</u> is greater than zero, print <u>AMOUNT</u>
     and read another card.
(g) If <u>ON-HAND</u> is less than zero, print a warning
     message and stop.
(h) Read another record.

- - - - - - - - - - - - - - - - - - -

Your flowchart should look something like this. The words you used may be different but the logic should be the same.

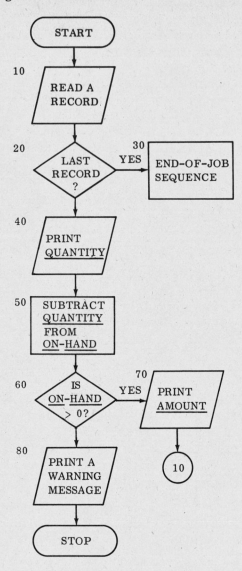

11. Now try to write a description of the flowchart at the top of the next page. Space is provided below the chart for your description.

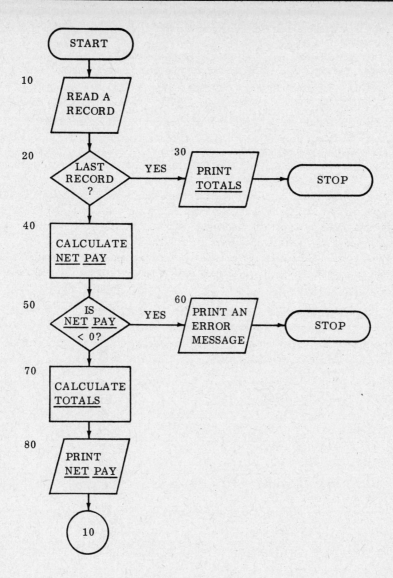

Your description should be something like this:
(a) Start.
(b) Read a record.
(c) If it is last record, print TOTALS and stop.
(d) If it is not last record, calculate NET PAY.
(e) If NET PAY is less than zero, print an error message and stop.
(f) If NET PAY is not less than zero, calculate TOTALS.
(g) Print NET PAY.
(h) Read another record.

12. Now we will look at some flowcharts made up mainly from conditional branches. As you will remember from Chapter 6, conditional branches are sometimes called logical decisions. A logical decision is simply one that says, "If such and such, do this; otherwise do that."

We will now draw a flowchart for part of a payroll program. This part involves the calculation of gross pay and requires logical decisions to be made. The specifications are:

(a) Read a record containing employee number, wage classification, and number of hours worked.
(b) Calculate gross pay using the following wage classification and the hourly wage:

Wage Classification	Hourly Wage
1	$2.65
2	3.05
3	3.45
4	3.90

(c) When the last record is read, go to an end-of-job sequence.
(d) If wage classification is not 1, 2, 3, or 4, print an error message.

The flowchart should begin with START and READ A RECORD, like this:

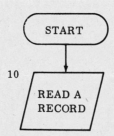

10

When a record is read we will have three numbers to work with—employee number (E), wage classification (C) and hours worked (H). When do we have to go to end-of-job sequence? _____

- - - - - - - - - - - - - - - - - - - -

when the last record is read

13. Which of these is the correct symbol for asking the question "Is this the last record?"

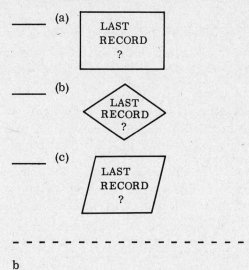

———— (a)

LAST
RECORD
?

———— (b)

LAST
RECORD
?

———— (c)

LAST
RECORD
?

- - - - - - - - - - - - - - - - - - - -

b

14. So the flowchart will now look like this:

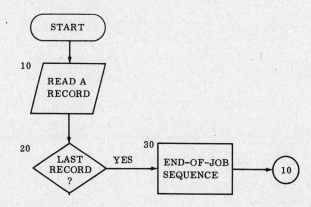

START

10

READ A
RECORD

20   30

LAST   YES   END-OF-JOB
RECORD   SEQUENCE   10
?

The end-of-job sequence to which the program moves when the last record has been read is a series of instructions that tell the computer what to do next. For this payroll program, the computer would probably go to another section where taxes on the gross pay are calculated.

If the record read is not the last record, then we have to begin the calculations of gross pay. The first thing to do is to ask if the wage classification

is "1." If it is, what will the hourly wage be? _____

- - - - - - - - - - - - - - - - - - -

$2.65

15. Knowing the wage rate and the hours worked, how do we calculate gross pay (that is, the total amount earned before any deductions are made)?

_____

- - - - - - - - - - - - - - - - - - - -

gross pay = hours worked × wage rate

16. If we ask the question "Is C = 1?" (where C stands for wage classification) and the answer is YES, then this calculation has to be performed: GROSS PAY = HOURS WORKED × $2.65. Once gross pay has been calculated for an employee we must return and read another record.

So now the flowchart looks like this:

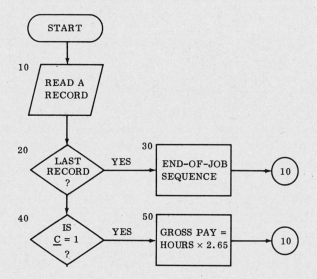

What should we do if the answer to step 40 is NO?

_____ (a) Print an error message saying that we have an invalid wage class-
          ification.

_____ (b) Ask if C = 2.

_____ (c) Read another record.

_____ (d) none of the above

- - - - - - - - - - - - - - - - - - - -

b

17. If C̲ is not 1, then we have to ask whether it is 2. If it is, what shall we do? _____

- - - - - - - - - - - - - - - - - -

Calculate gross pay using $3.05 as wage rate.

18. If C̲ is not 2, what should we do? _____

_____

- - - - - - - - - - - - - - - - - -

Ask if C̲ = 3.

19. Our flowchart now looks like this:

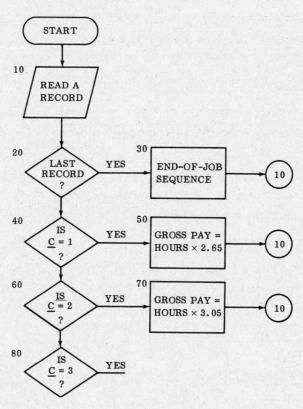

On a scrap of paper try to draw the next step after the YES answer to step 80 and the next two steps after the NO answer to step 80.

- - - - - - - - - - - - - - - - - -

Here are the next few steps you might have drawn. Don't worry if you didn't get them all, since this was a difficult question. However, be sure you understand why these steps are there.

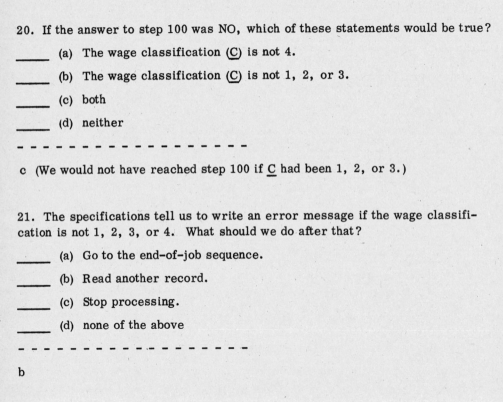

20. If the answer to step 100 was NO, which of these statements would be true?

_____ (a) The wage classification ($\underline{C}$) is not 4.

_____ (b) The wage classification ($\underline{C}$) is not 1, 2, or 3.

_____ (c) both

_____ (d) neither

- - - - - - - - - - - - - - - - - -

c (We would not have reached step 100 if $\underline{C}$ had been 1, 2, or 3.)

21. The specifications tell us to write an error message if the wage classification is not 1, 2, 3, or 4. What should we do after that?

_____ (a) Go to the end-of-job sequence.

_____ (b) Read another record.

_____ (c) Stop processing.

_____ (d) none of the above

- - - - - - - - - - - - - - - - - -

b

22. The completed flowchart is shown at the top of the next page.

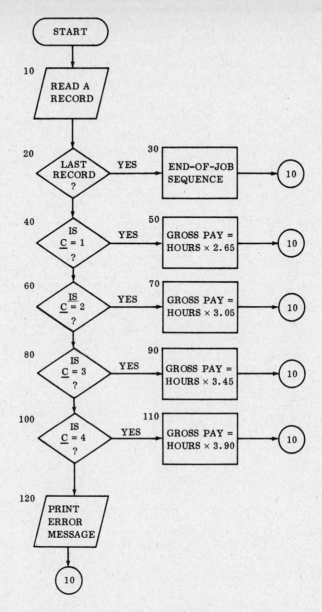

Here's another problem involving a series of logical decisions. See if you can draw a flowchart for it, using a separate piece of paper.

The program is to count the number of students in each class using their class code. You are to read a series of records and check column 9 for the presence of a 1, 2, 3, or 4. If there is a 1, add 1 to the field FROSH; if there is a 2, add 1 to the field SOPH; if there is a 3, add 1 to the field JUN; if there is a 4, add 1 to the field SEN; if none of these are present in column 9, add 1 to the field <u>OTHER</u>. When the last record has been read, print the contents of each field and then stop.

- - - - - - - - - - - - - - - - -

Your flowchart should look something like this:

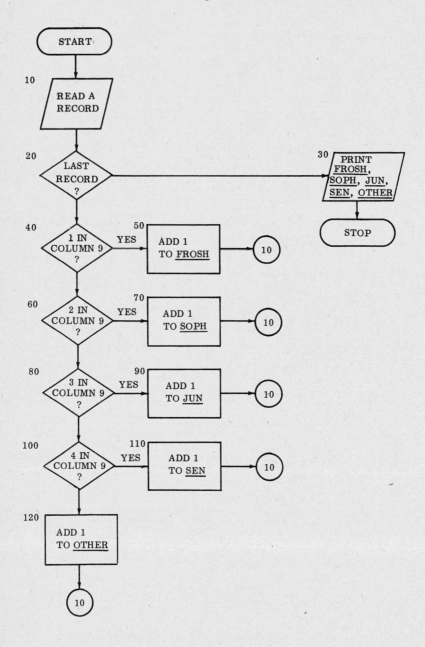

23. The flowchart below shows the processing steps required to select and print the names of people having certain features.

The records to be read have three fields to be used, and the data recorded in them is as follows:

SEX	HAIR	EYES
1 = male	1 = blonde	1 = brown
2 = female	2 = brown	2 = blue
	3 = other	3 = other

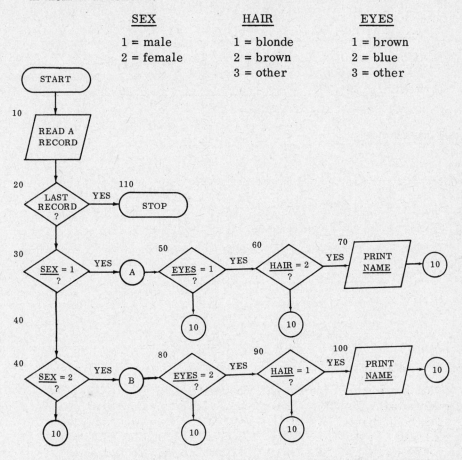

If <u>SEX</u> = 1 for a particular record, what are the first four steps of the flowchart that will be followed. (Write down the number of each step.)

- - - - - - - - - - - - - - - - - -

10, 20, 30, 50

24. If this particular male had blue eyes, what step would follow step 50?

- - - - - - - - - - - - - - - - - -

10 (Blue eyes are coded as 2. Step 50 asks if <u>EYES</u> = 1 (brown). If not, go to step 10.)

25. Would a male with brown eyes and brown hair have his name printed? If so, at what step? _____

- - - - - - - - - - - - - - - - - -

Yes, at step 70

26. What combination of eye and hair color must a female have, if her name is to be printed? _____

- - - - - - - - - - - - - - - - - - -

blue eyes and blond hair

27. Which of these would have their names printed?

_____ (a) a blue-eyed, brown-haired male

_____ (b) a brown-eyed, blond-haired female

_____ (c) a blue-eyed, brown-haired female

_____ (d) none of the above

- - - - - - - - - - - - - - - - - - -

d

28. Here's another flowchart for you to draw on a piece of scrap paper.

You are to read a record and check the field SALES. If SALES is greater than $1,000, then calculate the commission as COMM = SALES × 15 percent. If SALES is greater than $500, then calculate commission as COMM = SALES × 5 percent. After each calculation add COMM to TOT COMM, print COMM on a check, and read the next record. If SALES is less than $500, then read another record. When the last record is read, print TOT COMM and stop.

- - - - - - - - - - - - - - - - - -

Your flowchart should look something like the one at the top of the next page.

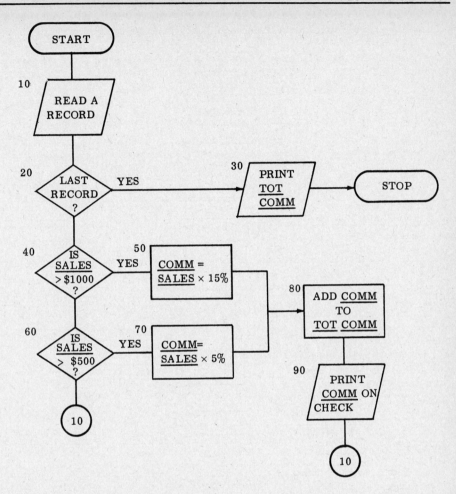

29. We will now draw a flowchart that will read three numbers, choose the largest, and print it. Imagine we have a magnetic tape with a long string of numbers on it. Then we must:

(a) read three numbers (in a record),
(b) choose the largest,
(c) print it, and
(d) read three more numbers.

We could draw a flowchart like the one at the top of the next page. But it doesn't tell <u>how</u> to select the largest number from the three. What we need is more detail for the second step.

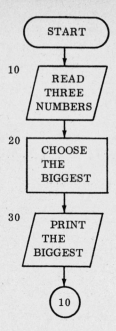

We shall start the flowchart like this:

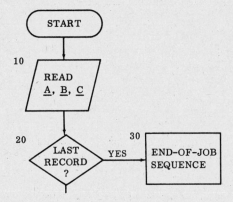

This says to read three numbers and to call the first one A, the second one B, and the third C. We will include the standard "LAST RECORD?" check.

There are several ways to go from here, but we will ask the question "Is A bigger than B?" The shorthand for "bigger than" is the special symbol >. The open end always points to the bigger number.

Which of these is correct use of the "bigger than" symbol?

_____ (a)   16 > 10

_____ (b)   22 < 14

_____ (c)   6 > 6

a

30. The first decision in our program, then, is this:

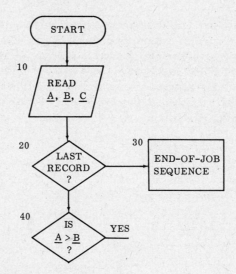

If the answer to this question is YES, then:

_____ (a) B is bigger than A.

_____ (b) A is bigger than B.

_____ (c) A is equal to B.

- - - - - - - - - - - - - - - - - -

b

31. Let's see where the YES answer leads. If A is bigger than B, do we know which of the three numbers is the biggest? _____

- - - - - - - - - - - - - - - - - -

no

32. We know that A is bigger than B, but we don't know the relationships between A and C, and B and C. So we should ask another question. Remember, we want to find the biggest number in the smallest number of steps. Which of these questions should we ask next?

_____ (a) Is A > C?

_____ (b) Is B > C?

_____ (c) Is C > A?

_____ (d) any of the above

- - - - - - - - - - - - - - - - - - -

a

33. Any of these questions would help us find the biggest number, but the question, "Is $\underline{A} > \underline{C}$?" is the best one to ask here. We always aim to ask the smallest number of questions to reach a solution. We know that $\underline{A} > \underline{B}$ (because we have taken the YES branch from the question "Is $\underline{A} > \underline{B}$?"); so a YES answer to "Is $\underline{A} > \underline{C}$?" tells us that $\underline{A}$ must be the biggest number. It is bigger than both $\underline{B}$ and $\underline{C}$. We should print it and then read three more numbers. The flowchart now looks like this:

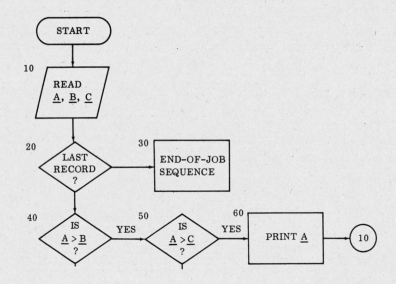

If the answer to "Is $\underline{A} > \underline{C}$?" were NO, would we know the biggest number? If so, is it $\underline{A}$, $\underline{B}$, or $\underline{C}$? _____

- - - - - - - - - - - - - - - - - -

yes, $\underline{C}$

34. The biggest number would be $\underline{C}$, because $\underline{A} > \underline{B}$, but $\underline{A}$ is not bigger than $\underline{C}$. (We'll talk in a moment about cases where the numbers are equal.) Now we can add another step to the flowchart, which is shown at the top of the next page.

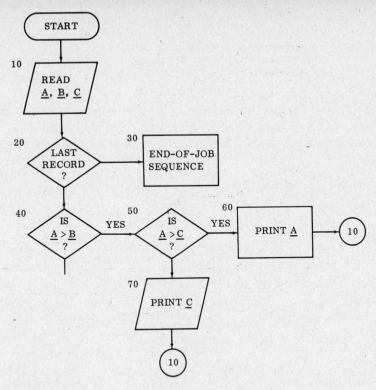

Let's go back to step 40. "Is $\underline{A} > \underline{B}$?" If the answer were NO, which would be the best question to ask next?

_____ (a) Is $\underline{A} > \underline{C}$?

_____ (b) Is $\underline{C} > \underline{A}$?

_____ (c) Is $\underline{B} > \underline{C}$?

- - - - - - - - - - - - - - - - - -

c

35. Again, we could ask any of those questions (and some other questions too) and eventually arrive at the largest number. But asking "Is $\underline{B} > \underline{C}$?" is the most efficient question. If the answer is YES, do we know the biggest number?

What is it? _____

- - - - - - - - - - - - - - - - - -

yes, $\underline{B}$

36. We know that $\underline{B}$ is bigger than $\underline{A}$ (since $\underline{A}$ is not bigger than $\underline{B}$); so if $\underline{B}$ is also bigger than $\underline{C}$, it must be the biggest number. Our flowchart showing

this result is shown below.

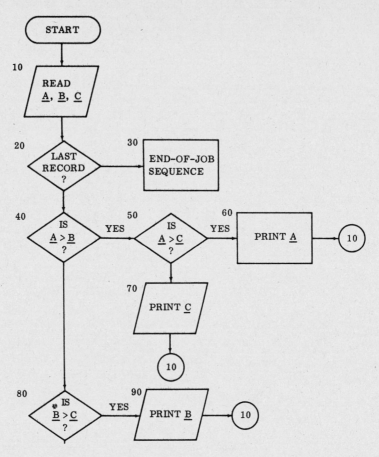

If the answer to step 80 is NO, which is the biggest number? _____

- - - - - - - - - - - - - - - - - -

<u>C</u>

37. Look at our completed flowchart at the top of the next page.

Let's see what happens when two of the numbers are equal. Taking the numbers <u>A</u> = 10, <u>B</u> = 15, and <u>C</u> = 15, we'll work through the flowchart step by step.

What is the answer to the question, "Is <u>A</u> > <u>B</u>?" _____

- - - - - - - - - - - - - - - - - -

NO

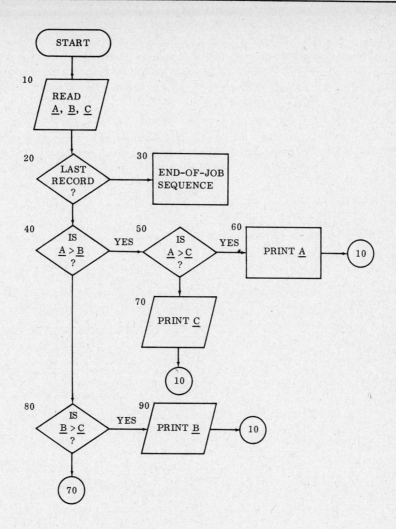

38. Which question will be asked next? _____

- - - - - - - - - - - - - - - - - -

Is <u>B</u> > <u>C</u>? (step 80)

39. What is the answer, and which step follows next? _____

- - - - - - - - - - - - - - - - - -

NO; step 70 (PRINT <u>C</u>)

40. If 10, 15, and 15 are read by the computer, 15 will be printed. And 15
is the biggest number of the three. Try working through a few other sets of
numbers and see if the largest number is always chosen.

The largest is always chosen, isn't it? We needn't worry about two numbers being equal, since everything works out by asking, "is something bigger than something else?" Now see whether you can modify the flowchart so that it selects the smallest number of the three. Ask exactly the same questions but in a different order. Draw your flowchart on a piece of scrap paper; then compare it with the one below.

- - - - - - - - - - - - - - - - - -

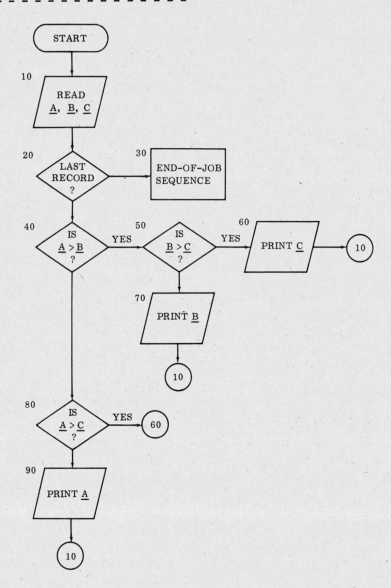

Your flowchart may be something like this one. If it isn't, check it with a few sets of numbers to see whether it is correct. It is possible to ask any of the questions first.

41. The rest of this chapter is optional. In it we will build a more complex flowchart using logical decisions. If you want to take the Self-Test now, turn to page 201. You will not miss any new material by doing so.

In this flowchart we want to read the three numbers and write them out in descending order. This means finding which number is the biggest and remembering it while finding the smallest number. We will do this by creating three special storage locations called HI, MED, and LO. As we find the largest, smallest, and middle numbers, we will put them in these storage locations and then print their contents when all three are filled. If at any time while drawing this flowchart, you're not sure what's going on, check it by picking three numbers that fit the decisions made to that point.

As an optional part of Chapter 8 we will write a program in BASIC for this flowchart that can be run directly on a terminal. When working on a terminal, the check for last record for this program will be replaced by a question at START, so we do not need a box for "LAST RECORD?"

So here is how we will begin:

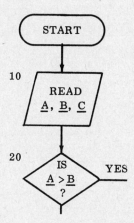

Do we know which numbers to put in HI, MED, or LO? If so, which ones?

- - - - - - - - - - - - - - - - - - -

no

42. The next question to ask is shown in the flowchart at the top of the next page. (Again, this isn't the only question that will lead to a solution, but it is the most efficient to ask here.)

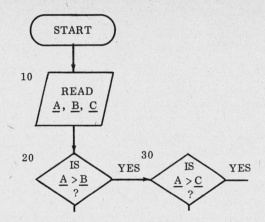

Consider the NO answer. Does this allow us to say which numbers are

HI, MED, or LO? If so, which ones? _____

- - - - - - - - - - - - - - - - - - -

yes; C is HI; A is MED; and B is LO (because A is bigger than B, but A is
not bigger than C)

43. The values of C, A, and B have to be placed, respectively, in the HI,
MED, and LO storage locations. Step 40 does this. C = HI means, "Put the
value of C in the location called HI." Step 900 is an instruction that will be
added later to print the numbers in order.

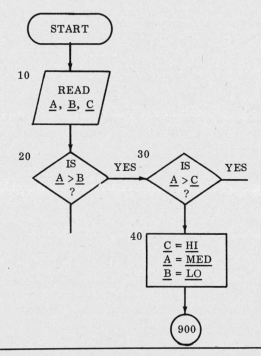

Now consider the YES answer to the question, "Is $\underline{A}$ > $\underline{C}$?" Can we assign $\underline{A}$, $\underline{B}$, or $\underline{C}$ to $\underline{HI}$, $\underline{MED}$, or $\underline{LO}$? If so, how? _____

- - - - - - - - - - - - - - - - - - -

yes; $\underline{A}$ = $\underline{HI}$ (since $\underline{A}$ is bigger than $\underline{B}$ and bigger than $\underline{C}$.)

44. So in step 50 we assign $\underline{A}$ to $\underline{HI}$.

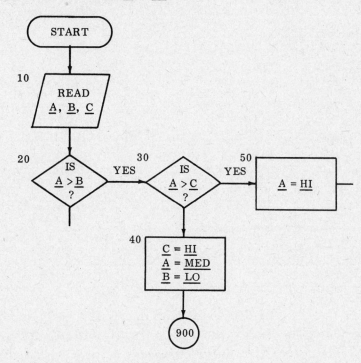

Which question should we ask after step 30?

_____ (a) Is $\underline{B}$ > $\underline{C}$?

_____ (b) Is $\underline{C}$ > $\underline{B}$?

_____ (c) either

_____ (d) neither

- - - - - - - - - - - - - - - - - - -

c

45. Either question will do. If we ask "Is $\underline{B}$ > $\underline{C}$?" and the answer is YES, which number should be assigned to $\underline{MED}$ and which to $\underline{LO}$? _____

_____

- - - - - - - - - - - - - - - - - - -

$\underline{C}$ = $\underline{LO}$, $\underline{B}$ = $\underline{MED}$

46. If the answer to "Is $\underline{B}$ > $\underline{C}$?" is NO, what assignments of $\underline{B}$ and $\underline{C}$ should be made? _____

- - - - - - - - - - - - - - - - - - -

$\underline{C}$ = $\underline{MED}$, $\underline{B}$ = $\underline{LO}$

47. The flowchart now looks like this:

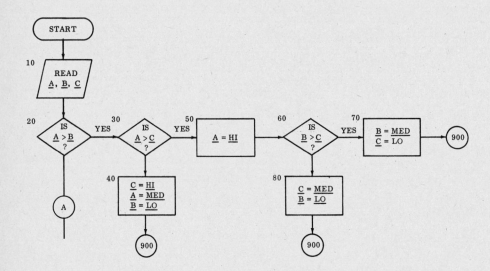

We have added a connector after step 20. This will enable us to draw the next part of the flowchart as a separate sequence.

Now let's go back to step 20. Which question should we ask next if the answer is NO?

_____ (a) Is $\underline{B}$ > $\underline{A}$?

_____ (b) Is $\underline{B}$ > $\underline{C}$?

_____ (c) either

_____ (d) neither

- - - - - - - - - - - - - - - - - - -

b (Choice $\underline{a}$ is the reverse of step 20, to which the answer is already known.)

48.

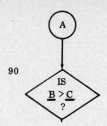

If the answer to the question, "Is $\underline{B} > \underline{C}$?" is NO, what assignments can we make to HI, MED, and LO? _____

- - - - - - - - - - - - - - - - - - - -

$\underline{C} = \underline{HI}$, $\underline{B} = \underline{MED}$, $\underline{A} = \underline{LO}$

49.

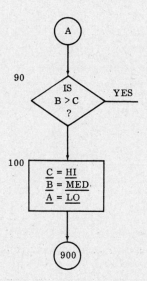

If the answer at step 90 were YES, which of these assignments could we make?

_____ (a) $\underline{A} = \underline{MED}$

_____ (b) $\underline{B} = \underline{HI}$

_____ (c) $\underline{C} = \underline{LO}$

_____ (d) none of the above

- - - - - - - - - - - - - - - - - - - -

b ($\underline{B}$ is bigger than $\underline{A}$, as shown in the second step; and $\underline{B}$ is bigger than $\underline{C}$.)

50.

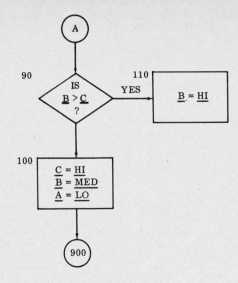

Which question should we ask next?

_____ (a) Is $\underline{A} > \underline{C}$?

_____ (b) Is $\underline{C} > \underline{A}$?

_____ (c) either

_____ (d) neither

- - - - - - - - - - - - - - - - - - -

c

51. If we ask "Is $\underline{A} > \underline{C}$?" and the answer is YES, which numbers are assigned to $\underline{MED}$ and $\underline{LO}$? If the answer is NO, what assignments should be made?

_____

- - - - - - - - - - - - - - - - - -

YES, $\underline{A}$ = $\underline{MED}$, $\underline{C}$ = $\underline{LO}$; NO, $\underline{C}$ = $\underline{MED}$, $\underline{A}$ = $\underline{LO}$

52. At the top of the next page is the completed flowchart, including step 900, which says print $\underline{HI}$, $\underline{MED}$, $\underline{LO}$ (in that order) and an instruction to read three more numbers. Try out the flowchart on some sets of numbers that include equals.

Remember, if we are ordering the numbers $\underline{A}$ = 20, $\underline{B}$ = 20, and $\underline{C}$ = 15, it does not really matter whether we put the number called $\underline{A}$ in $\underline{HI}$ and the number called $\underline{B}$ in $\underline{MED}$, or the other way around. All we are concerned about is printing the numbers in order, as: 20 20 15.

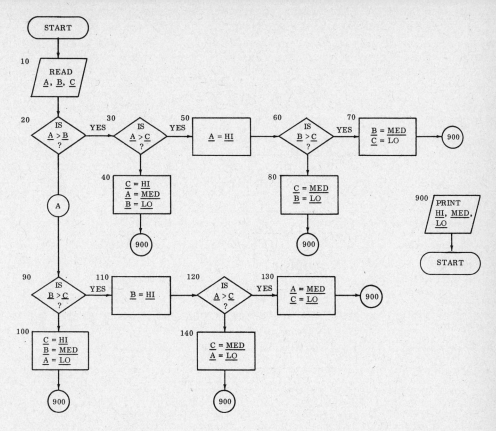

This is the end of Chapter 7. You should now work the Self-Test that follows.

SELF-TEST

Answer all the questions and then check against the answers that follow.

1. Match the following:

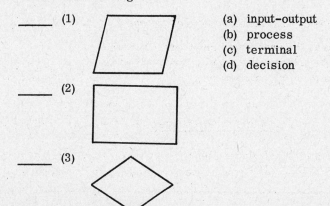

_____ (1)

_____ (2)

_____ (3)

    (a) input-output
    (b) process
    (c) terminal
    (d) decision

2. Here's part of a flowchart. Write a brief description of the operations shown. Use a separate sheet of paper.

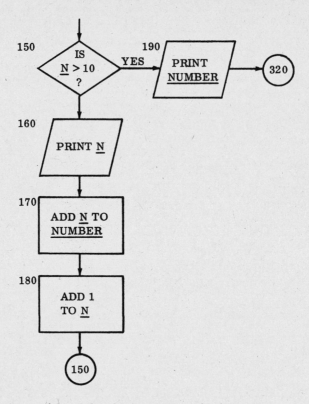

3. Draw a flowchart to describe this sequence of instructions:

   (a) Read a record.
   (b) Print COST.
   (c) Add COST to TOTAL .
   (d) Is TOTAL greater than BAL? If it is, print OVERDRAWN and stop.
   (e) If TOTAL is not greater than BAL, print BAL.
   (f) Read another record.

4. Draw the most efficient flowchart you can that will:

   (a) read three different numbers from a record,
   (b) select the middle-sized one and print it, and
   (c) read three more numbers.

Answers to Self-Test

The numbers in parentheses after each answer refer to the frames in the chapter where the appropriate answers can be found. If you have a wrong answer or are not sure why your answer is correct, read that frame again before going on to the next chapter.

1. (1) a; (2) b; (3) d   (frame 1)

2. Your description should be something like this:
    (a) Is N greater than 10? If it is, print NUMBER and go to instruction 320.
    (b) If N is not greater than 10, print N.
    (c) Add N to NUMBER.
    (d) Add 1 to N and go to instruction 150.   (frame 5)

3. Your flowchart should look something like this:

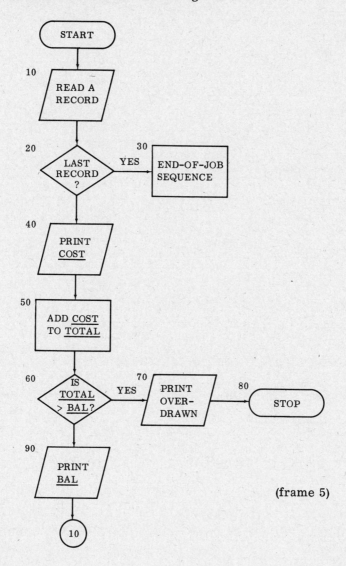

(frame 5)

4. Your flowchart could be something like this. However, if yours is different <u>and</u> <u>it</u> <u>works</u>, then consider it correct.

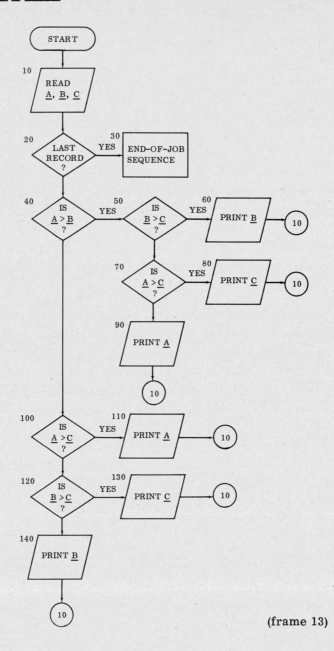

(frame 13)

CHAPTER EIGHT
Writing a Computer Program in BASIC

This chapter is designed to show you how programs are written. First, a few elementary concepts of the symbolic language called BASIC are introduced. Then we show how these concepts can be used to write programs from some of the flowcharts in Chapter 7. But a word of warning: this chapter is not intended to teach you how to write a complete program in BASIC or to teach all its rules.*

After completing this chapter you will be able to:

- identify simple statements written in BASIC which describe a given instruction; and
- interpret simple statements written in BASIC.

1. As we described in Chapter 6, BASIC stands for Beginners All-purpose Symbolic Instruction Code. As a beginning writer of programs you will see that BASIC is an easy language to learn. It is also particularly suited to time-sharing situations—that is, to telecommunications situations where a programmer is working through a terminal and sharing a central processing unit with many others.

To use BASIC a programmer simply sits at a terminal and writes a program in much the same way as one might write an essay. The programmer is able to correct errors and even insert instructions that were omitted earlier in the program.

Which of these statements is true?

_____ (a) BASIC is an advanced symbolic language that is very difficult to learn.

_____ (b) BASIC is best suited for batch processing use.

---

*If you would like to learn more about using BASIC, an excellent book (also a Self-Teaching Guide) is BASIC, 2nd edition, by Robert Albrecht, LeRoy Finkel, and Jerald Brown. If you would like to learn how to program a home minicomputer, see BASIC for Home Computers, by Robert Albrecht, LeRoy Finkel, and Jerald Brown. another Self-Teaching Guide.

_____ (c) both

_____ (d) neither

- - - - - - - - - - - - - - - - - -

d

2. A word of caution. In Chapter 6 we pointed out that BASIC has many versions. The programs shown in this chapter may not work on your computer (if you are lucky enough to have access to one). Although all versions of BASIC have the same general rules, the small differences between them can cause serious problems for beginning programmers when attempting to use a version not designed for the computer on which they are working.

Before starting on BASIC itself, we should look at one of the many ways of "logging on" to a computer from a terminal—that is, a way of establishing contact with the central processing unit from a terminal. Again, the specific techniques of logging on vary from one computer to another, so this may not be the correct way for yours.

We must first connect the terminal to the computer through a telecommunications system. There are basically three methods of getting on-line—first, from a terminal such as that in Figure 4-2 (page 86), which has a built-in modem. Here the user picks up the telephone, dials the computer's number, and, on hearing a steady, high-pitched sound, hangs up the phone and presses the appropriate button on the terminal, at which time input can be sent from the terminal to the computer. The second method involves a terminal such as that in Figure 4-8 (page 94). In this terminal the modem is in the carrying case beside the terminal. The user picks up a telephone, dials the computer's number, and, on hearing the high-pitched sound, places the telephone receiver firmly in the rubber cups of the modem. The terminal is then ready for use. The third method is from a terminal that is wired directly to the computer. Here all the user has to do to establish contact is switch on the terminal.

Having established contact with the computer in one of these ways, we might type

```
hi
```

In all the examples in this chapter what we type will be in lower case (small) letters, and the computer system response will be in upper-case (capital) letters. This is how most systems operate so that the user can easily see what was his or her input and what the computer responses were.

The "hi" tells the system that we are waiting to use it. So it responds by giving its name, the date and time, and then asks for our identification.

```
DOWNTOWN UNIVERSITY COMPUTER FACILITY
08/08/78                      10:45:27
ACCOUNT NUMBER?
```

The time shown on the right means 10:45 and 27 seconds. We then type in our account number.

ACCOUNT NUMBER?   z265

The account number is checked against a file of current account numbers that may be used on the system. If z265 is there the system responds:

KEYWORD?

The keyword is a private code word known only to the user and the computer. It is used to prevent unauthorized persons using our account—use for which we would be charged. So we enter our keyword:

KEYWORD?   ann

If this is the correct keyword for the account, we will be asked which part of the system we wish to use and we will respond with the name of the compiler, like this:

SYSTEM?   basic

The supervisor then loads the BASIC compiler into a main storage and signals that we can begin writing a program like this:

READY

Here is the entire conversation we have held with the computer since switching on:

```
hi
DOWNTOWN UNIVERSITY COMPUTER FACILITY
08/08/78                    10:45:27
ACCOUNT NUMBER?   z265
KEYWORD?   ann
SYSTEM?   basic
READY
```

We can now begin writing instructions in BASIC. You should realize that this conversation varies from computer to computer. If you want to try out the programs in this chapter, you must first find out how to log on to the computer you are going to use.

BASIC is written as a series of statements, each of which occupies one line. Each statement has a number, the numbering normally being 10, 20, 30, and so on. The length of each statement is determined by the system being used, but in this chapter we will assume a limit of 72 characters per line. That is, not more than 72 letters, numbers, spaces, or punctuation marks may be used on any one line.

Which of these statements is true?

_____   (a) With only minor changes a program written in BASIC for one system can be run on any other system.

_____   (b) Each line of a BASIC program contains one statement.

_____   (c) Each statement has a number.

_____ (d) all of the above

- - - - - - - - - - - - - - - - - - -

d

3. The simplest thing we can tell the computer to do is write something for us. For example, if we type line 10 like this followed by "run"

```
10 print "martin l harris"
run
```

the computer would print, on our terminal:

```
MARTIN L HARRIS
READY
```

The computer has interpreted the word "print" in line 10 to mean, "Print whatever there is on this line in quotation marks."

The word "run" tells the computer to go ahead and do whatever it has been told to do up to that point. After printing the output requested, the computer prints READY to show that we can write in a new set of instructions. The word "run" does not need a line number because it is an instruction to the computer system and not part of the BASIC program.

Merely writing one's name is not, of course, a very productive use of a computer system. (The first time I used a computer terminal, however, I felt very good telling that complex piece of machinery to print my name and then watching it obey me!! Perhaps you will feel the same way the first time you have the opportunity to use a computer.)

Let's try adding some numbers together. If we wanted to add 5, 6, and 7, we could type:

```
10 let c = 5 + 6 + 7
20 print c
run
```

The output would be:

```
18
READY
```

Why did we get 18 (which is 5 + 6 + 7) and not C? BASIC accepts any single letter or combination of one letter and one digit (for example, M, N, P3, X9) not in quotation marks as a variable.

A variable is the name given to a storage location, or field, in the central processing unit. No matter what we put into that field, it is still called by its variable name. So, when we typed

```
let c = 5 + 6 + 7
```

we were telling the system to create a field in storage called $\underline{c}$ and to store in that field 5 + 6 + 7. The system adds these numbers together and stores the result in the location called $\underline{c}$.

When we type <u>print</u> $\underline{c}$, the system prints the <u>contents</u> of $\underline{c}$, in this case 18.

Putting quotation marks around a letter, or combination of letters, tells the computer that this is not a variable but a <u>string</u> and is to be printed exactly as it is—just as my name was printed.

Which of these would BASIC accept as a variable?

_____ (a) "B3"

_____ (b) A9

_____ (c) D27

_____ (d) none of the above

- - - - - - - - - - - - - - - - - - -

b (Remember, a variable may have no more than two characters—a single letter or a letter and a digit.)

4.   If we typed the following, what would the computer print as output?

```
10 let x9 = 15 + 20 - 5
20 print x9
run
```

_____ (a)   X9
          READY

_____ (b)   15 + 20 - 5
          READY

_____ (c)   30
          READY

_____ (d) none of the above

- - - - - - - - - - - - - - - - - - -

c (Remember, the calculations will be performed before a number is stored in $\underline{x9}$.)

5.   Write three statements in BASIC that would tell the computer to perform this calculation and print the result: 37 + 5 - 27.

- - - - - - - - - - - - - - - - - - -

You may have a different variable name and different statement numbers, but otherwise your program should look like the one shown at the top of the next page.

```
10 let ml = 37 + 5 - 27
20 print ml
run
```

6. The computer would then print:

```
15
READY
```

What if we had a long series of groups of numbers to add together? Consider these eight groups of three numbers:

$$15 + 15 + 5$$
$$12 + 6 + 3$$
$$4 + 10 + 56$$
$$10 + 10 + 10$$
$$6 + 3 + 6$$
$$50 + 50 + 50$$
$$35 + 45 + 5$$
$$15 + 70 + 10$$

How would we do it? We could keep rewriting the three statements each time the computer gave us one answer.

```
10 let s = 15 + 15 + 5
20 print s
run

35
READY
10 let s = 12 + 6 + 3
20 print s
run

21
READY
```

We could continue this way six more times; but this is very time consuming, and we could do the calculations much quicker in our heads. When using BASIC, we can write a program that will give the computer all the sets of numbers that are to be added together, and then we can write just one set of instructions that will cause the sum of each group to be found in turn.

The first two statements in this program will be:

```
10 data 15,15,5,12,6,3,4,10,56,10,10,10,
20 data 6,3,6,50,50,50,35,45,5,15,70,10
```

These statements tell the computer to store this data somewhere for use later on. Now we want to take those numbers three at a time, so we type the following:

```
30 read a, b, c
```

This says, "Go to the data just stored and put the first number in a field called a, the second number in a field called b, and the third number in a field called _____."

- - - - - - - - - - - - - - - - - - - -

c

7. If we want to call the sum of these three numbers t, we would then type:

    30 let t = a + b + c

    The first three numbers in the data are 15, 15, and 5. What would be stored in the field t? _____

- - - - - - - - - - - - - - - - - - - -

35

8. Next we type a print statement; so the program looks like this:

```
10 data 15,15,5,12,6,3,4,10,56,10,10,10,
20 data 6,3,6,50,50,50,35,45,5,15,70,10
30 read a, b, c
40 let t = a + b + c
50 print t
```

After we have printed the sum of the first three numbers in the data list, we want to find and print the sum of the next three. So we type this statement:

```
60 go to 30
```

This means, "Now go to statement 30 and execute it." What is statement 30? _____

- - - - - - - - - - - - - - - - - - - -

read a, b, c

9. When executing statement 30 for the second time, the system reads the second set of three numbers in the data list. The fourth number in the list will be stored in field a, the fifth number in field b, and the sixth in field c. Statements 40, 50, and 60 are executed. Then the system goes back to statement 30 and begins again.

    By typing the word "list" we can instruct the computer to print back for us everything we have written so far. Here's what we would get:

```
10 DATA 15,15,5,12,6,3,4,10,56,10,10,10,
20 DATA 6,3,6,50,50,50,35,45,5,15,70,10
30 READ A, B, C
40 LET T = A + B + C
50 PRINT T
60 GO TO 30
```

If we now type the word "run" the computer will execute the program and print the output:

```
run
35      21      70      30      15      150     85      95
3273 OUT OF DATA
```

The last line of output indicates that the computer has discovered an error condition while working the program—it has run out of data to process. This is not really a serious error because all the data that we wanted processed has been processed. It is possible to avoid getting this error message, as we shall see later.

Now see if you can write the BASIC code that will read two numbers from the data in line 10 and 20, subtract the second number from the first, and then print the result.

- - - - - - - - - - - - - - - - - -

Lines 30 through 60 of your program should look like this, although you may have used different letters to represent the variables:

```
30 read x, y
40 let z = x - y
50 print z
60 go to 30
```

10. If we typed the word "run" after line 60, the following output would be produced when the program was executed;

```
run
0       -7      3       -6      46      0       3       -44
0       -10     -10     60
3273 OUT OF DATA
```

The "go to" statement in the programs above is an <u>unconditional</u> <u>transfer-of-control</u> instruction. It tells the computer to stop processing instructions in the order in which they are written, and it is unconditional because the branch to statement 30 will happen every time statement 60 is reached.

Which of these statements is true?

_____   (a) The word "list" instructs the computer to execute the program and list the output.

_____   (b) The word "run" instructs the computer to print all the statements written so far.

_____   (c) both

_____   (d) neither

- - - - - - - - - - - - - - - - - - -

d

11.   If we have now finished all we wanted to do at this time, we have to "log off" the computer. That is, we have to tell the computer that we are finished. Just switching off the terminal does not always work too well, so it is important to follow the correct procedure.

On this system we type:

    bye

and the computer responds:

```
Z265      LOGOFF      11:36:35
Z265      CPU      11.892 SEC
```

This tells us that we are logged off at 11:36 and 35 seconds—that is, after about 52 minutes of use (we logged on at 10:45:27). During this time, however, we used only about 12 seconds of CPU time. Remember, the CPU is used only to process the instructions we wrote in BASIC. The rest of the time is for our typing and thinking.

12. BASIC also allows us to write conditional transfer-of-control instructions, which we discussed in Chapter 6. For example, in the program above we could decide that the last number in the input would always be –1 and that the program was to end when –1 was read. To do this we would need to make these three changes to the program:

(a) add a new data line:

    21 data -1

(b) add a conditional transfer of control statement that would tell the computer "if a equals –1 then go to the end of the program, " like this:

    31 if a = -1 then 70

(c) add an "end" statement, like this:

    70 end

If, after we type these new instructions, we then type the word "list," the computer will take the original program, insert the new lines at the appropriate place, and then write out the old program and the new lines, like this:

```
10 DATA 15,15,5,12,6,3,4,10,56,10,10,10,
20 DATA 6,3,6,50,50,50,35,45,5,15,70,10
21 DATA -1
30 READ A, B, C
31 IF A = -1 THEN 70
40 LET T = A + B + C
50 PRINT T
60 GO TO 30
70 END
```

If we now type the word "run," the output will look like this:

```
35     21     70     15     150     85     95
READY
```

The "READY" shows that the program came to the "END" statement, stopped, and is now ready to receive further input.

Notice that because we numbered the lines in the original program by tens, we were able to add new lines to the program very easily. Had we numbered them 1, 2, 3, ..., the entire program would have to be retyped with new numbers and the new lines in exactly the right place.

A conditional transfer-of-control instruction is easy to write. For example:

IF (some condition) THEN (some statement number)

The IF... THEN... statement, as it is called, allows us to make logical decisions about the next processing step that is based on the condition of a piece of data. To see how this statement is used, let's program a problem for which you drew a flowchart in the last chapter. Figure 8-1 shows the flowchart we drew to explain how to count the number of students in each class. The only change is that the steps are renumbered to make the programming easier. Figure 8-1 is shown at the top of the next page.

First we will type some data statements. Because, in general, one step on the flowchart will become one line in the program, it is convenient to keep the flowchart step numbers and the statement numbers that represent them the same. Therefore we have to give the data statements numbers less than 10, the first step in the flowchart:

```
5 data 1,2,3,3,6,3,4,1,2,4,8,3,2,
6 data 4,3,2,1,3,2,1,1,3,4,3,8,-1
```

The -1 (minus 1) will be used to tell us when we have come to the end of the data list. Since these numbers represent the year in school, we'll call our variable y. The next statement will correspond to step 10 on the flowchart:

```
10 read y
```

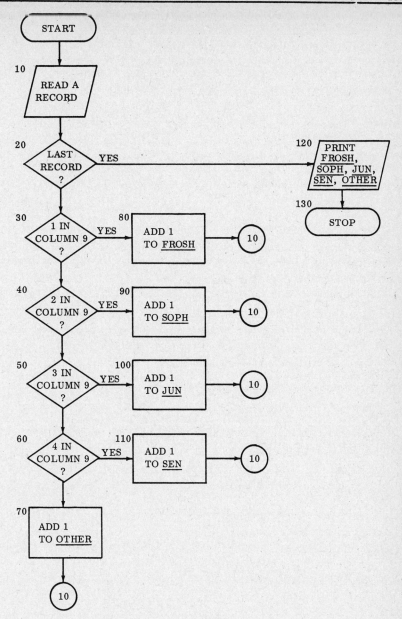

Figure 8-1.   Flowchart to Calculate the Number of
Students per Class

The next step on the flowchart, step 20, tells us to find out whether we
have reached the last record.   If so, we are to go to step _____.

- - - - - - - - - - - - - - - - - - -

120

13. We have arranged it so that the last value to be read will be -1. Which of these statements should we type next?

_____ (a) `go to 120`

_____ (b) `if y = -1 go to 120`

_____ (c) `if y = -1 then 120`

_____ (d) none of the above

- - - - - - - - - - - - - - - - - -

c (Remember, the conditional branch is IF... THEN... .)

14. If y is not equal to -1, then the next step on the flowchart is step 30. The computer interprets conditional BASIC statements the same way we do. If the test is false—that is, if the condition does not exist—the computer moves on to the next statement in sequence.

If the answer to the question at step 30 is YES, which step is next? _____

- - - - - - - - - - - - - - - - - -

step 80

15. We would type the following:

    `30 if y = 1 then  80`

See if you can write the statements that correspond to steps 40, 50, and 60 on the flowchart.

- - - - - - - - - - - - - - - - - -

```
40 if y = 2 then  90
50 if y = 3 then 100
60 if y = 4 then 110
```


16. The flowchart shows us that if y (the number in column 9 as it is referred to on the flowchart) is not 1, 2, 3, or 4, then we should add 1 to a field called OTHER. We can't call it OTHER because names of fields must consist of one letter or one letter and a digit. Let's call the field r. Statement 70 will then be:

    `70 let r = r + 1`

This means, "Take the number currently stored at r, and add 1 to it, and then put the result back in r." Every time statement 70 is executed, the number stored at r will increase by 1.

Once statement 70 has been executed, we have to return to statement 10 to read another number from the data list. The following statement will do this:

```
75 go to 10
```

Before we go any further, let's "list" the whole program so far.

```
5   DATA 1,2,3,3,6,3,4,1,2,4,8,3,2,
6   DATA 4,3,2,1,3,2,1,1,3,4,3,8,¬1
10 READ Y
20 IF Y = -1 THEN 120
30 IF Y = 1 THEN 80
40 IF Y = 2 THEN 90
50 IF Y = 3 THEN 100
60 IF Y = 4 THEN 110
70 LET R = R + 1
75 GO TO 10
```

Steps 80 through 110 are similar. We have to perform an addition and then go to step 10. Using these variable names, write the statements for steps 80 through 110: $\underline{f}$ = FROSH, $\underline{s1}$ = SOPH, $\underline{j}$ = JUN, and $\underline{s2}$ = SEN. (If you're not sure how to do it, go ahead and check the answer—it's a tough assignment.)

- - - - - - - - - - - - - - - - - - -

You may not have used the same numbers for the GO TO statements, but otherwise your statements should be like this:

```
80   let f = f + 1
85   go to 10
90   let s1 = s1 + 1
95   go to 10
100 let j = j + 1
105 go to 10
110 let s2 = s2 + 1
115 go to 10
```

17. Now we have to type statements telling the system to print the contents of $\underline{f}$, $\underline{s1}$, $\underline{j}$, $\underline{s2}$, and $\underline{r}$ after the last number has been read and to end execution:

```
120 print f, s1, j, s2, r
130 end
```

That is the completed program. What should we type next in order to have it executed? _____

- - - - - - - - - - - - - - - - - -

run

18. Here's the complete program and the output that would be produced:

```
5    data 1,2,3,3,6,3,4,1,2,4,8,3,2,
6    data 4,3,2,1,3,2,1,1,3,4,3,8,-1
10   read y
20   if y = -1 then 120
30   if y = 1 then 80
40   if y = 2 then 90
50   if y = 3 then 100
60   if y = 4 then 110
70   let r = r + 1
75   go to 10
80   let f = f + 1
85   go to 10
90   let sl = sl + 1
95   go to 10
100  let j = j + 1
105  go to 10
110  let s2 = s2 + 1
115  go to 10
120  print f, sl, j, s2, r
130  end

run

5    5    8    4    3
READY
```

Now we'll write a program that will select females with blue eyes and blond hair and males with brown eyes and brown hair. The data is written in this order—name, sex code, hair-color code, eye-color code. The flowchart shown at the top of the next page tells us what to do.

We will begin by entering the data that is to be used. The names must be entered in quotation marks and we will require more than one data statement.

```
5 data "harris",1,2,3,"jones",2,2,1,"pogrow",1,2,3,
6 data "smith",1,1,2,"alias",2,2,1,"marr",2,2,1
7 data "dunn",1,2,2,"heflin",1,2,1,"haffner",1,1,2,
8 data "oats",1,3,2,"end",0,0,0
```

We could get more than this on each line, but it is not important to do so. Neither is it important to have all the data for one person on one line, for the computer reads all the data in sequence and is not concerned about which statement it is in. The last statement will be used to indicate that we have come to the end of the data.

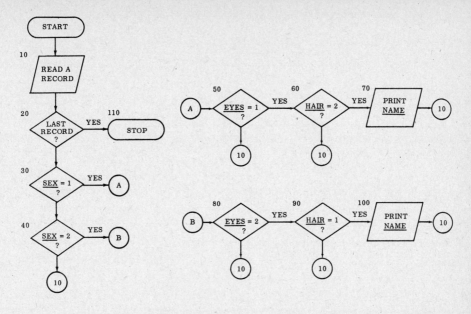

If we use these variable names—name, n; sex, s; hair, h, and eyes, e—what would statement 10 be? _____

- - - - - - - - - - - - - - - - - -

10 read n, s, h, e

19. What do we do at step 20 of the flowchart? _____

_____

- - - - - - - - - - - - - - - - - -

check to see whether we have reached the last record

20. If we have reached the last record, what is stored in the field n?

_____

- - - - - - - - - - - - - - - - - -

end

21. Write the statement that describes step 20. _____

_____

- - - - - - - - - - - - - - - - - -

20 if n = "end" then 110   (The quotation marks are necessary to show

that <u>end</u> is a string that is to be compared to the strings in the input.)

22. Now write statements for steps 30 and 40.

- - - - - - - - - - - - - - - - -

```
30 if s = 1 then 50
40 if s = 2 then 80
```

23. If neither statement 30 nor statement 40 is true, what should the computer do? _____
- - - - - - - - - - - - - - - - - -

read another record (go to step 10)

24. Write the statement that tells the computer to do that.

- - - - - - - - - - - - - - - - - -

```
45 go to 10
```

25. Which of these statements should we write for step 50?

_____ (a) if e = 1 then 10

_____ (b) if e = 1 then 60

_____ (c) if e = 1 go to 60

_____ (d) none of the above

- - - - - - - - - - - - - - - - - -

b (if e = 1 then 60)

26. That was tricky because the positions of the YES and NO branches on the flowchart have been reversed for step 50.
    If the computer doesn't branch to step 60 at step 50, what should it do? Write a statement telling the computer what to do.

- - - - - - - - - - - - - - - - -

```
55 go to 10
```

27. Here's the program as far as we have gone:

```
5   data "harris",2,2,3,"jones",2,2,1,"pogrow",1,2,3,
6   data "smith",1,1,2,"alias",2,2,1,"marr",2,2,1,
7   data "dunn",1,2,2,"heflin",1,2,1,"haffner",1,1,2,
8   data "oats",1,3,2,"end",0,0,0
10  read n, s, h, e
20  if n = "end" then 110
30  if s = 1 then 50
40  if s = 2 then 80
45  go to 10
50  if e = 1 then 60
55  go to 10
```

Now write statements for steps 60 and 70.

- - - - - - - - - - - - - - - - - -

```
60 if h = 2 then 70
65 go to 10
70 print n
```


28. Did you remember to include line 65, "go to 10." If you had forgotten it and had typed at the terminal

```
60 if h = 2 then 70
70 print n
```

how could you have "backed up" and put line 65 in? Here BASIC is very kind; we can type the missing statement like this:

```
60 if h = 2 then 70
70 print n
65 go to 10
```

When we type the word "list" the computer will arrange the statements in the correct order according to their sequence number. For example, if we did enter the lines above in the wrong order, then typed "list," we would receive a print out like the one shown at the top of the next page.

```
5    DATA "HARRIS",1,2,3,"JONES",2,2,1,"POGROW",1,2,3,
6    DATA "SMITH",1,1,2,"ALIAS",2,2,1,"MARR",2,2,1,
7    DATA "DUNN",1,2,2,"HEFLIN",1,2,1,"HAFFNER",1,1,2,
8    DATA "OATS",1,3,2,"END",0,0,0
10   READ N, S, H, E
20   IF N = "END" THEN 110
30   IF S = 1 THEN 50
40   IF S = 2 THEN 80
45   GO TO 10
50   IF E = 1 THEN 60
55   GO TO 10
60   IF H = 2 THEN 70
65   GO TO 10
70   PRINT N
```

The system allows us to make mistakes in the order that we type in statements, but as long as the statements have the correct sequence number, they will be executed in the correct order.

See if you can write the rest of the program on your own.

- - - - - - - - - - - - - - - - -

You may have different statement numbers, but otherwise your statements should be like this:

```
75   go to 10
80   if e = 2 then 90
85   go to 10
90   if h = 1 then 100
95   go to 10
100  print n
105  go to 10
110  end
```

29. At the top of the next page is the whole program as it would appear if we typed "list."

```
5    DATA "HARRIS",1,2,2,"JONES",2,2,1,"POGROW",1,2,3,
6    DATA "SMITH",1,1,2,"ALIAS",2,2,1,"MARR",2,2,1,
7    DATA "DUNN",1,2,2,"HEFLIN",1,2,1,"HAFFNER",1,1,2,
8    DATA "OATS",1,3,2,"END",0,0,0
10   READ N, S, H, E
20   IF N = "END" THEN 110
30   IF S = 1 THEN 50
40   IF S = 2 THEN 80
45   GO TO 10
50   IF E = 1 THEN 60
55   GO TO 10
60   IF H = 2 THEN 70
65   GO TO 10
70   PRINT N
75   GO TO 10
80   IF E = 2 THEN 90
85   GO TO 10
90   IF H = 1 THEN 100
95   GO TO 10
100  PRINT N
105  GO TO 10
110  END
```

If we now type the word "run," the following output will be produced:

```
run

JONES    SMITH    ALIAS    MARR    HAFFNER
READY
```

This has been a very brief look at BASIC and some of the things it can do. Of course, not all programs are as simple as this. Some require very sophisticated statements involving complex mathematical relations. But BASIC can handle many of them.

BASIC is a very useful language for beginners and for solving relatively small and simple problems in business and science. More complex problems, however, require the use of more complex symbolic languages such as FORTRAN or COBOL.

30. The rest of this chapter is optional and may be used to increase your understanding of BASIC. We will write a more complex program in BASIC—the sorting of numbers into descending order, which was an optional exercise in Chapter 7. If you would like to work at the program, it is recommended that you read the optional part of Chapter 7, beginning on page 195 (frame 41), if you have not already done so. If you choose not to read on, you will find the Self-Test on page 229.

Figure 8-2 at the top of the next page shows the flowchart drawn to sort three numbers into descending order. The only changes made here are the numbering of the boxes and the addition of step 990: "end." These changes have been made to simplify the programming.

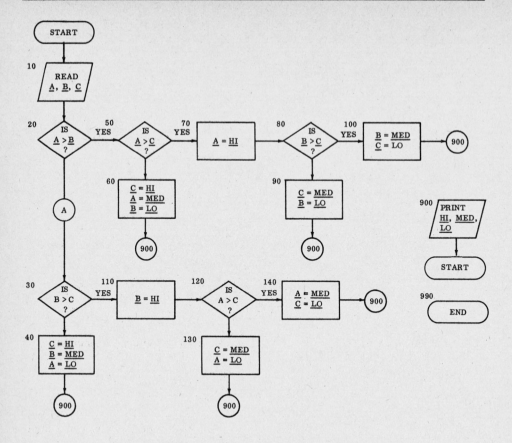

Figure 8-2. Flowchart for Sorting Three Numbers

The first box, step 10, tells us to read a, b, c. In the previous example "read" was used to get data from a tape file. But we will write this program so that the three numbers a, b, and c can be typed at the terminal, sorted, and printed back at the terminal.

To do this we will have more than one statement to represent step 10, like this:

```
10 input "are there any numbers to sort?";an$
11 if an$="no" then 990
12 input "type three numbers";a, b, c
13 h = 0: m = 0: l = 0
```

The input statement in line 10 will do two things. First, it will write at the terminal the words in quotes: "are there any numbers to sort?" You can then type "yes" or "no" and the computer will accept your response as data for the variable "an$."

Which of these statements is true about the meaning of step 11?

_____ (a) If "an$" is "no" the program will branch to statement 990.

_____ (b) If "an$" is "yes" the program will continue to statement 12.

_____ (c) both

_____ (d) neither

- - - - - - - - - - - - - - - - - - -

c

31. The input statement on line 12 will cause "type three numbers" to be printed at the terminal and accept the three numbers typed as data for variables a, b, c.

The program is going to sort the three numbers a, b, and c into descending order. The highest number will be assigned to variable h (for HIghest), the next highest to variable m (for MEDium), and the lowest number to l (for LOwest).

Line 13 of the program instructs the computer to put a 0 (zero) in each variable each time the program is run. This ensures that the values of h, m, and l do not carry over from one pass through the program to the next. (This is a difficult concept and is fully explained in texts on BASIC.)

We have now entered the three numbers to be sorted. Write the next two statements in the program.

- - - - - - - - - - - - - - - - - - -

```
20 if a > b then 50
30 if b > c then 110
```


32. If we arrive at step 40 on the flowchart, we know that a is the lowest number, b the medium, and c the highest. We could write three lines to make these assignments, like this:

```
h = c
m = b
l = a
```

However, some BASIC compilers allow more than one statement to be written on a line. The statements are separated by a colon (:). So step 40 could be written like this:

```
40 h = c : m = b : l = a
```

Having done this, we need a statement sending the program to the step at which the values of h, m, and l will be printed. Which of these statements will do that?

_____ (a) go to 990

_____ (b) go to 900

_____ (c) go to 10

_____ (d) none of the above

- - - - - - - - - - - - - - - - - -

b

33. Step 900 will print the values of <u>h</u>, <u>m</u>, and <u>l</u>. Write BASIC statements for steps 50 and 60.

- - - - - - - - - - - - - - - - - -

```
50 if a > c then 70
60 h = c : m = a : l = b
```


34. What will the next line of the program be?

- - - - - - - - - - - - - - - - - -

```
61 go to 10
```
(The statement number could be anything between 61 and 69.)

35. What should we type to get the computer to print the program so far?

_____ (a) run

_____ (b) list

_____ (c) print

_____ (d) any of the above

- - - - - - - - - - - - - - - - - -

b

36. Here's what we would get if we typed "list."

```
10 INPUT "ARE THERE ANY NUMBERS TO SORT?";ANS$
11 IF ANS$="NO" THEN 990
12 INPUT "TYPE THREE NUMBERS";A, B, C
13 H = 0: M = 0: l = 0
20 IF A > B THEN 50
30 IF B > C THEN 110
40 H = C: M = B: L = A
41 GO TO 900
50 IF A > C THEN 70
60 H = C: M = A: L = B
61 GO TO 900
```

Write the BASIC statements for steps 70, 80, and 90.

- - - - - - - - - - - - - - - - -

```
70 h = a
80 if b > c then 100
90 m = c : l = b
```

37. After step 90 we have to go to step 900 to print the values of h, m, and l, so we need this statement:

```
91 go to 900
```

Try to write the statements to cover the remaining steps to step 140.

- - - - - - - - - - - - - - - - -

```
100 m = b: l = c
101 go to 900
110 h = b
120 if a > c then 140
130 m = c: l = a
131 go to 900
140 m = a: l = c
```

(You may have written the statements on lines 130 and 140 on two lines each.)

38. Write statements for step 900 and the return to step 10.

- - - - - - - - - - - - - - - - -

```
900 print h, m, l
901 go to 10
```

39. Recall that at the beginning of the program we went to step 990 if the response to the question "are there any numbers to sort?" was "no." The statement should be:

```
990 print "end of program"
```

The computer will print this message and then go to the last statement:

999 end

The message printed at line 990 makes it clear to anyone using the program that the end has been reached as a result of responding "no. "
Here is the completed program:

```
10   INPUT "ARE THERE ANY NUMBERS TO SORT?";AN$
11   IF AN$="NO" THEN 990
12   INPUT "TYPE THREE NUMBERS";A, B, C
13   H = 0: M = 0: 1 = 0
20   IF A > B THEN 50
30   IF B > C THEN 110
40   H = C: M = B: L = A
41   GO TO 900
50   IF A > C THEN 70
60   H = C: M = A: L = B
61   GO TO 900
70   H = A
80   IF B > C THEN 100
90   M = C: L = B
91   GO TO 900
100 M = B: L = C
101 GO TO 900
110 H = B
120 IF A > C THEN 140
130 M = C: L = A
131 GO TO 900
140 M = A: L = C
900 PRINT H, M, L
901 GO TO 10
990 PRINT "END OF PROGRAM"
999 END
```

And here's how the program works. If we type "run, " the computer responds:

```
ARE THERE ANY NUMBERS TO SORT?
```

We have to answer "yes, " to which the computer responds:

```
ARE THERE ANY NUMBERS TO SORT?  yes
TYPE THREE NUMBERS
```

When we type in three numbers, the computer will sort them and ask if there are any numbers to sort:

```
ARE THERE ANY NUMBERS TO SORT?  yes
TYPE THREE NUMBERS 20 15 20
20     20     15
ARE THERE ANY NUMBERS TO SORT?
```

This will continue until we respond "no, " at which time the program will stop executing after printing the appropriate message:

```
ARE THERE ANY NUMBERS TO SORT?    yes
TYPE THREE NUMBERS 20 15 20
20      20      15
ARE THERE ANY NUMBERS TO SORT?    yes
TYPE THREE NUMBERS 14 7 21
21      14      7
ARE THERE ANY NUMBERS TO SORT?    yes
TYPE THREE NUMBERS 6 77 19
77      19      6
ARE THERE ANY NUMBERS TO SORT?    no
END OF PROGRAM
READY
```

You should now work the Self-Test that follows.

SELF-TEST

Answer all the questions and then check against the answers that follow.

1. How would this instruction be written in BASIC: "Add 50 to the data at M and put the result at A "?

   _____ (a) LET A = M + 50

   _____ (b) A = M + 50

   _____ (c) LET M + 50 = A

   _____ (d) none of the above

2. Which of these statements instructs the computer to execute statement 101 next if the data at Q is equal to the data at N?

   _____ (a) GO TO 101 IF Q = N

   _____ (b) THEN 101 IF Q = N

   _____ (c) IF Q = N THEN 101

   _____ (d) none of the above

3. Which of these statements is correct?

   _____ (a) The word "run" causes the computer to compile and execute the program.

   _____ (b) The statement "print a" will cause the letter A to be printed.

   _____ (c) The statement "print 15 + 6 + 2" will cause 23 to be printed.

   _____ (d) all of the above

4. What does this statement mean: IF W = 57 GO TO 36?

_____ (a) If the value of W is 57, change it to 36.

_____ (b) If the value of W is 57, execute statement 36 next.

_____ (c) If the value of W is 57, add 36 to it.

_____ (d) none of the above

5. What does this statement mean: PRINT X, Y, Z?

_____ (a) Write X, Y, Z at the terminal.

_____ (b) Write x, y, z at the terminal.

_____ (c) Write the values of the variables X, Y, and Z at the terminal.

_____ (d) none of the above

6. What will these three statements cause the computer to do?

```
100  IF X = Y GO TO 200
110  IF X > Y GO TO 210
120  PRINT X
```

_____ (a) If the value of X is equal to the value of Y, go to step 200, by-passing steps 110 and 120.

_____ (b) If the value of X is not equal to Y and the value of X is greater than the value of Y, go to step 210.

_____ (c) If the value of X is not equal to the value of Y and if the value of X is not greater than the value of Y, print the value of X.

_____ (d) all of the above

7. Read this BASIC program:

```
10    READ A, B, C
20    IF A = -1 GO TO 999
30    IF A = C THEN 100
40    IF B = C THEN 110
50    IF A = B THEN 120
60    PRINT "THERE ARE NO EQUAL NUMBERS?"
70    GO TO 10
100   PRINT "A = C"
105   GO TO 10
110   PRINT "B = C"
120   PRINT "A = B"
125   GO TO 10
999   END
```

Which of these statements is true for this program?

_____ (a) If the numbers 3, 7, and 5 are read, the program will execute steps 20, 30, 40, 50, 60 and return to step 10.

_____ (b) If the numbers 3, 7, and 3 are read, the program will execute steps 20, 30, 100 and return to step 10.

_____ (c) If -1, -1, and 6 are read, the program will go to step 999 and stop.

_____ (d) all of the above

8. What would the program in question 7 print if the three numbers read were 8, 8, and 8?

_____ (a) A = C

_____ (b) B = C

_____ (c) A = B

_____ (d) all of the above

Answers to Self-Test

The numbers in parentheses after each answer refer to the frames in the chapter where the appropriate answers can be found. If you have a wrong answer or are not sure why your answer is correct, read that frame again before going on to the next chapter.

1. a (frame 7)

2. c (frame 10)

3. d (frame 3)

4. d (frame 10)

5. c (frame 16)

6. d (frame 10)

7. d (frame 10)

8. a (frame 10)

CHAPTER NINE
Software

In Chapters 2, 3, 4, and 5 we discussed computer <u>hardware</u>—that is, the phys-ical devices that make up computer systems. In this chapter we will be look-ing at <u>software</u>, the programs that are an essential part of any computer sys-tem. We will discuss the various types of program that reduce the amount of programming that an individual must do and that increase the efficiency of computer systems.

After completing this chapter you will be able to:

- define <u>user-prepared</u> <u>programs</u>, <u>utility</u> <u>programs</u>, <u>applications</u> pro-grams, and <u>report</u> <u>generators</u>;
- define the term <u>operating</u> <u>system</u>;
- describe three major functions of the <u>supervisor</u>;
- describe the function of the <u>compiler</u> <u>library</u>, <u>program</u> <u>library</u>, <u>debugging</u> <u>routines</u>, and <u>housekeeping</u> <u>routines</u>;
- describe the use of <u>job-control</u> <u>language</u>;
- define the term <u>multiprogramming</u> and describe its advantages; and
- describe <u>structured</u> <u>programming</u> and <u>virtual</u> <u>memory</u>.

1. As you will recall, a computer program is a detailed set of instructions that tells the computer what types of input data it will receive, exactly what calculations to perform on it and in what order, and, finally, what type of out-put to produce. Not all programs are written by the organization that uses them. Many are supplied by the computer manufacturer while others are pur-chased from companies that specialize in writing programs.

Programs fall into one of four general categories—user-prepared program utility programs, applications programs, and report generators. These are very general categories, and it is not always easy to determine into which cate-gory a particular program might fall.

<u>User-prepared</u> <u>programs</u> are those written within the organization using the computer. They are generally designed to perform processing tasks that are peculiar to that particular organization. They are designed and written by people who work for that organization and have a detailed understanding of its data-processing needs.

Utility programs are supplied by the computer manufacturer and perform many of the routine tasks that are necessary in any data-processing situation. Examples of utility programs are: reading punched cards and writing the data in them onto tape; reading the data on tape and writing it onto disk; printing data that is stored on disk. Programs to sort records into, say, ascending order by customer number or to merge two files into one keeping the records in alphabetical order by customer name are also utility programs. To use these programs the programmer has only to name the program and give a few key pieces of information, such as the size of the records and the location of the customer name.

Applications programs are supplied by the computer manufacturer or by companies that specialize in writing computer programs. Applications programs are virtually ready to use and require only minor modifications, if any, to fit a particular organization's needs. The programmer concentrates on preparing the input data in the format called for by the application program. Typical applications programs are inventory control, bank-account processing, customer billing for gas and electric utilities, and payroll. The specifications for these programs vary little from organization to organization, so there is little sense in each preparing its own programs. As the use of computers spreads to smaller and smaller organizations, the use and value of applications programs is increasing.

Which of these statements is true?

_____ (a) A program to read punched cards to tape is a typical user-prepared program.

_____ (b) User programs are normally supplied by the computer manufacturer.

_____ (c) Applications programs are written to solve problems peculiar to one organization.

_____ (d) none of the above

- - - - - - - - - - - - - - - - - -

d

2. The final category of programs is that of report generators. These programs are used to produce reports from a data file, or a series of data files. They are generally supplied by the computer manufacturer and are fairly simple to use. Report generators do not require the same level of skill as is required to write programs from scratch. Report Program Generator (RPG) is one of the most popular report generators used in business for solving relatively simple reporting problems.

There are also report generators for producing statistical information. For example, the Statistical Package for the Social Sciences (SPSS) allows researchers and scientists who are not programmers to perform a wide range of statistical analyses. All that is necessary is to ensure that the data to be analyzed is put into the correct general format and to write some simple instructions telling the computer what analyses to perform on that data.

Which of these statements is true?

_____ (a) Report generators are written by each organization to meet their own peculiar data-processing needs.

_____ (b) Applications programs are designed to be used in many organizations to solve the same problem.

_____ (c) Utility programs perform routine functions necessary in almost any data-processing organization.

_____ (d) none of the above

- - - - - - - - - - - - - - - - - - - -

b, c

3. On early computer systems the human operator was responsible for loading each program into storage, loading the compiler, checking to see whether the compilation was successful, manually starting the processing run, unloading the output, and maintaining a record of jobs run. When a job was complete, the operator had to decide which job to run next and then repeat these same operations. All of these manual operations resulted in the computer being idle for considerable periods of time.

With the exception of physically loading and unloading cards, tapes, or disks from input and output devices, most of the operator's functions have been taken over by the <u>operating system</u> on recent computer systems.

As shown in Figure 9-1, an operating system consists of a supervisor, a compiler library, a program library, debugging routines, and housekeeping routines. The supervisor is always stored in the central processing unit when the system is in use. The other components may be stored on magnetic tape, disk, or drum and called into main storage by the supervisor as they are required.

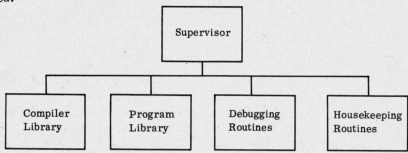

Figure 9-1. Major Components of an Operating System

Operating systems are designed by the computer manufacturer and are responsible for the control of most computer operations. As computers have become more complex and more expensive, it is essential to use them as efficiently as possible. The efficiency of a system is measured by the amount of time it is actually processing data. Operating systems are designed to maximize this efficiency by performing many of the operations that were formerly performed by the computer operator.

An operating system:

_____ (a) is designed by the computer manufacturer.

_____ (b) increases the efficiency of the system.

_____ (c) both

_____ (d) neither

- - - - - - - - - - - - - - - - - -

c

4. We will discuss each component of the operating system in turn. The
supervisor is a special program that controls the operation of the entire computer system. It performs the functions that were previously handled by the
operator—the loading of programs and data from the various input devices and
the scheduling of programs through the computer.

When a request to execute a program is received from a remote terminal,
for example, the supervisor determines how much storage is required and
which devices are needed. If the system has them it will also assign a pri-
ority to the program, indicating whether it can be executed immediately or
has to wait until some previously determined time of day. The supervisor then
schedules the program, along with all the others awaiting execution, so as to
make the most efficient use of the central processing unit.

All computer systems, whether or not they have complex operating systems, require human operators. The operator is responsible for loading and
unloading input and output devices and for intervening in the system's operation
either at the request of the operating system or in the event of a failure in the
system.

Systems and their operators communicate through the control console.
As shown in Figure 9-2 at the top of the next page, the control console consists
of a panel containing lights, switches, dials, and a terminal. The terminal
enables the system and the operator to "talk" to each other about the status of
the system.

The supervisor keeps the operator informed about what is happening by
listing information about each program on the console. It will tell the operator when the compilation of a program is complete and if there were any
errors detected. If a magnetic tape or disk pack has to be loaded onto a particular drive, the supervisor will request the operator to do it. When done,
the operator tells the supervisor that the tape or disk is now available for use.

Sometimes a part of the system or part of a program that is being run
will fail for some reason and the system stops. Messages will be printed on
the typewriter telling the operator what has happened. The operator will record the information in the rows of lights on the console. These are just like
the light bulbs we described in Chapter 5, and they are used to show the data
that is stored in particular addresses in the central processing unit. When an
error occurs that causes the system to stop, it is often useful to know the contents of these registers when determining what in fact happened. So the operator makes a note of their contents and then follows the instructions in the

manuals for starting the system again. This may involve typing some information on the console typewriter and setting dials and switches on the console
to predetermined positions.

Figure 9-2. UNIVAC 1100/40 Control Console

Which of these statements is true?

_____ (a) An operating system removes the need for an operator on a large
system.

_____ (b) A system and its operator communicate through the control console
and console typewriter.

_____ (c) The only function performed by an operator is loading and unloading
input-output devices.

_____ (d) none of the above

- - - - - - - - - - - - - - - - - - - -

b

5. The supervisor can call upon all the other components of the operating
system to accomplish its task of controlling the computer. It is able to call
compilers from the compiler library as they are required. A large system
would have compilers for as many as 10 or 12 different languages.

When the source program has been compiled, the resulting object program
would be stored in the program library. The program library is usually stored
on magnetic disk or magnetic drum and holds all the programs in regular use
on the computer system. The program library would also contain all the utility programs for the system.

Which of these statements is true?

_____ (a) When an error message is written on the control console, the supervisor corrects the error.

_____ (b) Compilers are not considered part of the operating system.

_____ (c) On a large computer system, the operator is responsible for scheduling programs through the central processing unit.

_____ (d) none of the above

- - - - - - - - - - - - - - - - - - -

d

6.   As you will recall from Chapter 6, when a programmer is preparing a program, an important step is debugging—that is, finding and correcting all the errors, both in logic and in the symbolic code. This can sometimes be difficult, especially in large or sophisticated programs. The debugging routines in the operating system are designed to help a programmer locate obscure errors that occur when the program is being tested.

The last major component of the operating system we will discuss is that containing the housekeeping routines. These routines are used by the operating system to protect accounts and files and to do the "bookkeeping." In large systems with many users and many data files, elaborate precautions have to be taken to ensure file security—that is, to prevent unauthorized people from gaining access to data files.

Also included in the housekeeping routines are procedures for keeping track of the amount of time a user is on the system and what devices have been used so that the user can then be billed accordingly. And, of course, there are housekeeping routines designed to prevent unauthorized use of user accounts.

Which of these statements is true?

_____ (a) Debugging routines are used by the supervisor to check that all devices in the system are working.

_____ (b) Housekeeping routines are used by the operating system for file protection and billing.

_____ (c) both

_____ (d) neither

- - - - - - - - - - - - - - - - - -

b

7.   Perhaps the best way to show how the operating system functions is to see how a programmer communicates with the system and how instructions are interpreted.

A programmer uses job-control language to communicate with the operating system.   Through the JCL the programmer identifies the user and describes the language in which the program is written, where the source program begins and ends, and where the data is located.   Job-control languages vary from computer system to computer system.

As an example, we will look at the basic requirements for a JCL that is to be used for inputting the source program and data on cards.

The programmer has two card decks—one contains the source program and the other the data.   The two decks have to be combined into one deck to be put through the card reader.   The cards cannot be fed through the reader on their own because the system will not know what to do with them.   So the programmer prepares job-control cards, which you might expect to be written in

_____ language.

- - - - - - - - - - - - - - - - - -

job-control

8.   The following examples are not real ones but will show what kinds of information the user might give to the system.   First, the user has to be identified through an account number (more about this later), a name, and a special password.   This information might be punched into two cards, like this:

ACC Z265 "HARRIS MARTIN L"
KEYWORD ANN

The keyword, or password, is used as protection for the user's account. The keyword is known only to the user and the system—it isn't recorded anywhere.   This protection is necessary to prevent an unauthorized operator from using an account without the owner's knowledge.   The keyword can be changed any time simply by using the appropriate job-control language to give the system the new keyword.

Which part of the operating system is responsible for protecting accounts?

_____   (a)   debugging routines

_____   (b)   program library

_____   (c)   housekeeping routines

_____   (d)   none of the above

- - - - - - - - - - - - - - - - - -

c

9. When the supervisor receives the account number and keyword, it calls a housekeeping routine into main storage. This particular routine, or short program, is designed to check a file containing all users' account numbers, names, and keywords. If the account number, name, and keyword match those assigned to a particular user, processing can continue. If these items don't match, a message such as INVALID ACCOUNT NUMBER or INVALID KEYWORD will be printed or displayed on a display terminal and processing will not continue. After this check has been made, the supervisor moves the housekeeping routine back to an auxiliary storage device to make room in main storage for another program.

Which of these is used as special protection for the user's account?

_____ (a) account number

_____ (b) user name

_____ (c) keyword

_____ (d) none of the above

- - - - - - - - - - - - - - - - - - -

c

10. We have now identified ourselves to the system, but it still doesn't know what language our source program is using. For the next step, we might punch a card with this information:

// EXEC FORTRAN

This card informs the supervisor that we are giving the system a program written in FORTRAN. The supervisor will then move the FORTRAN compiler from the compiler library in auxiliary storage into main storage.

The next card to be punched tells the system that it has reached the beginning of the source program. Thus, we punch:

%FORTRAN

We then insert the source-program cards and follow them with a card punched:

%DATA

This card tells the system that it has finished reading the source program and is about to begin reading _____ cards.

- - - - - - - - - - - - - - - - - -

data

11. We now insert the data cards and follow them with a card punched:

/ *

This signals the end of the data-input file.   Figure 9-3 shows how the whole deck might be set up.

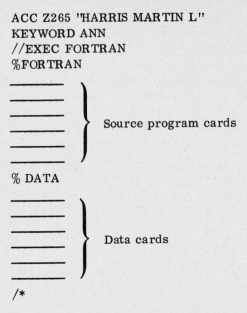

```
ACC Z265 "HARRIS MARTIN L"
KEYWORD ANN
//EXEC FORTRAN
%FORTRAN
```

} Source program cards

% DATA

} Data cards

/*

Figure 9-3. Use of Job-Control Cards

The log-on procedures described in Chapter 8 are an example of job-control language in a time-sharing, on-line situation. The introductory "conversation" looked like this.

```
hi
DOWNTOWN UNIVERSITY COMPUTER FACILITY
08/08-78                    10:45:27
ACCOUNT NUMBER?  z265
KEYWORD?  ann
SYSTEM?  basic
```

Which of these statements is true?

_____ (a) JCL allows a programmer to communicate with the operating system.

_____ (b) The operating system communicates with the operator using job-control language.

_____ (c) JCL can be inputted to the operating system from punched cards or from a remote terminal.

_____ (d) all of the above

- - - - - - - - - - - - - - - - - -

a, c

12. When a terminal session is complete, the programmer might type:

goodbye

This is accepted as the last statement in JCL, and the operating system will switch off the connection to the terminal. Before doing so, however, it may use another housekeeping routine to print some information about the programmer's usage of the system, like this:

```
Z265   LOGOFF   11:36:35
Z265   CPU      11.892 SEC
```

This tells the programmer that the terminal will be disconnected at 11:36 and 35 seconds and that 11.892 seconds of CPU time has been used. Notice that nearly one hour was spent using the terminal (10:45 until 11:36), but only about 12 seconds of CPU time were used to compile and run the program written.

The timing is done by an extremely accurate clock built into the system as part of a housekeeping routine. In addition to being printed on our output device, the time for our program is used by another housekeeping routine that maintains records of the jobs run on the system, the times they were run, and how long they took.

This information may be used in two ways. Users who have their own system need a record of jobs run and the time used in order to check on the system's efficiency. A complete record will enable the managers of the data-processing department to improve their service to other departments within the company.

On a time-sharing system, the records may be used for billing users. As mentioned, each user has an account that is charged for use of the system. Although methods of charging users vary, the charge is often based on a particular cost per hour for terminal time and cost per second for processing time.

On-line processing and time sharing are only possible with complex operating systems. There is no way human operators could control an efficient time-sharing system if they had to perform each of the operations described above for each user.

The basis of time sharing is the apparent simultaneous execution of several programs. In fact, however, only one program is controlling the central processing unit at any one time. The operating system transfers control of processing back and forth between programs so quickly that it seems as if the programs are being executed simultaneously. This process is sometimes called <u>multiprogramming</u>.

Time sharing is:

_____ (a) dependent on the concept of multiprogramming.

_____ (b) possible only through the use of complex operating systems.

_____ (c) both

_____ (d) neither

- - - - - - - - - - - - - - - - - - - -

c

13. To illustrate the concept of multiprogramming, consider three programs, A, B, and C, that are requested at the same time. For simplicity, assume that the system on which they are to be run has one card reader and one printer and that each of the programs needs to use both, as well as to do some processing. Further assume each program takes exactly the same length of time for each operation.

Figure 9-4, part 1, shows that the total time required to run the three programs consecutively is 27 units.

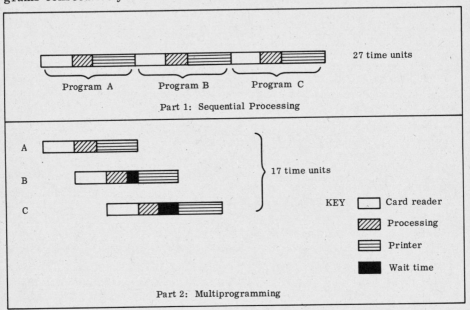

Figure 9-4. Illustration of the Advantage of Multiprogramming

Part 2 of Figure 9-4 shows how the programs could be executed in a multiprogramming system. Program A starts by using the card reader to input data. As soon as it begins to process the data, the card reader is free and the data for program B can be read. Before all the input data for B has been read, program A has finished processing and begin using the printer.

Notice that when program B has finished processing, it has to wait for 1 unit of time until program A has finished with the printer.

Program C reads its input data:

_____ (a) as soon as program B has finished with the card reader.

_____ (b) while program A is using the printer.

_____ (c) both

_____ (d) neither

c

14. Why does program B have to wait 1 unit of time after processing its data before printing the output?

_____ (a) Because program A is still using the printer.

_____ (b) Because program C is still using the card reader.

_____ (c) Because program C has not yet processed its data.

_____ (d) all of the above

- - - - - - - - - - - - - - - - - -

a (All statements are true, but a gives the reason for program B having to wait.)

15. Program C has to wait 2 units of time until program B has finished with the printer before printing its output. By multiprogramming, or overlapping, these three programs, the total time taken to execute all three is reduced from 27 units to 17 units, a saving of 37 percent.

In real applications, of course, the picture is much more complex, since programs typically perform input-output operations and processing operations more than once during their execution. Also, a computer system with an operating system supporting multiprogramming would have more than one input and one output device, so the overlapping of programs would be even more dramatic.

Another concept that has the potential to increase the efficiency of computer systems is called structured programming. Structured programming breaks large and complex programming tasks into a series of smaller, less complex ones. For example, a payroll program can be very complex and contain many thousands of instructions. Using structured programming techniques it might be broken down into a series of smaller, interrelated programs. One might read the various input files required, another calculate gross pay, another calculate taxes and then net pay, another write the checks, and another update the payroll files.

Once the overall design of all the programs is complete and a set of specifications for each is written, teams of programmers can work on all of them at the same time. Each can be debugged and tested independently of the others.

In addition to reducing the complexity of the individual programs, documentation is easier under the structured approach. Modification of the payroll system is also simplified.

Structured programming also allows for the processing of applications that would be too large for the central processing unit if written as a single program.

For example, suppose a program requires 76K of main storage, but the system on which it is to be executed has only 60K available. Then the program might be broken into three modules—input operations requiring 16K, processing operations requiring 40K, and output operations requiring 20K.

When the program is to be executed, the supervisor would load the input module and execute it, then load the processing module into the storage area used by the input module (plus some more), and then, when processing is complete, load the output module. Thus a program that is in one piece would require 76K can be executed using not more than 40K.

Which of these statements is true?

_____ (a) The supervisor controls the operations of the computer.

_____ (b) Structured programming breaks a large application into a series of small programs.

_____ (c) both

_____ (d) neither

- - - - - - - - - - - - - - - - - -

b

16. The final concept that we will discuss is that of <u>virtual storage</u>. Virtual storage allows the computer to behave as if the central processing unit were larger than it actually is. Let's say we have a program that requires 90K of main storage, but the computer we want to run it on has only 48K of available storage. An operating system that uses virtual storage will, when the program is loaded onto a disk pack, automatically <u>page</u> the program. That is, the program is divided into segments, called pages, that will easily fit the available main storage. When the program is executed, the supervisor reads it into main memory page by page, executing each page in turn. When a given page has been executed, it is returned to the disk pack and the next page is read in. The major limitation of virtual-storage techniques lies in the time taken to transfer pages into memory. Compared to the time taken to execute individual instructions, this time can be very long, and in many instances it reduces the overall efficiency of the system.

Which of these statements is true?

_____ (a) Virtual storage involves breaking large applications into a series of small programs.

_____ (b) Structured programming allows the computer to break a program into pages and thus act as if its main storage were larger than it actually is.

_____ (c) both

_____ (d) neither

- - - - - - - - - - - - - - - - - -

d

This is the end of Chapter 9. You should now work the Self-Test that follows.

SELF-TEST

Answer all the questions and then check against the answers that follow.

1. Which of these statements is true?

   _____ (a) Report generators are relatively simple to use and are generally supplied by the computer manufacturer.

   _____ (b) Utility programs are designed specifically for customer billing by gas and electric companies.

   _____ (c) Applications programs are designed to solve data-processing problems that are common to a large number of organizations.

   _____ (d) all of the above

2. Which of these statements is true?

   _____ (a) An operating system is the book that tells the operator how to run a particular program.

   _____ (b) An operating system is designed by the computer manufacturer.

   _____ (c) An operating system is inefficient, but saves the cost of having a human operator.

   _____ (d) none of the above

3. Which of these is a function of the supervisor?

   _____ (a) Loading programs and data into the CPU.

   _____ (b) Scheduling the flow of programs through the CPU.

   _____ (c) Communicating with the operator.

   _____ (d) all of the above

4. Which of these statements is true?

   _____ (a) Virtual storage allows a computer to operate as if it has more main storage than it actually has.

   _____ (b) The operating system communicates with the operator through the control console.

   _____ (c) The operator has only to load and unload input–output devices.

   _____ (d) none of the above

5. Job-control language:

   _____ (a) allows a programmer to communicate with the supervisor.

   _____ (b) allows the operating system to communicate with the operator.

   _____ (c) both

   _____ (d) neither

246 INTRODUCTION TO DATA PROCESSING

6. Multiprogramming:

_____ (a) allows the simultaneous execution of more than one program.

_____ (b) is possible only with complex operating systems.

_____ (c) is essential to time-sharing applications.

_____ (d) all of the above

7. Structured programming:

_____ (a) requires very complex operating systems.

_____ (b) breaks large applications into a series of small programs.

_____ (c) both

_____ (d) neither

Answers to Self-Test

The numbers in parentheses after each answer refer to the frames in which the appropriate answers can be found. If you have a wrong answer or are not sure why your answer is correct, read that section again before going on.

1. a, c (frame 1)

2. b (frame 3)

3. d (frame 3)

4. a, b (frames 4, 16)

5. a (frame 7)

6. d (frame 13)

7. b (frame 15)

CHAPTER TEN
Systems Analysis

Systems analysis is the study of the various components of a business organization with the purpose of refining their operation and of improving the relationships among them. It is a very complex subject and this chapter is designed to give only a brief over view.

After completing this chapter you will be able to:

- state the two major objectives of systems analysis;
- describe the use of a feasibility study;
- describe how a systems analyst gathers the information required for an analysis;
- describe how a new computerized system is tested and implemented; and
- describe the purpose of management-information systems.

1. Any business organization can be thought of as a series of related components or systems. Each system is an organized method of accomplishing some goal or objective. Figure 10-1 shows some typical business systems and their objectives.

SYSTEM	BASIC OBJECTIVES
Payroll	To provide periodic pay checks to employees and to maintain payroll information on each employee for processing of tax reports, etc.
Accounts Receivable	To maintain records on money owed by customers and to send out monthly statements to each customer.
Accounts Payable	To maintain records on money owed to various suppliers.

(continued on following page)

Inventory	To maintain records on the various types of merchandise and the quantities that are on hand for each.
Personnel	To maintain records on all personnel working for the company so that various "profile" reports can be readily prepared for management review.

Figure 10-1. Typical Business Systems and Their Objectives

The term analysis means to break something down into its individual components and study them. Systems analysis is the breaking down of an organization into its component parts and studying them. Through the study of each component and the relationships between them, systems analysis allows us to see how an organization works and, hopefully, the ways to improve it.

Systems analysis in data processing has two major objectives. The first aim is to provide greater efficiency within the organization. Efficiency might be improved through more up-to-date reports to management, better customer service, or a reduction in overlapping operations with the organization.

Second, systems analysis attempts to improve the economy of the organization. This can be done by eliminating unnecessary tasks, increasing the productivity of certain departments, or reducing the cost of clerical operations.

Ideally these two objectives combine to produce greater efficiency at lower cost. However, greater efficiency may sometimes result in increased costs. In this case, management has to decide whether the increased efficiency is worth the cost. The opposite may also occur: an increase in economy leading to a decrease in efficiency. For example, adding six more people to a customer-service department that is unable to cope with the number of queries from

customers would increase the _____ of the department while reducing its _____ .

- - - - - - - - - - - - - - - - - -

efficiency, economy

2. Of course, increasing the efficiency of the customer-service department could result in an increase in sales, thus increasing the economy of the organization as a whole. That is the kind of judgment made by management on the basis of information from a systems analysis. (It could also be that extra cost is necessary to prevent sales from falling and further damaging the economy of the organization.)

Banning all overtime in the accounting department might result in an improvement in the _____ , but lead to a reduction in

_____ because reports are not prepared on time, checks are written late, and so on.

- - - - - - - - - - - - - - - - - -

economy, efficiency

3.   A <u>systems</u> <u>analyst</u> is a person who analyzes systems. There are a wide range of procedures and techniques available to the systems analyst, but this chapter will present only a general overview of them.
     Systems analysis refers to the examination of the:

_____   (a) individual components of the organization.

_____   (b) relationships between the components of an organization.

_____   (c) both

_____   (d) neither

- - - - - - - - - - - - - - - - - - -

c

4.   Which of these are objectives of systems analysis?

_____   (a) A reduction in the number of personnel performing clerical functions.

_____   (b) An increase in the economy of an organization.

_____   (c) The installation of data-processing equipment.

_____   (d) An improvement in the efficiency of an organization.

- - - - - - - - - - - - - - - - - - -

b, d (Choices a and c may be courses of action recommended by a systems analyst in a particular situation, but they are not the objectives of systems analysis in general.)

5.   Which of these statements is true?

_____   (a) An increase in efficiency always leads to an increase in the economy of an organization.

_____   (b) An improvement in the economy of an organization always leads to a decrease in the efficiency.

_____   (c) It is not always possible to increase both the economy and the efficiency of an organization at the same time.

- - - - - - - - - - - - - - - - - - -

c

6.   A critical factor in systems analysis is the degree to which analysts and management communicate with each other. Historically the two groups have had quite different, and separate, training; one talked the language of systems and computers while the other talked the language of business. The gap in

understanding was very wide, and considerable amounts of time and money were wasted when the gap was not adequately bridged.

Today most people training to be managers take courses in data-processing principles, and most systems analysts and programmers take courses in business principles. This gives both sides an understanding of the other's language and problems. The major responsibility for bridging the gap between managers and data-processing personnel, however, lies with the systems analyst.

The major task of a systems analyst is to investigate the data-processing operations of an organization with a view toward increasing their efficiency and economy. This may involve modifying an existing system for handling data or designing an entirely new system. In either case the analyst will be concerned to automate the processing of data as much as possible, by installing new equipment if necessary. This is, of course, an expensive thing to do.

If the analyst believes that new equipment should be installed, a <u>feasibility study</u> is conducted. The feasibility study compares the cost of obtaining the equipment and changing operating procedures with the long-term expected benefits of the new system—both in efficiency and economy.

A feasibility study:

_____ (a) is done if only minor changes to a data-processing system are being considered.

_____ (b) is done if the installation of automated data-processing equipment is being considered.

_____ (c) compares the benefits of automated data processing with its costs.

_____ (d) none of the above

- - - - - - - - - - - - - - - - - -

b, c

7.   A feasibility study applies specifically to situations where the installation of computer equipment is being considered. However, the analyst uses the same techniques that are used to improve the efficiency and economy of an existing automated data-processing system.

The analyst considers how to change in one or more components of the system will affect the organization as a whole. Suppose the production department wants to change the format of the job cards that its employees complete every day. The change will reflect current operating procedures. It will not only make the cards easier to fill out but also reduce the number of errors made. This may seem a very reasonable thing to do; nevertheless, the systems analyst has to study the effects of this change on other parts of the system.

Although fairly minor in itself, this change may have serious consequences elsewhere. Clerical personnel will have to be trained to work with the new cards; forms used in other departments may have to be changed; or computer programs may have to be changed because the data on the new cards is arranged in a different format. All these changes may be too expensive to be worthwhile. Or, the changes may more than pay for themselves in terms of more accurate management reports, decreased clerical work, and the like. The systems study should indicate which alternative will be the case.

How does the systems analyst go about this work? To analyze a system, the analyst has three major sources of information—the systems objectives as described by management, the procedures manuals that tell how the system is supposed to operate, and the people who actually operate the system from day to day.

It is, of course, essential that the analyst have a clear understanding of management's objectives; these, after all, are the objectives that must be met with maximum efficiency and economy.

After the analyst understands what the system is intended to do, the procedures manuals must be studied to find out how the existing system operates. These manuals indicate where the input data comes from, what forms the data is recorded on, how it is processed, what the output is like, and where the output goes. The manual tells the analyst how the system is <u>supposed</u> to operate, but systems have a tendency to change somewhat as time goes by.

To find out how the system <u>actually</u> operates, the analyst interviews all the staff involved in actually running the system. This is perhaps the most difficult part of the job: the analyst has to convince staff that they will not be penalized for not following the procedures manual to the letter. On the one hand, the system may be running more efficiently because some employees are <u>not</u> following the manual! On the other hand, the efficiency of the whole system could be greatly reduced because one or two people do not follow the instructions.

Once the analyst knows what the system is intended to do and how it is actually doing it (or failing to do it), the next stage of the job begins—the design of a new system.

Which of these statements is true?

_____ (a) The analyst finds out what the system's objectives are by talking to the staff who run it.

_____ (b) The analyst finds out how the system is actually run by talking to management.

_____ (c) The run manuals tell the analyst how the system is supposed to operate.

_____ (d) none of the above

- - - - - - - - - - - - - - - - - - -

c

8.   At the design phase of the job, the analyst may have to design new forms for recording input and output, new files to store data, new computer programs to process data, and new ways of transmitting data from its source to the data-processing department. In designing new procedures for handling data, the analyst makes use of <u>systems</u> flowcharts. Systems flowcharts are similar to program flowcharts, as you can see from Figure 10-2 at the top of the next page. They use more symbols than program flowcharts and show the flow of forms and data through the system.

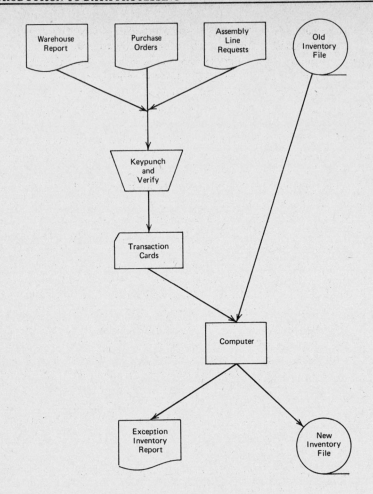

Figure 10-2. A Systems Flowchart

An analyst frequently designs two new systems: perhaps one will use existing data-processing equipment, and the other will call for new equipment. The cost of each system will then be estimated. Cost estimates show how much each system will cost over, say, the first five years of operation and the savings that will result. Management can then make a decision as to which system to implement.

At the design phase, the analyst:

_____ (a) specifies what the system is to do.

_____ (b) details how the new system is to work.

_____ (c) estimates costs involved in introducing the new system.

_____ (d) all of the above

- -

b, c

9. Once management decides which system changes are to be made, the analyst works with a computer programmer, or programmers, to design the programs that will be needed to implement the system. The analyst is responsible for specifying for the programmer what the input will be, what processing has to be performed, and what the output will be like.

The programmer will then:

_____ (a) write the source programs in symbolic code.

_____ (b) test and debug the programs.

_____ (c) prepare procedures manuals for the programs.

_____ (d) all of the above

- - - - - - - - - - - - - - - - - - - -

d

10. When all the programs are written, the systems analyst then <u>tests</u> and <u>implements</u> the new system. Testing the system involves preparing sample data that covers all the possible situations that might arise and running the data through the system. The output is then checked against a hand calculation of what the output should be. If there are any errors, the source is found and corrected.

Implementation of the new system can be done in two ways. If the changes to the system are relatively minor and/or simple to follow, then it may be possible merely to abandon the old ways and establish the new. However, there are dangers in this approach. If for some reason the implementation doesn't go well, valuable data and information may be lost forever. For this reason, with major changes in particular, a <u>parallel run</u> is performed. This means that both the old and the new methods are used until the new system is clearly working smoothly. The parallel run ensures that nothing is lost (except time and some money) if the new system develops implementation problems. The old method is still there.

Another important part of the implementation is the training of personnel in the operation of the new system.

Which of these statements is true?

_____ (a) A parallel run is usually performed if major changes are being made to the system.

_____ (b) A parallel run is used to test the system before it is implemented.

_____ (c) both

_____ (d) neither

- - - - - - - - - - - - - - - - - - - -

a

11. Figure 10-3 is a summary of the steps involved in systems analysis and the people involved in it.

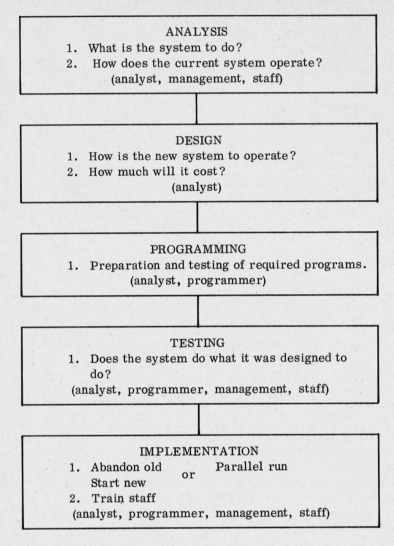

Figure 10-3. Summary of Systems Analysis

Most large companies have had data-processing systems designed to perform specific tasks. For example, the accounts-receivable department will have its own data-processing system to keep track of who owes the company money and for what. The accounts-payable department also has a system to ensure that money owed by the company is paid at the correct time to the correct people. Each department supplies management with periodic reports of the status of accounts payable and accounts receivable. However, if management wants to get an overall picture of how money flows in and out of the company, it has to wait for the latest reports from each department and then integrate the findings of those reports.

If management wants to know the total worth of the company at a particular time, it has to study reports from the two departments mentioned above, and an inventory showing the value of raw materials and finished goods in stock, as well as a production report showing the worth of the goods that are in various stages of completion. By the time all these reports have been gathered and analyzed, the data may be worthless because it is no longer current.

Because of the vast storage capabilities of modern computer systems and random-access techniques, it is possible to rectify this problem. Through the creation of a vast, company-wide storage facility that stores all the data used by all departments, <u>management-information systems</u> may be designed and implemented. In a management-information system, each department continues to produce its reports, but all departments use common data files instead of maintaining their own files. These common data files are called <u>data bases</u>. When management wants a report it can use the data-base files to produce the report directly and much more quickly.

Which of these statements is true?

_____ (a) A management-information system uses a common data-storage area for all departments.

_____ (b) A management-information system will allow management to receive more up-to-date reports on the company's total operations.

_____ (c) both

_____ (d) neither

- - - - - - - - - - - - - - - - - -

c

12. While management-information systems have the potential to provide better and more up-to-date information and reports, they are not for every organization.

In addition to requiring a large and sophisticated central computer, management-information systems also need an extensive telecommunications system. The development time can be considerable, with a large team of analysts and programmers working for several years to design and implement a system. Design problems can be greatly complicated by the difficulty that management often has in defining exactly what the system is to do for it.

All these factors make management-information systems extremely expensive. The design of a system may cost several million dollars, with the equipment on which it is to be implemented costing another million dollars.

This is the end of Chapter 10. You should now work the following Self-Test.

SELF-TEST

Answer all of the questions and then check the answers that follow.

1. Which of these is an objective of systems analysis?

   _____ (a) A reduction in the number of clerical employees.

   _____ (b) An increase in the efficiency of an organization.

   _____ (c) An increase in the economy of an organization.

   _____ (d) all of the above

2. Which of these statements is true?

   _____ (a) A systems analyst looks at the individual components of an organization and their relationships.

   _____ (b) An increase in the economy of an organization usually leads to a decrease in its efficiency.

   _____ (c) both

   _____ (d) neither

3. A feasibility study is conducted:

   _____ (a) to see if a systems analyst is required.

   _____ (b) if the installation of data-processing equipment is being considered.

   _____ (c) both

   _____ (d) neither

4. Where do analysts obtain their information when analyzing a system?

   _____ (a) the staff who operate the system

   _____ (b) management

   _____ (c) the systems manuals

   _____ (d) all of the above

5. When the systems design is completed, the analyst:

   _____ (a) has a series of system flowcharts showing how documents are processed.

   _____ (b) writes the specifications for the required programs.

   _____ (c) both

   _____ (d) neither

6. A new system may be implemented by:

    _____ (a) running small amounts of data through the system and checking the output against hand calculations.

    _____ (b) using both old and new systems in parallel until it is clear that the new system is working.

    _____ (c) both

    _____ (d) neither

7. Management-information systems:

    _____ (a) make use of the vast storage capacities of the computer systems.

    _____ (b) are designed to provide management with up-to-date reports on the company's operations.

    _____ (c) both

    _____ (d) neither

Answers to Self-Test

The numbers in parentheses after each answer refer to the frames in which the appropriate answers can be found. If you have a wrong answer or are not sure why your answer is correct, read that frame of the chapter again before going on to Chapter 11.

1. b, c (frame 1)

2. a (frame 2)

3. b (frame 6)

4. d (frame 7)

5. c (frame 8)

6. b (frame 9)

7. c (frame 10)

CHAPTER ELEVEN
The Impact of Computers

This chapter is designed to put into some perspective what you have learned in the first ten chapters. In describing the physical equipment used in data processing, we have made many references to its application in everyday life. We now will focus on the applications and how they affect our lives. There are no questions to be answered as you go, nor is there a Self-Test. Rather, we hope that this chapter will help get you thinking about broad questions and concerns about data processing and help you form some opinions as to how you think computers might best be used—or perhaps misused.

Let's look at some aspects of everyday life that we take for granted, but that would be quite different without computers.

The financial institutions—banks, savings and loans, credit unions, and credit-card companies—would be unable to operate at the same speed or with the same volume of business without computers. Consider the processing of a check. A customer writes a check in a store and at the end of the day the merchant deposits all the checks received at the bank. That part hasn't been changed by computers. What has changed is the speed with which the amount of the check is credited to the merchant's account and debited to the customer's. Before computers, the check was credited to the merchant's account by hand, the checks were then sorted and mailed, or sent by courier, to the bank of the person writing the check where the amount was debited by hand. All of this could take three or four days if checks had to go to another town. Now the accounting part—crediting and debiting—is done overnight, so a check deposited before a certain time in the afternoon has been processed by eight o'clock the next morning. The check itself might still take several days to reach the writer's bank for filing, but that's not too important. Telecommunications and the high speed of computers have reduced the time necessary to process a check and at the same time have increased the volume of transactions that can be handled.

The telephone system as we know it would not be possible without computers. It has been estimated that to handle the number of calls being made today if manual switching were required would use one-half of all adults in the country and would not offer as efficient a service. Computers determine the best way to route calls across country, avoiding busy areas. Many large telephone exchanges also have computers that monitor their performance and regularly print out a list of problems for engineers to fix. Thus, your telephone could be out of order for a few hours and then be fixed without your knowledge.

It is possible that airlines would be unable to offer all the flights they do without computerized reservation systems. How could one determine if there were passenger space available on a flight leaving in an hour and make a reservation without a computerized system? As you can see, the nation's travel habits would certainly be different without computers.

If you are unfortunate enough to be hospitalized in an intensive-care unit, there is a good chance that you will be monitored by a computer. Patient-monitoring systems make continuous readings of vital signs and, in addition to creating a continuous record of changes in these signs, can alert nursing staff when vital signs exceed some predetermined limits. Such systems not only provide better monitoring than could be performed by a nurse at bedside, but allow more patients to be cared for by a fixed number of staff.

Hospitals are also using computer-information systems to help with the assignment of patients to beds, maintenance of critical medical information about patients, monitoring drug usage, and scheduling patients for specialized treatment and follow-up visits.

Finally, consider the role the various governments—local, state, and federal—play in our lives, through collecting tax money and then disbursing it in various ways. The biggest collector, of course, is the Internal Revenue Service. It is inconceivable to think of the IRS processing tax returns without the use of computers, unless returns were submitted on a year-round basis and were less complex. The social-security system is the largest disburser of federal funds. Again, it is hard to imagine how it could keep track of all the contributors to, and recipients of, its funds without computers.

There are, of course, hundreds of other ways in which computers impinge on our lives, and there is a tendency to accept all the applications of computers as good. It is important to take a balanced view of their impact, however, for there is always some cost involved in computerizing a system that was previously manual. And these costs have to be balanced against the benefits.

Take, for example, the use of the universal product code and point-of-sale terminals. Zebra codes, as the universal product code is called, now appear on practically all goods. But consider just supermarkets. In the past, every item placed on a shelf had the price marked on it so that the customer and the checkers knew what it cost. But to mark every item is a labor-intensive task, and therefore expensive. With the zebra codes, the price of each item can be displayed on the shelf where the items are found. Checkers do not have to know the price of each item because that is programmed into the terminal. All the checker does with the system in Figure 11-1 (at the top of the next page) is slide the item across the rectangular scanner, "zebra" mark down. The scanner reads the code and transmits it to the terminal. Special discounts, such as $.25 each but 5 for $1.00, can also be programmed into the terminal. The terminal will then print out an itemized bill giving the name of each item bought, its price, the sales tax, and total amount owed.

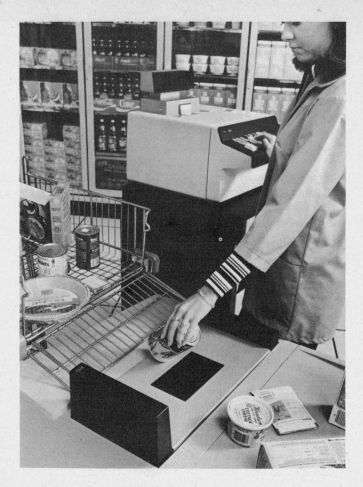

Figure 11-1.   The IBM 3660 Supermarket Check-out System

Large supermarkets think the universal product code is a great idea because it reduces the number of people who are employed to stock shelves. The savings can result either in greater profits, in lower prices, or a combination of both. Great savings can also be made in inventory control. However, the labor unions who are affected by this change oppose it because it will result in fewer people being employed. Many customers object because they are used to having each item marked and fear that supermarkets may misplace items on shelves so that it is not easy to find out how much an item costs. Added to customer concerns is a fear that "the computer" will ring up the wrong amount for an item or incorrectly total the bill.

The issue of labeling versus the use of the universal product code is complex, and there are good arguments to be made for and against it. But who should make the final decision: the supermarket managers, the labor unions, or the customers? In California, the issue has been debated in the State Legislature with solutions ranging from "go ahead and do it and make all the savings possible" to "use it but also put the price on every item" (a nice political compromise), to "use it but don't reduce the number of employees and don't label each item. " As you might imagine, the Legislature was unable to decide on the issue, so the decision is now up to the supermarkets. Many are trying the system on a limited scale and, after having time to get used to it, most customers forget their concerns and appreciate the increased speed of the checkout process. So we should look for a gradual introduction of the universal product code used in conjunction with point-of-sales terminals, and only expect to find it in markets belonging to fairly large chains.

An extension of the computerization of the banking and credit-card systems is being discussed that is causing much more controversy than the use of the universal product code. This new development, called Electronic Funds Transfer (EFT), refers to the transfer of funds (money) solely by means of data-processing systems. It is intended to make banking more efficient by increasing the speed with which funds are debited and credited and by almost eliminating paper documents such as checks.

The basic intent of EFT is to make the telephone a computer terminal and every individual a data-entry clerk. When you receive, say, a utility bill, you would no longer write a check and mail it to the utility company. Rather, you would dial your bank's computer and, with the aid of an audio-response system, use the buttons on the telephone to enter your account number, your own secret code to identify yourself, the account number of the utility company, and the amount you want to pay them. The bank computer would probably verify all those numbers by "reading" them back to you using its audio-response capability and then tell you to hang up. And that's all you would have to do! The charge would be immediately debited to your account. Perhaps once a day the bank computer would accumulate all the credits for the utility company and transfer them, via a telecommunications system, to the utility company's bank for crediting.

It is not difficult to visualize the elimination of checks and bills altogether. If all purchases were made with credit cards through intelligent terminals in a telecommunications network, everything would be done electronically. The customer could have a receipt, but the merchant would not have to send copies to the bank—the terminal would transmit all the necessary data. And, instead of mailing the credit-card user a monthly bill, the credit-card company would debit the user's account directly. Many banks have moved in the direction of EFT by providing systems whereby salaries can be deposited directly to employee bank accounts, and regular monthly payments, such as those for mortgages, insurance, etc., are made automatically. Full implementation of EFT could lead to the situation where the only cash you might need would be to pay the kid across the street for babysitting!

Of course, the widespread use of such a system may never occur, and even minor variations of it are some time away. But the development work on EFT has begun and we have the technical know-how to implement the system. What then would prevent its implementation?

Apart from customer resistance (always a major factor in new developments in any field), the major concerns are cost and security. Such a system would have an enormous cost not only in machinery but in development time. As the demand for skilled systems analysts and programmers increases, so do their salaries. Also, EFT systems require thousands of person-years to develop and test. While EFT systems may cut paper and data-entry personnel costs, they will be more expensive to maintain. It is unlikely that the widespread use of EFT would reduce banking costs. At best it might prevent those costs from rising as rapidly as they might otherwise. (Another consideration the government must make before giving general approval to EFT is the economic effect EFT will have on the postal service as the system will cause the loss of millions of bills a day flowing through the mails.)

But security is the most serious problem. There are three types of security problems—security of data from catastrophic equipment failure, security against unauthorized access to accounts, and security of the computer installation from terrorist activity.

A large-scale equipment failure could be overwhelming if appropriate safeguards were not incorporated into the design of the system because data would be lost. Imagine losing all the data on, say, 1,000 accounts. With present banking systems, most of the data could be reconstructed from the original documents. But with EFT there are no documents. Thus elaborate backup systems would be required. For example, data about an account might be maintained on two or three magnetic drums, each in a different location and under the control of a different computer. If the main computer malfunctioned and erased the data on its magnetic drum, the account information could be retrieved from one of the others. Such systems, of course, are expensive. (All good data-processing departments now maintain copies of important files to protect against loss of data.)

The major security problem, however, is that of protecting accounts from unauthorized access. Although each user of an account would have his or her own code or keyword as identification, such codes are typically not very complex. Most of us would have it written down somewhere, making our accounts vulnerable to thieves. A skillful thief could move money through a series of accounts in ways that would make it very difficult, if not impossible, to trace.

Finally, the entire computer center needs to be secure from seizure by terrorists. The takeover of a computer of a very large bank could have serious and widespread effects. Even if the data files were not tampered with, to close down the computer would bring the bank's business to a halt, perhaps affecting the financial affairs of hundreds of thousands of people.

Crimes involving computers have become more common and can involve very large sums of money. While computer use in accounting may have made it more difficult for the average employee to "fix the books," highly trained analysts and programmers can now do so. And because their methods are so complex, there is less chance of their being caught.

While many earlier schemes—such as to round up the results of calculations and put the difference into a special account known only to the programmer—can now be avoided by careful supervision, skilled and dishonest personnel can still program methods to steal money. And as we mentioned above, it is possible to learn the keywords that give access to accounts.

There have also been court cases involving the theft of computer programs that were extremely expensive to develop. Other computer crimes have involved the use of a terminal to send shipping orders directly to the warehouse, with no corresponding instructions to bill the person receiving the goods.

Finally, it is possible to steal data from telecommunications lines. More and more information is being transmitted by commercial organizations that is valuable to competitors and vulnerable while being transmitted.

There are now people who specialize in computer security and whose job it is to anticipate ways in which computer crimes might be committed. They then design systems to prevent those methods being used. New coding schemes for transmitted data are being designed that are practically unbreakable. These coding schemes will be programmed on chips and inserted into the terminals within a telecommunications network. Users will have their own chips—one for encoding and one for decoding.

Before looking at expectations for the future of data processing, we should consider one more very important issue—privacy. Commercial and government organizations have a great deal of information about each one of us, most of which is already or will soon be computerized. Local government has information on when I was born, when I was married, how many children I have, and how much I paid for my house. The university has a record of my grades and previous education. The bank has a record of how I spend my money. The local credit bureau knows what loans I have and what my record of repayment is. The state and federal governments have my tax returns, which also offer clues as to how I live. The prepaid health-care group to which I belong has a record of my medical history. The Department of Motor Vehicles has personal information about me and the vehicles I own. Because I am an immigrant, the Commissioner of Immigration and Naturalization has information about me. And, had I committed any crimes, the local police and maybe even the FBI would have computerized information about me!

If someone were able to put all that information together they would know nearly as much about me as I do! But luckily it is in many different computers and maintained under different coding schemes. In some, it is by an account number, in some by social-security number, and in some by name. The likelihood of anyone being able to retrieve all that information about me is very small—so small that it is not worth thinking about.

What about an individual computer file, though? How secure from unauthorized access is the local credit-bureau data? They need the information but they also have a responsibility to protect it from misuse. The same responsibility lies with all other agencies who maintain computer files.

One great fear many people have about computers is that they will increase the chances of a "Big Brother" society, one in which the government is able to keep track of everyone's movements and transactions. Even if all the agencies listed above had their information about me organized by social-security number, to retrieve it all would be extremely expensive. To design and build a system specifically to make all that data for everyone readily accessible would be so expensive that no government agency or private organization could do it secretly. And that is probably the greatest safeguard against such a system being built—cost.

The development of large-scale computer systems will continue in the future, as they are essential to the improved efficiency of business and government. It is in the area of personal use, however, that computers are likely to have their greatest impact on us as individuals.

As we saw in Chapter 4, microcomputers can be bought for as little as $600, and the price is continuing to fall. Small computers for cars that will calculate and display average speed, fuel consumption, estimated arrival time, etc., at the touch of a button can be purchased for less than $100. Increasingly, microwave ovens and other appliances are being marketed with computer controls. There are even light switches that contain, in addition to a digital clock, a computerized system that will turn lights on and off—at times determined by the user—in order to discourage burglars. Computerized games using a TV set as the display unit have become extremely popular.

Of all these applications of computers (and many not yet thought of), the microcomputer is likely to have the greatest impact in making everyone a data-processing user. The use of microcomputers in the home is limited only by the imagination of programmers. Since most people cannot write programs, and probably don't want to learn, the market for programs will be enormous. Programs for household finances, maintaining address lists and recipes, teaching math, calculating taxes, and, of course, playing games are already being sold on cassettes just like music tapes.

As the cost of equipment falls further, we can expect to see the microcomputer used as part of a telecommunications system on regular telephone lines. Friends can exchange programs and data and even play games together.

Already under development and use in some organizations are electronic mail systems. In these systems memos and letters can be typed at a terminal, edited and corrected until perfect, and then distributed through a telecommunications system. "Copies" can be sent to the appropriate people and, with a good security system built into the network, only the intended recipients can have access to them. Although such systems are expensive, they represent considerable savings in paper and duplicating costs as well as in personnel used to distribute the mail. Of course, if a copy is needed, it can be obtained with a touch of a button on the terminal.

Imagine receiving your mail at home on your microcomputer! With the cost of computer equipment and telephone calls falling and the cost of postage—not to mention delivery time—increasing, we are likely to see such an electronic mail system operating nationwide within the next 15 to 20 years.

The computerization of routine tasks has often been linked to the fear of mass unemployment. When computers were first introduced these fears were especially high but proved to be largely unwarranted for two reasons. First, many clerical personnel were retrained to work with computers. Second, the economy was expanding at a rapid rate, creating more jobs than were being replaced by computers. However, the impact of some of the systems on an economy unlikely to expand again at the rate it did in the 1960's may well have serious consequences for employment in many industries.

Severe labor-relation problems have already arisen in newspaper publishing, for example. Many publishers have electronic type-setting equipment. This is how it works: a reporter writes a story at a terminal, an editor edits it at a terminal, and the computer prepares the final typed copy for the printing press. This process results in the loss of many jobs—and there are no other jobs in publishing for which displaced personnel can be trained. The use of EFT, electronic mail, and the universal product code may lead to serious unemployment and retraining problems in the near future.

To summarize, computer systems play a large role in our lives and are likely to play an even larger role in the future. As we have seen, there are problems associated with their widespread use—security of data and the protection of individual rights to privacy among the most serious. It is the responsibility of each of us to understand something of the operation of computers and to insist that they be used to the ultimate benefit of us all.

APPENDIX I
Punched-Card Data Processing

This appendix is optional, and you may choose not to read it. If so, turn now to the Final Test on page 289.

Data-processing systems using punched cards and electronic accounting machines (EAM's) were once very common but have now been largely replaced by the computer systems described throughout this book. Many of these devices, however, are still used as peripheral devices in many data-processing departments to ease the burden of computer processing of cards.

After completing this appendix you will be able to:

- define the functions of the <u>reproducer</u>, <u>sorter</u>, <u>collator</u>, <u>calculating punch</u>, and <u>accounting machine</u>;
- identify the operations of <u>sorting</u>, <u>selecting</u>, <u>sequence checking</u>, <u>match-merging</u>; and
- identify the operations of <u>accumulating</u>, <u>detail printing</u>, <u>group printing</u>, and <u>summary punching</u>.

1. The key punch is the primary method of recording data from source documents. However, it is frequently necessary to duplicate the data in a punched card on one or more different cards. Although the card punch could be used for this duplication, it is not very efficient. Also, the location of a data field may have to be changed. That is, a customer number might be in columns 1 through 5 of one card, but have to be punched into columns 31 through 35 of another card. All of these operations can be performed by the IBM 519 Reproducing Punch shown in Figure A-1 at the top of the next page.

This machine is sometimes called a <u>document-originating</u> machine. Its operation is controlled by a <u>control panel</u> such as that shown in Figure A-2, the second photograph on the next page. All the EAM devices shown in this chapter (with the exception of the sorter) have control panels similar to this. The control panel is wired by the operator for each job done on the reproducer. In effect, the panel instructs the reproducer which columns to read and which columns to punch.

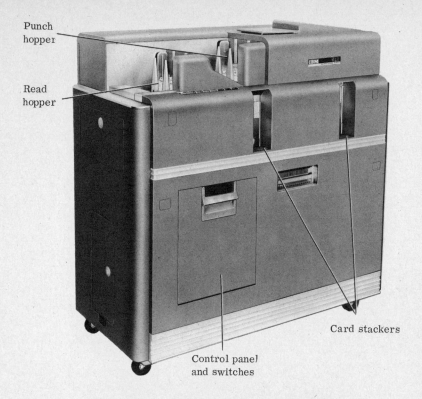

Punch hopper

Read hopper

Card stackers

Control panel and switches

Figure A-1. The IBM 519 Reproducing Punch

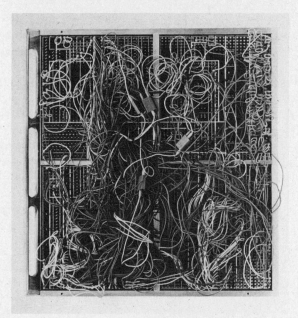

Figure A-2. A Control Panel Wired for Use

To punch data from one card into more than one card, the punched cards and blank cards are arranged as shown in Figure A-3. There can be as many blank cards as the application calls for. This deck of cards is placed in the punch hopper and the appropriately wired control panel is installed.

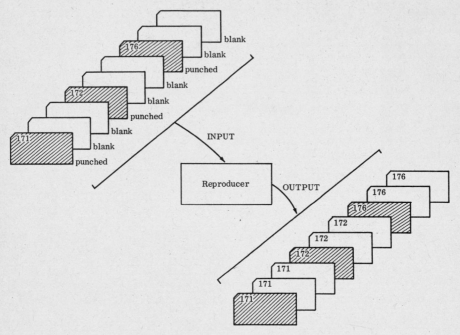

Figure A-3. Arrangement of Cards for Gang-Punching

The first card into the reproducer is a punched card. The columns to be reproduced are read and punched into each of the blank cards that follow the punched card. When a new punched card is fed into the reproducer, the appropriate columns are read and punched into as many blank cards as follows it, and so on through the deck. This operation is called gang-punching. Gang-punched cards are fed into an output stacker in the order in which they pass through the reproducer.

It should be pointed out that the cards to be punched do not have to be entirely blank. The only requirement is that the columns to be punched are blank. The reproducer does not interpret columns at the top of the card.

The reproducer can copy data from specified columns in one card into:

_____ (a) the same columns of another card.

_____ (b) different columns of another card.

_____ (c) both

_____ (d) neither

- - - - - - - - - - - - - - - - - - -

c

2. Gang-punching refers to the operation of:

_____ (a) punching data from one card into only one other card.

_____ (b) punching data from one card into two or more new cards.

_____ (c) both

_____ (d) neither

- - - - - - - - - - - - - - - - - - - -

b

3. The reproducer also performs three other useful functions. The operator may wire the control panel so that characters may be punched into the new cards that were not read off the existing card. This operation is called <u>emmit-ting</u>. The emitting operation can be performed at the same time as reproduc-ing or gang-punching. It is useful in such applications as reproducing employee time cards. Most of the data—name, department, number, and so forth—can be copied from this week's time card, but the date has to be for next week. So the date would be emmitted onto a new card, not copied from an existing card.

The reproducer can also <u>end-print</u> data onto a card. End-printing is simi-lar to interpreting, except that instead of characters being printed above the 12 row, they are printed across the end of the card, as shown in Figure A-4. This operation is useful as it provides a quick method of referring to selected data in the card.

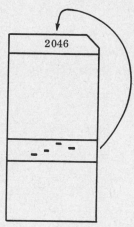

Figure A-4. An End-Printed Card

Through appropriate wiring of the control panel, end-printing may be done at the same time as reproducing or gang-punching.

Finally, the reproducer can read <u>mark-sensed cards</u>, an example of which is shown in Figure A-5 at the top of the next page.

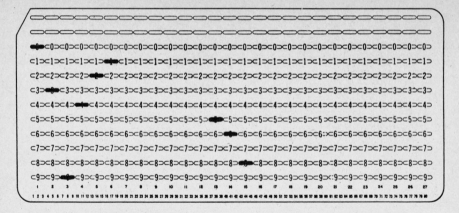

Figure A-5. A Mark-Sensed Card

The mark-sensed card is a source document that can be used directly in machine data processing.

Data is recorded by marking the appropriate portions of the card with a special pencil. Mark-sensed cards are set up with fields just like regular cards. The reproducer can read these pencil marks and convert them into punched holes in the card. The holes may be punched anywhere in the card, and do not have to be in the same columns as the pencil marks or the data. Figure A-6 shows a mark-sensed card before and after passing through the reproducer.

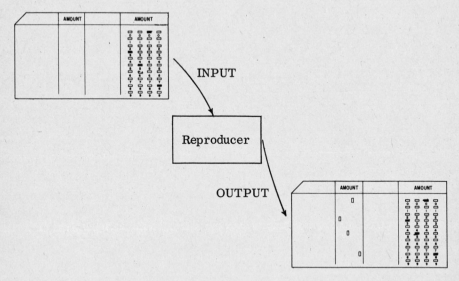

Figure A-6. Reproducing Mark-Sensed Data

Match the following:

_____ (1) emitting

_____ (2) gang-punching

(a) copying data from one card into two or more new cards

(b) copying data from one card into just one other card

(c) punching into a card characters that are not being copied from another card

- - - - - - - - - - - - - - - - - -

(1) c; (2) a

4. Data can be recorded by hand on a _____ card and automatically converted into punched holes on a _____.

- - - - - - - - - - - - - - - - - -

mark-sensed, reproducer

5. One more machine is commonly used in the preparation of punched cards. This is the <u>interpreter</u>. Cards that have been punched on the reproducer are not interpreted, making it difficult for people to read them. There are several types of interpreters in use, but here we shall discuss the IBM 557. This machine can interpret up to 60 characters per line in any one of 25 lines on the face of an IBM card. A control panel is wired by the operator to determine which characters are printed where.

The interpreter can read card columns and interpret the characters on the same card. Or it can read columns on one card and print data on another card. This latter application is useful in maintaining up-to-date records as, for example, in installment-loan accounting. Figure A-7 shows how the data from a payment card can be interpreted onto a master card that records all payments. This enables an easy check to be made on the history of an account, since most of it may be recorded on one card. Figure A-7 is shown at the top of the next page.

Because the interpreter prints only 60 characters to a line, the printed characters do not correspond to the columns in which they are punched. The type is somewhat larger on the interpreter than on the card punch.

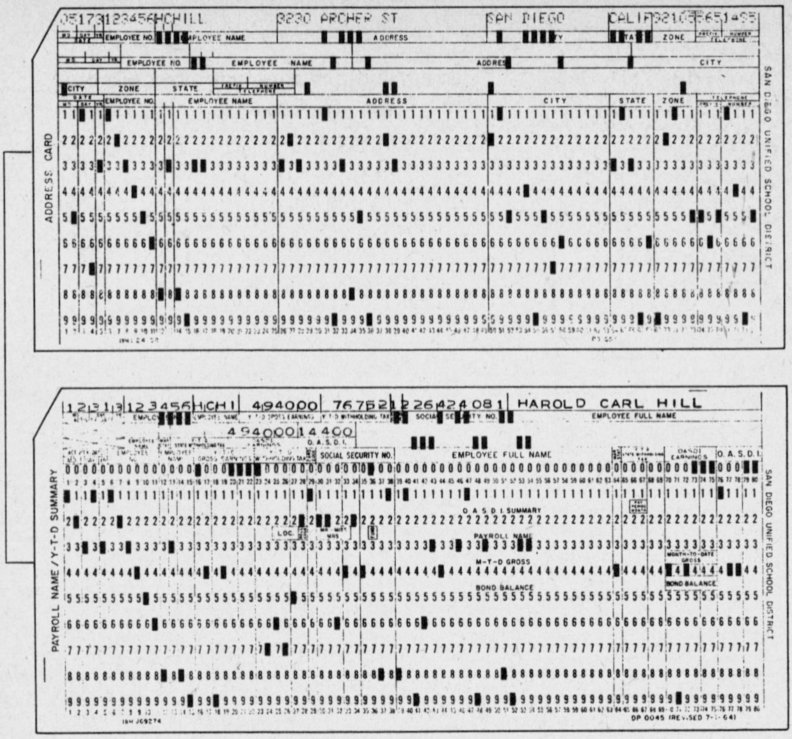

Figure A-7. Interpreting Data from One Card to Another

Match the following:

_____ (1) key punch

_____ (2) reproducer

_____ (3) interpreter

(a) cannot interpret characters at the top of
    of a card
(b) can print a character above each of the
    80 columns on a card
(c) can print characters across the end of a
    card
(d) can print characters on any of 25 lines
    on the face of the card

- - - - - - - - - - - - - - - - - -

(1) b; (2) a, c; (3) d

6. As you will recall from Chapter 2, when data has been recorded in punched cards from source documents, it is then _____ to ensure correct conversion.

- - - - - - - - - - - - - - - - - -

verified

7. Since source documents are rarely arranged in any special sequence before punching and verifying, they are frequently sorted into some predetermined sequence before further processing.

Sorting is done on a sorter, like the IBM 083 Sorter in Figure A-8. Numeric fields (those with only numbers in them) may be sorted with one pass per column through the sorter. Alphabetic fields, however, have to be passed through the sorter twice for each column. The first pass sorts on the digit portion of the character and the second pass sorts on the zone portion.

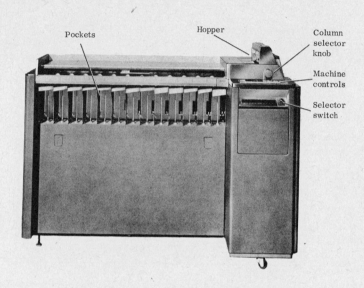

Figure A-8. The IBM 083 Sorter

A sorter may also be used to select certain records from a file. For example, if records for females are coded with a 12 punch in column 80 and records for males with a blank, they could easily be separated on a sorter. The sorter would be set to detect a 12 punch in column 80; records for females would fall into one pocket and the records for males into another.

Which of these statements is true?

_____ (a) The control panel is wired for each job to be done on a reproducer.

_____ (b) The reproducer can select certain records from a file.

_____ (c) The sorter can sort cards only on numeric fields.

_____ (d) none of the above

- -

a

8. Once a file has been arranged in numeric order, it may be <u>sequence checked</u>. Sequence checking is done on a <u>collator</u>. There are many types of collators, and Figure A-9 shows the IBM 088 Collator, which handles only numeric data.

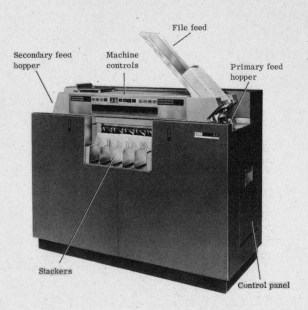

File feed

Secondary feed hopper

Machine controls

Primary feed hopper

Stackers

Control panel

Figure A-9. The IBM 088 Collator

Sequence checking is performed to check that the records in a file are in numeric order. If a file had been sorted but then stored for a few days, someone may have taken a card from it for some purpose and then put it back in the wrong place. This could cause problems in later processing of the file.

Many punched-card applications require the use of two files—a master file of records with customer name, number, address, and the like, and a detail file with records containing information on individual transactions. To produce a report showing which customers purchased something during a given period, master records of the customers who bought nothing are not required. There may also be transaction records for new customers who have no master records as yet. To produce the report, it is convenient to have only those master records that have corresponding transaction records, and vice versa.

The collator can be used to <u>match</u> the two files. Figure A-10 on the next page shows how two files are matched. The master file is placed in the

_____ hopper, and the transaction file is placed in

the _____ hopper.

- - - - - - - - - - - - - - - - - -

primary, secondary

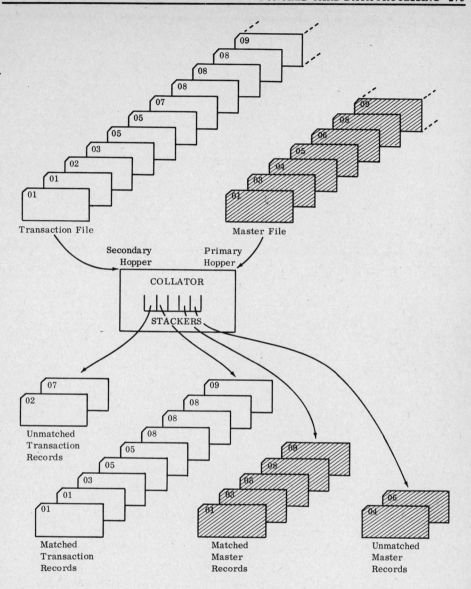

Figure A-10. Matching Two Files on a Collator

9. Unmatched master records are:

_____ (a) placed in a separate stacker.

_____ (b) placed in the same stacker as the unmatched detail records.

_____ (c) put in the same stacker as the matched masters.

— — — — — — — — — — — — — — — — — —

a

10. Both files should be arranged in the same numeric order, usually ascending order. Cards are fed simultaneously from each hopper and their control fields are compared. The result of the comparison determines the stacker to which each card is directed.

When two files are to be used in a job, they are frequently combined into a single file. This operation is called <u>merging</u> and is also performed on the collator.

Figure A-11 shows how the files that were matched in Figure A-10 are merged.

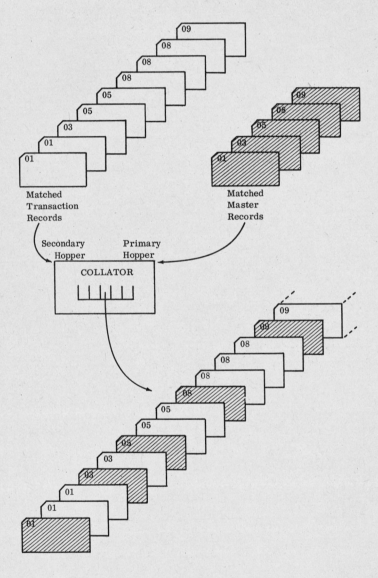

Figure A-11. Merging Two Matched Files

The collator considers the cards in the primary hopper to be more important than those in the secondary hopper. When cards come from two hoppers that have equal control fields, the card from the primary hopper falls into the stacker first and is followed by a card from the secondary hopper. This means that in a merged file:

_____ (a) each master record is followed by its matching detail record(s).

_____ (b) each detail record is followed by its matching master record.

_____ (c) each unmatched master record is placed at the end of the file.

- - - - - - - - - - - - - - - - - - -

a

11. Match the following:

_____ (1) matching

_____ (2) merging

(a) making one file from two while maintaining sequence
(b) selecting out records in one file that do not have matching records in another
(c) selecting records from a file on the basis of a character in a particular column

- - - - - - - - - - - - - - - - - -

(1) b; (2) a

12. Both matching and merging are very common in punched-card data processing, and the control panel of the collator can be wired to perform both procedures at the same time in the <u>match-merge</u> operation. The master file goes in the primary feed hopper, and the detail files goes in the secondary hopper. Figure A-12 on the next page shows how the match-merge operation would be performed on the files from Figure A-10.

In addition to match-merging two files, the collator can also sequence each file as it is processed. The collator will usually be wired to stop if either file is out of sequence; the operator can then decide how to remedy the situation.

Two files can be merged on a collator without matching them. In this case, the merged file may contain master records with no matching detail records and vice versa.

Sequence checking may be performed the same time as:

_____ (a) matching.

_____ (b) match-merging.

_____ (c) both

_____ (d) neither

- - - - - - - - - - - - - - - - - -

c

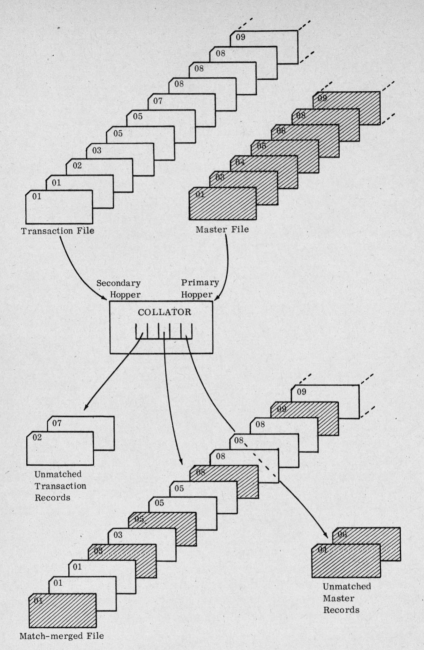

Figure A-12. Match-Merging Two Files

13. For which of these operations should both files be in the same sequence?

_____ (a) matching

_____ (b) match-merging

_____ (c) both

_____ (d) neither

- - - - - - - - - - - - - - - - - - - -

c

14. We have seen how files are sorted into a particular sequence and how two files may be merged. Once files have been sorted and merged, they may be further processed by punched-card calculators and accounting machines. Figure A-13 shows the IBM 609 Calculator.

Figure A-13.   IBM 609 Calculator

This machine reads data from punched cards, performs calculations on it, and punches the result into cards. For this last reason, it is sometimes called a <u>calculating punch</u>.

The calculator is controlled by the wiring of its control panel. As a card passes through the calculator, certain fields are read, calculations are performed on the data in the fields, and the results are punched into a predetermined field in the card. For example, the card at the top of the next page contains data about a transaction.

The calculator can be wired to read three fields—unit price, quantity, and discount. For each card, the following calculation is performed:

quantity × unit price × discount = total price

(The wiring of the calculator will avoid the problem of discount being equal to zero.) The result, the total price, is then punched into the appropriate columns of the card.

The calculator may be wired to perform addition, subtraction, multiplication, and division—in any order. Each operation may be performed more than once on the same data.

The calculator:

_____ (a) is sometimes known as a calculating punch.

_____ (b) can read data from a card and perform calculations on it.

_____ (c) can punch data into a card.

_____ (d) all of the above

- - - - - - - - - - - - - - - - - - -

d

15. Data may be read from one card and used with data from the card immediately following it, the result being punched into the second card. For example, in processing payments on a loan account, a detail file containing data on individual payments is merged with a master file containing the outstanding balance on the account. As the cards are processed through the calculator, the outstanding balance is read from a master record, and a payment made is read from the following detail record. A subtraction is performed, and the new outstanding balance is punched into the detail record. At the same time, the rest of the data from the master record is read and punched into the detail record, creating a new, up-to-date master record for that customer.

Match the two lists on the following page.

_____ (1) sorter

_____ (2) calculator

_____ (3) collator

(a) performs calculations on data read from cards
(b) can be used to sequence check a file
(c) can punch results of calculations into cards
(d) does not have a wired control panel
(e) can be used to match-merge files

- - - - - - - - - - - - - - - - - - - -

(1) d; (2) a, c; (3) b, e

16. The calculator is useful for performing large numbers of repetitive calculations on data recorded in cards, but it does not produce readily comprehensible reports.

The punched-card machine that does this is the accounting or tabulating machine. Figure A-14 shows the IBM 407 Accounting Machine. The accounting machine, or tabulator, is able to accumulate totals and print reports. Its actions are determined by the wiring of the control panel and by a special paper tape that controls the printer mechanism.

Figure A-14. IBM 407 Accounting Machine

The accounting machine can produce two different types of output—a printed report or punched summary cards.

The two types of printed reports that can be produced are detail-printed or group-printed. Detail-printed reports contain data from every record that was processed. Figure A-15 at the top of the next page shows such a report from an inventory application. Each individual transaction is shown as well as totals for each item.

PART NUMBER	PART NAME	UNIT	UNIT COST	TRANS DATE	T C	OPEN. BAL.	TRANSACTIONS REC-EIPTS	ISSUES	ON HAND
11124	TRANSISTOR BG	EA	12 65	228	1	68			
11124	TRANSISTOR BG	EA	12 65	303	4			36	
11124	TRANSISTOR BG	EA	12 65	307	4			18	
11124	TRANSISTOR BG	EA	12 65	310	2		144	40	
11124	TRANSISTOR BG	EA	12 65	314	4			12	
11124	TRANSISTOR BG	EA	12 65	321	5		1		
11124	TRANSISTOR BG	EA	12 65	322	3			1	
11124	TRANSISTOR BG	EA	12 65	328	4			24	
11124	TRANSISTOR BG	EA	12 65	330	4	68	145	131	82
11211	LENS 777	EA	8 33	228	1	84			
11211	LENS 777	EA	8 33	304	4			6	
11211	LENS 777	EA	8 33	307	4			15	
11211	LENS 777	EA	8 33	321	6			1	
11211	LENS 777	EA	8 33	325	4			36	
11211	LENS 777	EA	8 33	329	4			6	
11211	LENS 777	EA	8 33	330	2	84	156	18	
11211	LENS 777	EA	8 33			84	156	82	158
11381	CONNECTORS XX1	EA	1 99	228	1	148			
11381	CONNECTORS XX1	EA	1 99	303	4			24	
11381	CONNECTORS XX1	EA	1 99	312	2		180	36	
11381	CONNECTORS XX1	EA	1 99	314	4			12	

Figure A-15. A Detail-Printed Inventory Report

A group-printed report shows only the totals for any particular item. Figure A-16 shows a group-printed report for the same inventory job. Notice that each item occupies only one line of the report.

STOCK STATUS SUMMARY

DATE 3 / 31 /19--

PART NUMBER	PART NAME	UNIT	UNIT COST	OPENING BALANCE	TRANSACTIONS REC-EIPTS	ISSUES	ON HAND
11124	TRANSISTOR BG	EA	12 65	68	145	131	82
11211	LENS 777	EA	8 33	84	156	82	158
11381	CONNECTORS XX1	EA	1 99	148	180	175	153
11382	CONNECTORS XX2	EA	1 38	75	288	184	179

Figure A-16. Group-Printed Inventory Report

Match the following:

_____ (1) detail-printed report   (a) contains only summary for each group

                                     (b) contains only detail information

_____ (2) group-printed report   (c) contains both detail and summary information for each group

- - - - - - - - - - - - - - - - - - -

(1) c; (2) a

16. By linking the accounting machine to be a reproducer, we can punch this summary data, plus the item number, into a blank card at the same time the total line is printed on the detail report. Figure A-17 shows what the summary card might be like. The part name and unit will be punched into the summary card later.

The reproducer cannot print data on a card, so the summary card in Figure A-17 is interpreted in a separate operation on an interpreter.

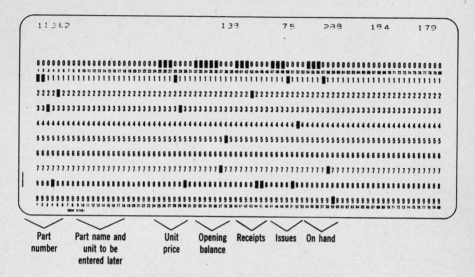

Figure A-17. A Summary Punched Card

Figure A-18 on the next page is a summary of the flow of cards in a punched-card system. All the operations shown, as well as the output, could be produced on a computer system. The punched cards from the key punch would be input through the card read-punch and all the intermediate files (sorted, merged, etc.) would be stored on magnetic disk or tape.

This is the end of Appendix I. You should now do the Self-Test which follows Figure A-18.

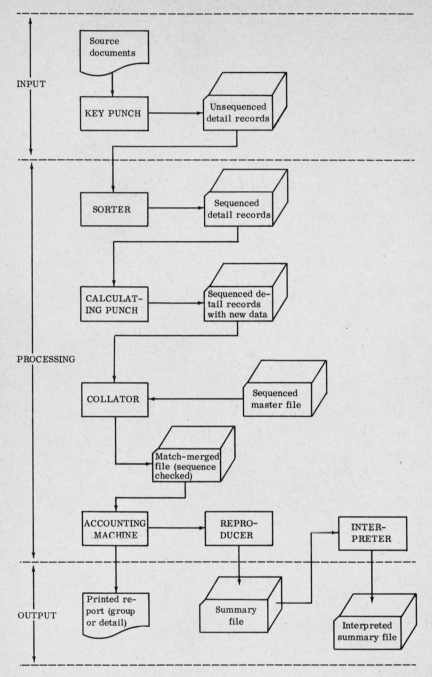

Figure A-18.   Summary of a Punched-Card System

(Not all devices and operations are required for every application.)

SELF-TEST

Answer all the questions and then check against the answers that follow.

1. Which of these statements is true?

_____ (a) A control panel is wired for each job to be performed on the reproducer.

_____ (b) The reproducer can only copy data from one card to another.

_____ (c) Gang-punching refers to the production of summary cards from an accounting machine.

_____ (d) all of the above

2. Match the operation with the equipment required to perform it:

_____ (1) reading mark-sensed   (a) sorter
        cards   (b) collator

_____ (2) selecting records   (c) reproducer

3. Which of these operations is performed on the collator?

_____ (a) matching

_____ (b) sequence checking

_____ (c) match-merge

_____ (d) all of the above

4. The calculating punch can read data from a card, perform calculations on it, and punch the results into:

_____ (a) same card.

_____ (b) following card.

_____ (c) either

_____ (d) neither

5. Match the operation with the equipment required to perform it:

_____ (1) emitting   (a) calculating punch
                          (b) collator
_____ (2) detail printing   (c) accounting machine

_____ (3) summary punching   (d) reproducer
                          (e) sorter

286 INTRODUCTION TO DATA PROCESSING

Answers to Self-Test

The numbers in parentheses refer to the frames in which the appropriate answers can be found. If you have a wrong answer or are not sure why your answer is correct, read Appendix I again before going on to Appendix II and the Final Test.

1. a (frame 1)

2. (1) c; (2) a (frames 1, 7)

3. d (frame 8)

4. c (frame 14)

5. (1) d; (2) c; (3) c, d (frames 1, 15)

APPENDIX II
Characteristics of Selected Computer Systems

This appendix consists of the reference table on the following page.

Type	CPU Storage Capacity*	Operating System	Time-Sharing Capability	SOFTWARE Multi-programming	BASIC	COBOL	FORTRAN
Commodore PET	8K	No	No	No	Yes	No	No
Radio Shack TRS 80	8K	No	No	No	Yes	No	No
Burroughs B300	19K	Yes	Yes	No	Yes	Yes	Nos
IBM System/3 Model 10	48K	Yes	No	No	No	Yes	No
Sperry Univac 9400	131K	Yes	No	Yes	No	Yes	Yes
Honeywell 440	256K	Yes	Yes	Yes	Yes	Yes	Yes
IBM 370 Model 145	524K	Yes	Yes	Yes	Yes	Yes	Yes
Varian V74	512K	Yes	Yes	Yes	Yes	No	Yes
Control Data Cyber 70	1310K	Yes	Yes	Yes	Yes	Yes	Yes

*CPU storage capacity can vary—the size shown here is for the most typical system.

Final Test

1. List the five main steps in the extended data-processing cycle

2. Data is verified in order to:

   _____ (a) arrange it in a suitable format for processing.

   _____ (b) check its accuracy after recording.

   _____ (c) ensure that it is available if required for further processing.

   _____ (d) none of the above

3. Coding of data:

   _____ (a) takes place at the input stage.

   _____ (b) is done on a verifier.

   _____ (c) refers to the substitution of letters, numbers, or letter-number combinations for data on a source document.

   _____ (d) none of the above

4. On a standard punched card:

   _____ (a) alphabetic characters are represented by one zone punch and one digit punch.

   _____ (b) numbers are represented by zone punches only.

   _____ (c) there are 96 columns.

   _____ (d) none of the above

5. Match the following:

_____ (1) field

_____ (2) unit-record

_____ (3) mark-sensed card

    (a) a record that contains all the data for one transaction

    (b) a card that is printed across one end

    (c) a card that has data recorded on it by means of a special pencil

    (d) the space in a record allocated to one particular type of data

6. Match the following:

_____ (1) verifier

_____ (2) reproducer

_____ (3) interpreter

    (a) prints data onto previously punched cards

    (b) end-prints card

    (c) punches data from one card into two or more new cards

    (d) punches a notch into the right-hand edge of correctly punched cards

7. Which of these statements is true?

_____ (a) A detail record contains data that is relatively constant.

_____ (b) A file is a collection of related data that is recorded in a single card.

_____ (c) A master record contains data generated by the processing of two or more records.

_____ (d) none of the above

_____ (e) all of the above

8. Match the following:

_____ (1) control unit

_____ (2) input-output device

_____ (3) storage component

    (a) found in the central processing unit

    (b) interprets instructions and issues commands

    (c) performs calculations on data

    (d) magnetic disk unit

9. Which of these statements is true?

_____ (a) An optical character-recognition machine can be used for both input and output.

_____ (b) A magnetic tape drive is an input-output device and may be used as an auxiliary storage device.

_____ (c) A card read-punch can be used to store data.

_____ (d) none of the above

_____ (e) all of the above

10. Which of these statements is true?

_____ (a) Optical character-recognition equipment can read only data that is recorded in magnetic ink.

_____ (b) A key-to-disk data-entry device records data from a keyboard directly on magnetic tape.

_____ (c) both

_____ (d) neither

11. Which of these statements is true?

_____ (a) Batch processing is the processing of a large number of records at a given time.

_____ (b) On-line processing requires random access to stored programs and data.

_____ (c) both

_____ (d) neither

12. Which of these statements is true?

_____ (a) A light pen is used to read the universal product code.

_____ (b) Telecommunications is the exchange of data between remote terminals and a computer.

_____ (c) A modem is a device used to convert data on a magnetic disk into a form that can be stored on magnetic tape.

_____ (d) all of the above

_____ (e) none of the above

13. Which of these statements is true?

_____ (a) Audio-response units are very difficult to use.

_____ (b) An intelligent terminal is one that can perform editing functions on data before it is transmitted to a central computer.

_____ (c) Remote job entry refers to the transmission of a request for batch processing from a remote terminal.

_____ (d) all of the above

_____ (e) none of the above

14. Convert 627 to binary and 101011010 to decimal.

15. Which of these statements is true?

_____ (a) The EBCDIC bit contains eight bytes.

_____ (b) The EBCDIC byte contains eight bits.

_____ (c) A parity bit is used to indicate where a new data field begins.

_____ (d) none of the above

_____ (e) all of the above

16. Data is represented:

_____ (a) in magnetic-core storage by the direction of magnetization of each core.

_____ (b) on magnetic tape by the presence of magnetized spots.

_____ (c) both

_____ (d) neither

17. The semiconductor chip:

_____ (a) contains a large number of transistors.

_____ (b) can be used as a storage device.

_____ (c) can contain a complete central processing unit.

_____ (d) all of the above

_____ (e) none of the above

18. Which of these statements is true?

_____ (a) An unconditional transfer-of-control instruction is made regardless of the condition of data.

_____ (b) An editing instruction tells the computer system where to find its next instruction.

_____ (c) both

_____ (d) neither

19. Match the following:

_____ (1) source program

_____ (2) object program

_____ (3) compiler

(a) converts a source program into an object program
(b) written in machine language
(c) written in symbolic language
(d) written in grammatical English

20. Which of these statements is true?

_____ (a) Debugging is the process of writing a program in coded form.

_____ (b) Execution-time diagnostics indicate grammatical errors in a source program.

_____ (c) Compilation-time diagnostics indicate errors that occur when data is run with the object program.

_____ (d) all of the above

_____ (e) none of the above

21. A run manual contains:

_____ (a) the information about a computer system that the operator needs.

_____ (b) the information about a program that the operator needs to run it.

_____ (c) both

_____ (d) neither

22. Match the following:

_____ (1) BASIC

_____ (2) COBOL

_____ (3) FORTRAN

(a) is particularly suited to time-sharing applications

(b) used primarily for the preparation of business reports

(c) used primarily for simple scientific and business applications

(d) used primarily for solving scientific problems

23. Write a brief description of the following flowchart.

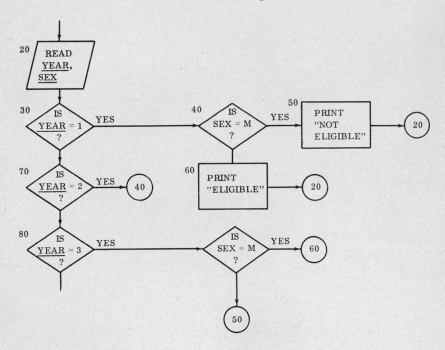

24. On separate paper, draw the most efficient flowchart you can that will read three numbers, A, B, C, and:

> Let T1 = A × 10
> Let T2 = B ÷ 3
> Let T3 = C + 150
> If T1 = T2 then print JACKPOT
> If T1 = T3 and T2 = T3 then print JACKPOT
> Otherwise print FORFEIT and read three more numbers

25. Which of these is a conditional statement?

_____ (a) GO TO 360

_____ (b) IF X = 47 GO TO 360

_____ (c) IF X = 47 THEN 360

_____ (d) none of the above

26. Match the following:

_____ (1) applications programs   (a) prepared by manufacturer to perform routine processing functions

_____ (2) utility programs   (b) prepared by user to meet his or her own particular needs

_____ (3) operating systems   (c) programs that meet the needs of many users with little modification

     (d) prepared by manufacturer to maintain control over the system

27. Which of these statements is true?

_____ (a) Job-control language is used by the programmer to communicate with the system being used.

_____ (b) The supervisor interprets the JCL and controls the operating system.

_____ (c) both

_____ (d) neither

28. A major aim of systems analysis is:

_____ (a) the reduction of the work force.

_____ (b) an improvement in the efficiency of an organization.

_____ (c) the preparation of a feasibility study.

_____ (d) none of the above

29. Which of these statements is true?

_____ (a) Management-information systems are being replaced by computer systems.

_____ (a) Implementation of a new system often involves using both old and new systems together until it is clear that the new system works well.

_____ (c) The primary concern of a systems analyst is maintaining the components of a computer system in efficient working order.

_____ (d) none of the above

Answers to Final Test

The numbers in parentheses after each answer refer to the chapter in which each answer can be found.

1. data entry, input, processing, output, storage (Chapter 1)

2. b (Chapter 1)

3. a, c (Chapter 1)

4. a (Chapter 2)

5. (1) d; (2) a; (3) c (Chapter 2)

6. (1) d; (2) c; (3) a (Chapter 2)

7. d (Chapter 3)

8. (1) a, b; (2) d; (3) a (Chapter 3)

9. b (Chapter 3)

10. b (Chapter 3)

11. c (Chapter 4)

12. b (Chapter 4)

13. b, c (Chapter 4)

14. $627 = 1001110011$
    $101011010 = 346$ (Chapter 5)

15. b (Chapter 5)

16. c (Chapter 5)

17. d (Chapter 5)

18. a (Chapter 6)

19. (1) c; (2) b; (3) a (Chapter 6)

20. e (Chapter 6)

21. b (Chapter 6)

22. (1) a, c; (2) b; (3) d (Chapter 6)

23. Your description should be something like this:

   Read <u>SEX</u> and <u>YEAR</u>
   If <u>YEAR</u> is 1 or 2 and <u>SEX</u> is male, print "NOT ELIGIBLE" and return to step 20
   If <u>YEAR</u> is 1 or 2 and <u>SEX</u> is female, print "ELIGIBLE" and return to step 20
   If <u>YEAR</u> is 3 and <u>SEX</u> is male, print "ELIGIBLE" and return to step 20
   If <u>YEAR</u> is 3 and <u>SEX</u> is female, print "NOT ELIGIBLE" and return to step 20   (Chapter 7)

24. Your flowchart should look something like this:

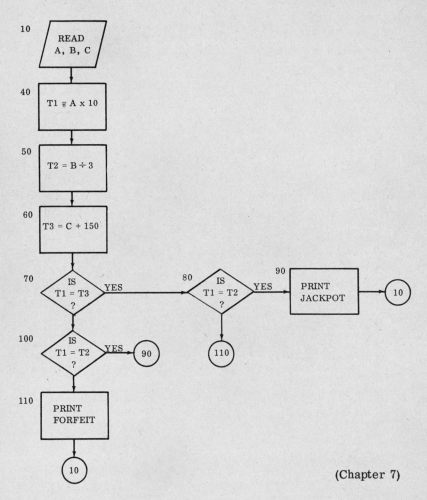

(Chapter 7)

25. c (Chapter 8)

26. (1) c; (2) a; (3) d (Chapter 9)

27. a (Chapter 9)

28. b, c (Chapter 10)

29. b (Chapter 10)

Glossary

ABSOLUTE MACHINE LANGUAGE—the language that is understood by a computer; each statement has two parts: a storage address and an operation code.

APPLICATIONS PROGRAM—a program that requires little or no modification for use in many organizations performing the same types of data processing; e.g., utility billing, bank account processing.

ARITHMETIC-LOGIC UNIT—that part of the central processing unit in which arithmetic and logical operations are performed.

AUDIO-RESPONSE UNIT—a device that allows a computer to "talk" using synthesized speech.

AUXILIARY STORAGE—storage that is external to the central processing unit in which data and programs are stored until required for processing.

BASIC—Beginners All-purpose Symbolic Interchange Code, the simplest symbolic language; designed primarily for the solution of scientific problems and to be used conversationally via telecommunications.

BATCH DATA PROCESSING—the gathering together of large amounts of data for processing at a given time.

BIT—a Binary digIT; the basic building block for representation of characters in computer storage.

BYTE—a series of eight bits that are used to represent characters in EBCDIC.

CARD PUNCH—a device for punching output data from the computer into punched cards.

CARD READER—an input device for reading data from punched cards into the computer.

CARD READ-PUNCH—a device that can both read input data from punched cards into the computer and punch output from the computer into punched cards.

CENTRAL PROCESSING UNIT—the heart of a computer system; contains the control unit, storage unit, and arithmetic-logic unit.

COBOL—COmmon Business-Oriented Language, the most commonly used language for business data processing; designed to perform relatively simple operations on large amounts of data.

COMPILER—a program supplied by a computer manufacturer to translate a source program in symbolic language into absolute machine language.

COMPUTER INPUT FROM MICROFILM—the technique for reading data on microfilm directly as input to a computer.

COMPUTER OUTPUT TO MICROFILM—the technique for recording output data from a computer directly on microfilm.

DATA CELL—a device used to store very large amounts of data that have to be available for processing at all times; a combination of magnetic tape and magnetic disk technology.

DATA-PROCESSING CYCLE—the basic sequence of events in the processing of any data; the five major steps are: data entry, input, processing, output, and storage.

DETAIL RECORD—a record that contains data related to only one transaction or event.

DISPLAY TERMINAL—a device used for both input and output on which data is shown on a screen.

EBCDIC—Extended Binary-Coded Decimal Interchange Code, a data representation scheme widely used in computer systems; it can represent 256 characters, using eight bits to a byte.

FEASIBILITY STUDY—a study to compare the cost of obtaining automated data-processing equipment and changing procedures with the expected long-term benefits of the new system.

FILE—a collection of related records.

FLOWCHART—a "picture" of a computer program and how it is intended to operate.

FORTRAN—FORmula TRANslator, a symbolic language designed especially for solving scientific problems; suited to the performance of complex operations on relatively small amounts of data.

GRAPHICS TERMINAL—an intelligent terminal designed specifically for the display of graphs, charts, and technical drawings.

INTELLIGENT TERMINAL—a remote terminal that can perform editing and data-checking functions before data is transmitted to the main computer.

INTERPRETER—a peripheral device that is used to read punched cards and print the appropriate characters above each column.

JOB-CONTROL LANGUAGE—the language used by a programmer or a terminal operator to communicate with the operating system.

KEYBOARD TERMINAL—a device, similar to a typewriter, used as an input and output device; both input and output data are written on paper.

KEY PUNCH—a device for recording data from source documents in punched cards.

KEY-TO-DISK—a method of data entry in which data is recorded directly from a keyboard onto magnetic disk.

KEY-TO-TAPE—a method of data entry in which data is recorded directly from a keyboard onto magnetic tape.

LINE PRINTER—the most common output device in business data processing; used for printing single or multiple copies of reports one full line at a time; characters are formed by the contact of keys on a carbon ribbon.

MAGNETIC-CHARACTER READER-SORTER—a device that can read and sort documents on which data is recorded using special symbols written in magnetic ink; primarily used to read checks.

MAGNETIC DISK DRIVE—the device used to read data from and write data on magnetic disks; input and output operations may be performed simultaneously.

MAGNETIC DISK PACK—a storage medium on which data is recorded as magnetic spots on a thin metal disk.

MAGNETIC DRUM—a large metal cylinder on which data is recorded in the form of magnetic spots; able to store more data and read and write it faster than the magnetic disk drive.

MAGNETIC-INK CHARACTER RECOGNITION—the technique used in the magnetic-character reader-sorter; numbers of a specific size and shape are printed in an ink that can be magnetized and read by special reading heads.

MAGNETIC TAPE—a medium on which data is recorded in the form of magnetic spots on thin plastic tape.

MAGNETIC TAPE DRIVE—a device used to read input from, and record output data on, magnetic tape; only one operation may be performed at one time.

MAGNETIC THIN-FILM MEMORY—a storage medium consisting of small pieces of nickel-iron alloy stuck on sheets of glass; used for main storage in some central processing units.

MANAGEMENT-INFORMATION SYSTEMS—the maintenance of large amounts of data in data banks accessible in real-time to provide for rapid decision making by management.

MASTER RECORD—a record that contains data that is relatively permanent.

MICROCOMPUTER—a computer normally having less than 16K of CPU storage and designed primarily for home use.

MINICOMPUTER—a computer having a CPU storage of 16K to 64K.

MODEM—a device that converts computer code into telephone code and vice versa in order to transmit and receive data through a telecommunications network.

MULTIPROGRAMMING—the ability of a central processing unit to execute more than one program at a time.

NONIMPACT PRINTER—a printer that forms characters on paper through the use of heat, electrostatic energy, or a laser beam.

OBJECT PROGRAM—a program in absolute machine language.

ON-LINE DATA PROCESSING—the processing of data as soon as it is received from a remote terminal.

OPERATING SYSTEM—a series of programs supplied by the computer manufacturer to control all operations of the computer; designed to maximize the efficiency of the system.

OPERATOR—a person who is responsible for monitoring the operation of a computer system and for loading and unloading tape drives, disk packs, etc.

OPTICAL-CHARACTER RECOGNITION—a technique for reading typewritten data and converting it to electrical impulses for direct input to a computer.

PERIPHERAL DEVICES—equipment that is used primarily for the processing of punched cards; these devices are not connected to the computer and are used to reduce the burden of card processing on the computer.

PL/1—Programming Language One, a symbolic programming language designed to incorporate the best features of COBOL and FORTRAN.

POINT-OF-SALE TERMINAL—an intelligent terminal specifically for use by checkers and sales clerks for the preparation of customer bills; often used in conjunction with the universal product code.

PROGRAM—a detailed set of instructions telling the computer what types of input data it will receive, exactly what operations to perform on it and in what order, and what type of output to produce.

PUNCHED CARD—a standard-sized data-recording medium made of strong, durable paper.

RANDOM ACCESS—the process by which a specific record in a file may be accessed without reading all the records that precede it; used with magnetic disk and magnetic drum.

REAL-TIME DATA PROCESSING—the processing of data from remote terminals fast enough for it to be used immediately for decision making; e.g., airline-reservation systems.

RECORD—a collection of related records.

REMOTE JOB ENTRY—the transmission of a request for batch processing from a remote terminal.

REPORT GENERATORS—programs supplied by computer manufacturers to produce a wide variety of simple reports; require less skill to use than symbolic programming languages.

RUN MANUAL—a book telling the computer operator how to run a particular program, which devices will be required, etc.

SEMICONDUCTOR CHIP—a tiny component containing a large number of transistors and used to store data or as a central processing unit.

SEQUENTIAL DATA PROCESSING—the process by which records in a file are accessed in the order in which they are written.

SOURCE PROGRAM—a computer program written in a symbolic language.

STORAGE UNIT—that part of the central processing unit in which data and instructions are stored for immediate use; computers are classified by the size of their storage units, measured in thousands of bytes.

STORED PROGRAM—a source or object program that is in the storage unit in the central processing unit or in auxiliary storage and available for use.

STRUCTURED PROGRAMMING—the breaking down of a large, complex data-processing task into a series of interrelated and relatively less complex programs.

SUPERVISOR—a special program supplied by the computer manufacturer that is always in the central processing unit when the computer is in operation; it controls the entire operation of the computer.

SYMBOLIC PROGRAMMING LANGUAGE—a language that can be understood by people but that has to be translated into absolute machine language for use in a computer; e.g., FORTRAN, COBOL.

SYSTEMS ANALYSIS—the breaking down of an organization into its component parts for study; the major objective of systems analysis is the improvement of the economy and efficiency of an organization.

TELECOMMUNICATIONS—the exchange of data between a computer and remote terminals using telephone lines or microwave links.

TIME SHARING—a technique by which many users may simultaneously share the central processing unit of a computer.

UNIVERSAL PRODUCT CODE—the "zebra" stripes now printed on most merchandise, which used in conjunction with a wand or special reader and an intelligent terminal speeds up the recording of sales.

UTILITY PROGRAMS—manufacturer-supplied programs for performing many of the routine tasks of data processing; e.g., card-to-tape data transfer, disk-to-disk data transfer, and disk-to-printer data transfer.

VERIFYING—the checking of data recorded in any medium to ensure its accuracy.

VIRTUAL STORAGE—a technique allowing a computer system to behave as if it has a larger central processing unit than it actually has; pages of the program being executed are brought into the CPU from auxiliary storage as required.

Index